Intelligent Decision Systems

SAMUEL HOLTZMAN
Strategic Decisions Group

ADDISON-WESLEY PUBLISHING COMPANY, INC.
Reading, Massachusetts•Menlo Park, California•Don Mills, Ontario
Wokingham, England•Amsterdam•Sydney•Singapore•Tokyo•Bonn
New York•Madrid•San Juan

The programs and applications presented in this book have been included for their instructional value. They have been tested with care, but are not guaranteed for any particular purpose. The publisher does not offer any warranties or representations, nor does it accept any liabilities with respect to the programs or applications.

Epigraph credits: "A Friend of Kafka" from A FRIEND OF KAFKA AND OTHER STORIES by Isaac Bashevis Singer. Copyright © 1968, 1970 by Isaac Bashevis Singer. Originally appeared in *The New Yorker*. Reprinted by permission of Farrar, Straus and Giroux, Inc., and Jonathan Cape Ltd., p. 11. *The Tao of Physics* by Fritjof Capra, © 1975. Reprinted by permission of Shambhala Publications, Inc., Boston, MA, and Gower Publishing Group, U.K., p. 78. COMPUTER POWER AND HUMAN REASON by Joseph Weizenbaum. Copyright © 1976. Reprinted by permission of W. H. Freeman and Company, p. 90. *God and Golem* by Norbert Wiener, copyright © 1964. Reprinted by permission of the MIT Press, p. 109. *Understanding Computers and Cognition: A New Foundation for Design*, Winograd, T. & Flores, F. (1986). Ablex Publishing Corporation, Norwood, NJ. Reprinted with permission. p. 152.

LIBRARY OF CONGRESS
Library of Congress Cataloging-in-Publication Data

Holtzman, Samuel, 1955-
    Intelligent decision systems/by Samuel Holtzman.
      p. cm.
    Bibliography : p.
    Includes index.
    ISBN 0-201-11602-2
1. Decision analysis
2. Expert systems (Computer science)
3. Artificial intelligence.
4. Medicine—Decision-making—Data processing.   I. Title.
QA76.76.E95H66 1989
006.3'3—dc 19

88-2184
CIP

BCDEFGHIJ-HA-89

The Teknowledge Series in Knowledge Engineering

Frederick Hayes-Roth, *Managing Editor*
Teknowledge Inc.

Books in the Teknowledge Series

Building Expert Systems
  Frederick Hayes-Roth, Donald A. Waterman, and
  Douglas B. Lenat (eds.), 1983

A Guide to Expert Systems
  Donald A. Waterman, 1986

Intelligent Decision Systems
  Samuel Holtzman, 1989

Contents

Table of Illustrations

Foreword

The success to date of knowledge engineers in building expert systems has been remarkable. The Teknowledge Series in Knowledge Engineering has helped fuel this development by providing high-quality, timely, and relevant books on expert systems technology. In the future, we expect not only to publish additional texts on expert systems but also to offer books of a broader sort, reporting on other ways that researchers and developers have exploited the power of computer-activated knowledge. The current book, by Sam Holtzman, exemplifies this broadening of focus.

The author's aim is to stimulate the development of "Intelligent Decision Systems." These systems would combine the knowledge-based reasoning methods of expert systems with formal methods of decision analysis. To date, practitioners of knowledge engineering have learned to focus their energy on automating high-value, routine, but challenging tasks. In contrast, decision analysts have focused on manually formulating mathematical representations of high-value special-case problems. To combine these two techniques, Holtzman proposes using the methods of knowledge engineering to automate the task of the decision analyst. He illustrates these ideas in a demonstration program that addresses personal problems arising in human infertility.

The Editors are enthusiastic about this book for several reasons. First, it brings together two fields that address closely related and complementary concerns. Second, it provides enough background so readers in either area, or readers new to both areas, can understand the thesis. Finally, the book's illustrative application addresses a compelling problem of general interest where we can easily see the forecasted benefits of intelligent decision systems.

Through this series we hope to provide an effective channel for informing and educating people interested in understanding knowledge processing and in performing knowledge engineering. We will identify needed works, encourage their development, and editorially manage their publication. Our intended audience includes practicing knowledge engineers, students and scientists in related disciplines, and technical managers assessing the potential of these systems. Readers with criticisms or suggestions for needed books are encouraged to contact the managing editor or a member of the editorial board.

Preface

A PERSONAL NOTE

Shortly after finishing my formal training as a decision analyst, I joined Strategic Decisions Group, a consulting firm offering professional decision analysis services to major business organizations. Since then, several of my friends, who learned of my interest and skills, have asked me to analyze their own personal decisions and to help them develop a simple, logical solution to their problems. Their concerns have included such things as changing careers, planning for retirement, selecting a permanent place to live, and designing a medical treatment strategy.

However, realizing that responsibly analyzing a significant decision usually involves over a hundred hours of intense work, I have had little choice but to turn down my friends' requests. While I have offered to discuss their problems and to try to clarify their decisions informally, I have also explained that a professional decision analysis is a major effort that is, unfortunately, beyond their means.

Although my friends have invariably understood my position (and, indeed, allowed me to help them informally), I was left with a strong desire to understand why the process of decision analysis was so costly. Underlying this curiosity was the hope that there might be a way to simplify the process to make it more accessible to the general public—a hope that was nurtured by several ideas I had developed a few years earlier when I became interested in artificial intelligence.

As a first step, I tried to model the process of decision analysis with sufficient accuracy to allow some of its components to be automated, hoping this would reduce the cost of the overall process. I soon realized, however, that this modeling effort would challenge even the most advanced computer programming techniques available. Despite this difficulty, I felt the goal could be attained with current technology as long as the resulting system could be designed to focus on a very specific decision domain. Furthermore, regardless of whether the task of modeling the decision analysis process was successful as a design technique for computer-based decision aids, it promised to yield major insights into the field of decision analysis itself, insights that could help to significantly advance decision analysis methodology.

As the concept of computer-aided decision analysis evolved, I began to consider specific application fields. Based on discussions with friends, I realized that medical treatment decisions, when compared to such other major personal decisions as selecting a job, buying a house, or designing an investment strategy, are particularly difficult to make. In dealing with this difficulty, patients commonly delegate the decision-making authority to their physician. However, this puts physicians in an awkward situation, because despite their extensive medical knowledge, they have no simple way of effectively incorporating their patients' knowledge and preferences into their own decision-making process. The result is a strained relationship between physicians and patients, one that ultimately increases the likelihood that poor decisions will be made.

This difficulty often occurs because physicians and patients cannot satisfactorily deal with uncertainty. In fact, human reasoning is notoriously poor at dealing with uncertain information. Daily life has plenty of simple examples where our intuition fails miserably in this arena. The abundance of sweepstakes and the existence of many types of insurance are evidence of this feature of human cognition. Moreover, everyday language is deplorably ambiguous concerning uncertainty. Terms such as *likely* and *probably* mean very different things to different people and can be the source of tremendous confusion. In particular, the uncertainty associated with many medical decisions can be overwhelming. The inability of the medical profession to effectively deal with uncertainty has led to an overabundance of diagnostic procedures that impose an unwarranted inconvenience on patients and burden our whole economic system.

In addition, medical decision-making is hampered by conspicuous communication barriers. On the one hand, physicians find it difficult to explain their medical conclusions to patients because of the economic and time pressures common in modern medical practice. On the other hand, patients cannot easily attach a value to the possible outcomes of their choices, since these outcomes are usually unfamiliar and involve such highly distinct attributes as financial effects, pain, and death. Many of these outcomes are difficult to quantify and to combine into a meaningful measure.

Furthermore, current trends in medical research are likely to increase the difficulty of making treatment selection decisions. In the past, the treatment selection was often simplified because there was only a small set of available alternatives. For example, in many cases, there used to be a single pertinent treatment, and the corresponding decision consisted of accepting or rejecting it. However, advances in medical research are creating many new alternatives, which, in turn, make it increasingly difficult to make decisions.

Given my focus on medical decisions, I explored the possibility of developing a computer-based tool for decision-making by codifying a large portion of what is commonly known as the "art" of decision analysis. As it matured, this effort became the basis of a computer program that analyzes significant decisions with little or no intervention by a human analyst.

The resultant program, called Rachel, deals with the decisions faced by infertile couples seeking medical help. Although it is experimental and has not been validated for clinical use, Rachel deals with realistic situations and interacts with patients and physicians to analyze their decisions and to guide them from a confusing decision situation toward a clear plan for action. Thus, Rachel constitutes the first instance of an *intelligent decision system* [Holtzman, 1985a, 1985b].

While implementing a general decision analysis system capable of handling all decision problems, and medical ones in particular, would have considerable value, it is beyond the reach of current technology. However, knowledge engineering has created an exciting opportunity for applying decision analysis to narrowly defined classes of decisions. The attractiveness of this opportunity hinges on the idea that a set of decisions having some degree of similarity between them can be effectively treated as a whole. Individual analyses would then be considered as instances of the collective analysis.

THE SCOPE OF THIS BOOK

This book serves as an introduction to the theory and practice of intelligent decision systems. Beginning with a broad view of decision-making, the book focuses on using knowledge engineering methods to design effective decision-making tools. For clarity, the book is divided into two parts. Part I—Foundations—presents the philosophical and theoretical underpinnings necessary to understand the concept and technology of intelligent decision systems. Part II—Applications—describes Rachel in detail and discusses how intelligent decision systems can be used in medicine and in industry. An annotated listing of a consultation with Rachel is included as an appendix.

Intelligent decision systems significantly challenge and extend the technology of expert systems to provide effective automated decision-making assistance. The key technical and practical implications of this new approach for building decision tools are discussed, respectively, in Chapters 6 and 9. In addition, Chapter 9 discusses the new possibilities created by intelligent decision system technology and illustrates how it could be applied in fields far beyond medicine. In particular, this technology could greatly facilitate and improve decisions in such diverse arenas as investing, law, bidding, marketing, real estate, power generation, and space exploration.

The presentation assumes some familiarity with the fields of decision analysis and applied artificial intelligence (e.g., knowledge-based systems), but it does not require proficiency in either. Readers who have been exposed to decision trees and sensitivity analysis and who know the difference between an inference engine and a knowledge base have enough preparation to understand most of this discussion.

As a guide to the reader, each chapter (except for Chapter 1) begins with a highlighted summary paragraph. This summary is preceded by an epigraph that at least partially captures the chapter's philosophical theme.

Since the book addresses three distinct fields of endeavor—decision analysis, artificial intelligence, and infertility medicine—special care has been given to the use of technical language. Technical terms defined in the book are printed in boldface when they are first used. When additional definitions can add clarity to the presentation, they are included in a glossary at the end of the book.

ACKNOWLEDGMENTS

The ideas presented in this book owe much to the help and guidance of many people. Foremost among them is Professor Ronald A. Howard, whose pioneering work led decision analysis from its academic origins to its current status as a professional discipline. I have also greatly benefited from the friendship, professional guidance, and many ideas of Dr. James E. Matheson. Their insights on the philosophy and technique of good decision-making underlie much of the material discussed here.

I am also grateful to Dr. Emmet J. Lamb and Dr. Robert Kessler, who taught me the medical fundamentals of human reproduction and provided me with firsthand exposure to the realities of clinical decision-making; to Professor Michael R. Genesereth, who helped me understand the principles and practical application of artificial intelligence technology; and to Professor Herbert A. Simon, who kindled my enthusiasm in the field of computer-aided decision-making.

I would also like to acknowledge Dr. Jack Breese, Dr. Frank Polansky, James E. Smith, Keh-Shiou Leu, Léonard Bertrand, Dr. Thomas W. Keelin, Professor Ross Shachter, Professor Edward H. Shortliffe, Dr. Emilio Navarro, Richard M. Catlin, Jr., and my friends and colleagues at Strategic Decisions Group for their many contributions, comments, and suggestions.

I am also grateful to Dr. Paul Steinberg for his editorial assistance in transforming the text of my doctoral dissertation into a book, and to Helen Goldstein of Addison-Wesley for her diligence and guidance. Finally, I would like to thank my wife, Judy, who commented on extensive portions of the book and whose emotional support, personal energy, and patience were invaluable throughout this project.

Menlo Park, California   S.H.

Part I

Foundations

1

Introduction

The Unknown Isle

Say, oh pretty maiden,
Where do you want to go?
The sail bellies its wing,
The wind is about to blow!

The oar is of ivory,
The flag of fine silk,
The rudder of fine gold;
For ballast I've an orange,
For sail, an angel's wing,
For ship's boy, a seraph.

Say, oh pretty maiden,
Where do you want to go?
The sail bellies its wing,
The wind is about to blow!

Is it within the Baltic,
In the Pacific sea,
In the isle of Java?
Or else is it in Norway,
To pluck the snow flower,
Or the flower of Angsoka?

Say, oh say pretty maiden,
Say, where do you want to go?

Take me, said the young beauty,
To the faithful shore
Where love lasts forever.
Alas, that shore, my dear,
Is scarcely known
In the land of love.

Where do you want to go?
The wind is about to blow!
—"The Nights of Summer,"
  Théophile Gautier

A HISTORICAL BACKGROUND ON DECISION SYSTEMS

Designing and implementing effective decision tools have been active areas of research since World War II, when the military urgency of the war directed a substantial amount of resources toward developing two fields—operations research and computer science. These two fields together constitute the foundation of most research in normative decision sciences. A close relationship between these academic areas continues to this day.

From their early days, operations research and computer science have relied on each other. Operations research concerns the application of mathematics (in particular, optimization theory) for managing scarce resources, usually to satisfy complex requirements. To accomplish their objectives, operations researchers have always required substantial computational facilities. In many instances, these computational needs have motivated major advances in the capacity and functionality of computers. Similarly, computer scientists have relied heavily on the results of operations researchers. The computational, storage, and communications resources in most computers are managed by operating systems that incorporate many algorithms developed by operations researchers.

As the two fields have matured, their original narrow focus on numerical computation has widened. Computer scientists have become increasingly concerned with symbolic manipulation, particularly in their attempts to emulate human cognitive and perceptual abilities. The concepts of **artificial intelligence** and **expert systems** are intimately related to this broader focus of computer science. Along a similar direction, operations researchers have directed some of their efforts at representing real problems in mathematical terms and away from the algorithms needed to evaluate the resulting mathematical descriptions. This focus on problem representation has been particularly strong (and quite successful) in the field of **decision analysis**, which grew out of operations research and systems science.

Since the early 1970s, decision and computer scientists have become attracted to the idea of constructing powerful computer-based decision tools, referred to as **decision systems**. Much of the current enthusiasm stems from the possibility of automating a large part of what is considered to be the "art" of designing mathematical models for decision problems.

Around 1965, research into artificial intelligence experienced a shift in approach. The old approach held that intelligence resulted almost entirely from the existence of highly sophisticated reasoning procedures that were believed to be essentially independent of the domain in which they were used. The new approach evolved from the realization that much of what we loosely refer to as "intelligent behavior" appears to depend on large amounts of domain-specific knowledge. The difference between the two views can be illustrated by contrasting the class of general problem-solving algorithms, such as GPS [Newell, et al., 1960; Newell and Simon, 1963] and STRIPS [Fikes and Nilsson, 1971; Fikes et al., 1972], which are based on domain-independent problem-solving procedures, with the set of task-specific systems, such as DENDRAL [Buchanan and Feigenbaum, 1978; Lindsay et al., 1980] and MYCIN [Shortliffe, 1976], which incorporate a large collection of domain-specific knowledge.

This shift in emphasis, away from domain independence in favor of a reliance on knowledge specific to the domain in which target problems are to be solved, led the way to the birth of the applied subarea of artificial intelligence known as **knowledge engineering**. The main concern of knowledge engineering is designing and implementing expert systems—large computer programs capable of exhibiting expert behavior. The expertise of such systems is generally concentrated on a narrowly defined class of problems. For example, the list of successful expert systems developed in the last decade includes DENDRAL [Lindsay et al., 1980], MACSYMA [Moses, 1975], the various HEARSAY systems [Erman et al., 1980; Erman and Lesser, 1980], MYCIN [Shortliffe, 1976] and its descendants (e.g., PUFF [Aikins et al., 1982], NEOMYCIN [Clancey and Letsinger, 1981], EMYCIN [Van Melle et al., 1981], and ONCOCIN [Shortliffe et al., 1981]), PROSPECTOR [Duda et al., 1977, 1978, 1979; Duda and Reboh, 1984], QMR (also known as CADUCEUS and INTERNIST) [Pople, 1977, 1982], CASNET [Kulikowski and Weiss, 1982], AM [Davis and Lenat, 1982], EURISKO [Lenat and Brown, 1983], and XCON (also known as R1) [McDermott, 1980a, 1980b, 1980c, 1982].

The shift in artificial intelligence from generality to a strong dependence on domain-specific knowledge was an important element in the process that helped turn the theoretical foundations of artificial intelligence into practical applications and, more recently, into commercial products. This shift was paralleled by a roughly simultaneous occurrence in decision sciences, which had a similar effect. The seminal works on formal decision theories [von Neumann and Morgenstern, 1947; Dantzig, 1951, 1963; Bellman, 1957] established a set of formal representations for large classes of complex decision problems and a corresponding set of algorithms to solve the formalized problems. However, these theories said little about the process of modeling real problems in formal terms and told us virtually nothing about how to validate and use the results of their deductions to allocate real resources.

The need to develop methodologies for translating real decision problems into a formal language and for interpreting the results of manipulating these formal representations led some decision scientists to focus their attention on applying decision theories to real problems rather than on the theories themselves. A particularly important consequence of this shift was the formation of the academic and professional discipline of decision analysis [Howard, 1966]. Decision analysis combines aspects of systems analysis [Howard, 1973; Luenberger, 1979] and statistical decision theory [von Neumann and Morgenstern, 1947; Howard, 1966; Keeney and Raiffa, 1976] to form a body of knowledge that can deal practically and generally with the logic of making choices in complex, dynamic, and uncertain situations [Howard and Matheson, 1983–1984].

However, with the exception of work that has led to the concept of the decision analysis cycle [Matheson and Howard, 1968] and its professional application [Howard, 1980b, 1983, 1987b; Howard and Matheson, 1983–1984], most research in normative decision sciences during the last two decades has concentrated almost exclusively on computational techniques, attempting to increase their generality and efficiency. Consequently, most researchers have devoted little attention to the processes within which these techniques are used to deal with real problems [Holtzman, 1981; Ackoff, 1987].

Since the early days in the mid-1960s, decision analysis and knowledge engineering have shared a common interest in developing computer-based decision systems. Many of the expert systems previously mentioned provide their users with a recommendation for action. For instance, MYCIN proposes antibiotic therapies for dealing with cases of meningitis, XCON suggests configurations for (VAX) computer installations, and QMR (as well as MYCIN) requests a variety of possibly toxic and invasive tests to help determine the nature of a patient's disease. Similarly, decision analysts have developed several systems to automate parts of the decision analysis process. These systems include ONRODA [Howard et al., 1975], CADMUS [Miller et al., 1976], SUPERTREE® [Olmsted, 1982; McNamee and Celona, 1987], SUPERID [Breese and Holtzman, 1984], DAVID [Shachter, 1986b], Analyst™ [Holtzman, 1986], and others [Freedy et al., 1976; Korsan and Matheson, 1978; Merkhofer et al., 1979; Merkhofer and Leaf, 1981]. The electric utility industry has been particularly active in developing computer-based tools for decision-making. A well-known example of these tools is the "Over/Under" model [Cazalet *et al.*, 1978] for making capacity planning decisions.

However, despite considerable effort, neither decision analysts nor knowledge engineers have been particularly successful in developing a comprehensive methodology for creating decision systems that truly assist decision-makers in all aspects of the decision-making process. Generally, decision analysts have succeeded in developing either general-purpose computer-based decision tools for experienced analysts (e.g., decision-tree processors [Olmsted, 1982; McNamee and Celona, 1987]) or parametric analyses of very narrowly defined (albeit sometimes quite complex) types of decisions (e.g., the Over/Under model [Cazalet *et al.*, 1978]). In contrast, the systems designed by knowledge engineers, although aimed at giving relatively customized assistance to novice users, have only been successful when the level of uncertainty in the problem is low and when the decision-maker's preferences are very simple to model (e.g., MYCIN [Shortliffe, 1976] and XCON [McDermott, 1980a, 1980b, 1980c]). Beyond this category of decision problems, knowledge engineering has been unable to provide much guidance in designing useful decision systems.

Thus, although some progress has been made, no one has produced computer-based decision systems that can interact with the decision-maker to actively formulate, evaluate, and appraise a customized model of the decision at hand that reflects his available alternatives, his best information, and his genuine preferences. As we will discuss at length in this book, a decision system must be able to do these things to produce the insight decision-makers need to take action.

The need to develop insight is one of this book's central themes. Specifically, the book is based on the belief that effective decision systems must concentrate on assisting the decision-maker to gain insight into the decision problem at hand rather than on merely supplying a somehow "right" answer. This belief implies that to help individuals facing difficult decision problems, a decision system must concentrate on formulating the problem clearly and understandably rather than exclusively on solving the problem or on producing a somehow "correct" model of the decision. Given the necessary insight, a "best" course of action should become obvious.

A major challenge for designers of decision systems is how to represent and use uncertain knowledge, because uncertainty requires us to represent and reason about multiple possible scenarios. As the size of the problem grows, the number of ways in which the uncertainty can be resolved becomes unmanageably large. Attempting to explicitly represent the detailed uncertainty of all but the simplest problems is thus a gargantuan task.

Almost without exception, knowledge engineering approaches to dealing with uncertainty have led researchers to use nonprobabilistic calculi [Shortliffe, 1976; Zadeh, 1983] and, in a few cases, to use probability under unrealistically strong independence assumptions [Duda *et al.*, 1976, 1977, 1987]. However, although they are appealing at first glance, these approaches can be shown to lead to highly undesirable decision-making behavior [Lindley, 1982]. (We will discuss this issue in more detail in Chapters 3 and 6.) In contrast, decision analysis methods for reducing the size of explicit probabilistic models are based on sensitivity analysis [Howard, 1968], which limits the combinatorial growth of probabilistic models by distinguishing those parts of a model worthy of extensive modeling from those that are not. Hence, explicit probabilistic representation can be restricted to the subset of model elements that would truly benefit from such luxurious description. Furthermore, sensitivity analysis does not require modelers to make independence assumptions, although, of course, complex dependencies do somewhat increase the difficulty of the procedure.

Recently, researchers in decision analysis have developed a new notation for representing decision problems—**influence diagrams** [Miller *et al.*, 1976; Howard and Matheson, 1981]—that promises to have a significant impact on how decisions are modeled. Influence diagrams (described in detail in Chapter 4) are useful because they are well-defined mathematical structures that are also intuitively appealing [Owen, 1978]. In addition, unlike decision trees, influence diagrams grow linearly with the size of the problem and clearly and simply represent probabilistic and informational dependencies among problem variables. Finally, the recent development of algorithms to solve decision problems directly from their influence diagram representation [Olmsted, 1983; Shachter, 1986a] has made this new notation even more attractive.

In summary, the field of decision systems has grown, quite independently, within the fields of decision analysis and knowledge engineering. And while these two approaches to designing computer-based decision tools have yielded important methodological contributions, they have each encountered significant barriers to forming a comprehensive body of knowledge to guide such design. However, that each field has taken a complementary (though different) route to solving these problems makes the possibility of combining these disciplines very attractive.

APPLYING DECISION METHODOLOGIES TO MEDICAL DECISION-MAKING

Because complex medical decisions are often made when major uncertainties are present and when the stakes are extremely high, they are ideally suited for decision analysis [Sox, 1987]. Unfortunately, medical problems have been the subject of decision analysis almost exclusively in an academic environment. Thus, most physicians and patients have been unable to benefit from this new decision technology. As mentioned in the Preface, the high cost of professional decision analysis is one important reason there is so little of it in the realm of medicine. A responsibly performed analysis can currently cost tens (and sometimes hundreds) of thousands of dollars, which is, of course, far beyond the reach of most individuals. It is therefore not surprising that industry and government are the primary users of decision analysis.

Decision analysis is also not used in the field of medical decisions because it is generally quite difficult to measure an individual's preferences over the wide range of possible medical outcomes. These outcomes are usually described in terms of their associated morbidity, financial cost, length of life, and quality of life, which are difficult to quantify and combine into a meaningful measure. Furthermore, the stakes in a medical decision can be so high (e.g., life and death) that strong emotions commonly play a significant role in the decision-making process. While this strong emotional involvement encourages medical decision-makers to spend the time and effort necessary to decide well, such strong feelings also often hinder the ability of physicians and patients to think clearly about the problem. In addition, many aspects of institutionalized medicine—particularly the fears most physicians have of being too controversial in the eyes of their peers and of being sued for malpractice—greatly reduce the role that patient needs and desires play in medical decision-making and stand in the way of the widespread medical use of decision analysis.

Despite the cost of professional decision analysis, the difficulty of modeling patient preferences, and the awkward social structure of institutionalized medicine, some progress has been made in applying decision analysis to medical problems. In particular, for about a decade, a small but influential group of physicians has offered a clinical decision consultation service based primarily at the New England Medical Center of the Tufts University School of Medicine in Boston, Massachusetts [Plante et al., 1986]. However, while the service has addressed a very wide range of medical decision situations documented by a voluminous literature (comprehensively reviewed in Kassirer et al., [1987] and Pauker and Kassirer [1987]), it has failed to provide the kind of assistance professional decision analysis typically offers in a corporate setting. The assistance is limited by the service's strong focus on solving the decision problem at hand rather than on actively formulating it with the patient to produce insight and by a notable disregard for the patient's unique preferences and circumstances ("*If necessary*, the patient also is interviewed" [Plante et al., 1986, p. 1170, emphasis added]). In addition, the service uses only a small fraction of available decision analysis techniques and has incorporated few of the many fundamental methodological advances decision analysis research has produced since the service's inception.

The limitations of current medical decision analysis practice are understandable when one realizes the considerable effort required to thoroughly analyze a decision—typically several hundred person-hours—and the level of training needed to produce skilled professional decision analysts—typically, a Ph.D. in decision analysis followed by several years of practical experience. The economics of this situation make it infeasible to offer full decision analysis assistance to individual patients and their physicians without the aid of automation. However, by greatly reducing the cost and time required to analyze decisions, intelligent decision systems can potentially make professional-quality clinical decision analysis widely available.

A critical factor in producing effective medical decision tools is developing effective models of patient preferences. This development effort has been slow, although some initial contributions have begun to raise pertinent issues and have proposed plausible patient preference models [McNeil *et al.*, 1978; Sackett and Torrance, 1978; McNeil and Pauker, 1979; Pliskin *et al.*, 1980; McNeil *et al.*, 1981; Eraker and Sox, 1981; McNeil *et al.*, 1982; Beck *et al.*, 1982a, 1982b; Ciampi *et al.*, 1982; Harron *et al.*, 1983; Holtzman, 1983b; Christensen-Szalanski, 1984; Read *et al.*, 1984]. Furthermore, recent work in multiattribute value theory [Keeney and Raiffa, 1976; Keelin, 1977, 1981] and in using decision analysis for health and safety decisions [Howard 1979, 1980a, 1984; Owen *et al.*, 1978] is directly applicable to designing medical preference models.

For completeness, it is worth noting that several methodologies besides decision analysis have been used in developing medical decision tools. For example, simple algorithmic methods have been designed to deal with straightforward medical situations [Sox *et al.*, 1973; Kunz, 1982]. In addition, classical and Bayesian statistical methods have been used, primarily in a diagnostic setting [Warner *et al.*, 1961; Hall, 1967; Gorry and Barnett, 1968; Leaper *et al.*, 1972; Goldman *et al.*, 1977]. Knowledge engineering has also been applied to medical decision-making, producing interesting results that show that expert systems can be effective clinical assistants in narrow domains [Shortliffe, 1976; Pauker *et al.*, 1976; Davis *et al.*, 1977; Pople, 1977; Szolovitz and Pauker, 1978]. A comprehensive review of this work can be found in the literature [Shortliffe *et al.*, 1979; Clancey and Shortliffe, 1984]. However, as we will discuss in Chapters 3, 6, and 7, most of this research in medical decision-making has not dealt effectively with uncertainty and has failed to incorporate the patient's preferences into the decision-making process.

2

Using Formal Decision Methods

"Didn't you once ask what makes me go on, or do I imagine that you did? What gives me the strength to bear poverty, sickness, and, worst of all, hopelessness? That's a good question, my young friend. I asked the same question when I first read the Book of Job. Why did Job continue to live and suffer? So that in the end he would have more daughters, more donkeys, more camels? No. The answer is that it was for the game itself. We all play chess with Fate as partner. He makes a move; we make a move. He tries to checkmate us in three moves; we try to prevent it. We know we can't win, but we're driven to give him a good fight. My opponent is a tough angel."

—"A Friend of Kafka,"
Isaac Bashevis Singer

Formal decision methods lie at the heart of the theory and practice of intelligent decision systems. This chapter discusses their nature and develops a general framework for using them to provide real help. A key point made is that effective decision-making assistance consists mostly of helping decision-makers understand their decisions and develop the insight necessary for action. Such assistance must recognize and break through the ignorance often at the source of much decision-making difficulty—a notion in sharp contrast with more traditional views that focus on answering complex decision problems with little regard for how well the decision being answered has been formulated.

ALTERNATIVE APPROACHES TO DECISION-MAKING

When making a decision, people usually rely on their common sense—the large body of knowledge they have gained through experience. Unfortunately, common sense only applies to familiar problems [Simon, 1976, 1982]. As people confront situations they have never previously encountered, the task of making a choice becomes increasingly difficult.

Our ability to make decisions intuitively is further hindered by the fact that the way most people go about making decisions comes from a time when information was scarce. Abraham Lincoln, we are told [Simon, 1982], walked many miles to borrow books so he could tap the world's knowledge. He lived in a society where information was scarce and dear. In those days, any obtainable piece of it was treasured and, if possible, copied into human memory. In his age, then, most decision-makers had adequate means to absorb the information they managed to acquire.

Today, by contrast, a decision-maker must deal with a flood of data, and his primary problem is to determine which portions, if any, of this flood are important to his decision. Living, as we do, in an information-rich world, we must devote our decision efforts to managing attention, which has now become the scarce resource. That we have not learned to properly manage attention rather than information should be apparent to anyone who has recently applied for a loan at a bank or who has been subjected to an unnecessarily long (and costly) battery of medical tests.

Imagine, for instance, trying to decide which house to buy by first surveying all the easily available information on houses. A visit to any good realtor would soon show that even if we restrict our survey to a specific neighborhood, the task would be both formidable and wasteful, since much of that information (e.g., about houses far outside our price range) would not affect our decision anyway. It is interesting that realtors rarely show a client more than a few houses at a time—far fewer than they have access to.

Unfortunately, since most of our intuitive decision-making capabilities were developed to deal with a scarcity of information, they perform poorly when there is an abundance of it. We must therefore consider new decision-making procedures that reflect our current, unfamiliar needs. For instance, we can sometimes solve a new problem by generalizing it, answering the resulting broader question, and then providing the desired solution as an instance of the more general result. A second approach involves representing the unfamiliar decision problem in the language of a formal decision method such as linear optimization, dynamic programming, or decision theory. Algorithmic techniques can then be used to answer the formalized problem, and the resulting answer can be interpreted in the terms of the original problem to provide a solution. A third technique for solving an unfamiliar decision problem is to find a familiar situation in which a similar problem occurs and then translate the known solution method to the new domain. People's extraordinary ability to find analogies, even among such abstract entities as decision problems, makes this technique quite appealing.

Our focus in this book will be almost exclusively on the second type of decision-making procedure—formal decision methods. Such methods are particularly attractive for solving difficult decisions because, ignoring issues of efficiency, they are typically insensitive to the size and complexity of the problem. Thus, formal decision methods can be used to address decision problems that are too large and complex to be dealt with by intuition [Holtzman, 1984]. However, formal methods do have the significant shortcoming of requiring that real problems be formalized. Thus, one important objective here is to describe this formalization process and to simplify it.

FORMAL DECISION METHODS

Basic Assumptions About Using Formal Decision Methods

To appropriately use formal methods for decision-making, we must explicitly state some important assumptions that are often overlooked in similar discussions. Central to our discussion is the assumption that the decision-maker desires to make choices based on a consistent line of reasoning. Moreover, we assume the reasons underlying his decisions should not be formulated to explicitly conflict with his perception of reality.[1]

It is also important to note that for a formal decision methodology to be useful in solving real problems, its conclusions must ultimately make intuitive sense to the decision-maker. It is unreasonable to assume that the decision-maker will allocate valuable resources merely because of a logical argument. Thus, the decision-maker must develop an intuitive understanding of the validity of any successful recommendation for action, even if he or she does not have detailed knowledge of the underlying formalism that led to the recommendation. This requirement, in turn, makes it essential that the decision-maker clearly understand how the formal methodology is interpreted in terms of its implications for real action.

---

[1]This assumption is at the root of the concept of a normative theory, which follows directly from the fundamental notion of preferences.

Some Important Definitions About Formal Decision Methods

The study of decision-making differs significantly from most other academic endeavors because although it deals with very nonacademic problems, it provides solutions that rely on highly sophisticated formal techniques. As a result, there is a considerable communication gap between academicians and decision-makers that isolates the former from the issues that most concern the latter [Ackoff, 1987]. Thus, we need to carefully state the problem of making decisions from a perspective that reflects the questions that trouble decision-makers. We will do so by defining several important terms.

Making a **decision** means designing and committing to a strategy to irrevocably allocate valuable resources. Thus, as defined here, the decision-making process does not include the actual allocation of resources, which we will refer to as an **action**. This definition of a decision deliberately excludes choices that involve resources of low value, where the difference between alternative courses of action is insignificant. Furthermore, we are only concerned with irrevocable resource allocations. Hence, we assume that returning to the situation that existed prior to an irrevocable action is only possible, if at all, at considerable cost to the decision-maker.

When we talk about a decision, we can talk about its **domain** of discourse. Thus, we can distinguish medical decisions from business or military decisions, and decisions within these domains can be further grouped into subdomains. Consider the purchase of an automobile as an example. For this purchase, it is useful to know that cars typically have either two or four doors, can run on either gasoline or diesel fuel, and may or may not have a rear-window defogger. These facts belong to the domain of discourse of car purchases and enter into this type of decisions regardless of who is making the purchase. In general, the domain of a decision is, by definition, *generic* in nature—in other words, many decisions share the same domain.

We will have more to say about decision domains in Chapter 5 when we discuss classes of decisions. In particular, we will see that although it may be tempting at first to view the definition of a decision domain as a given feature of nature, we should view it instead as the product of a design effort aimed at exploiting natural similarities among decisions. Well-designed decision domains should help to simplify thinking about the decision at hand. However, for now, we can begin to think of the decision domain as the collection of all the decision elements that are generic—those that also concern most other decision-makers.

In contrast to its generic elements, we refer to the *unique* aspects of a decision as the **situation** in which it is made. Thus, the decision situation consists of all factors that are specific to the particular decision-maker and that may, therefore, not be present in another decision in the same domain. A decision situation can be further broken down into the decision-maker's **circumstances** and **preferences**.

Every decision-maker has a unique set of circumstances that can greatly affect the availability and the attractiveness of various choices. These circumstances include the decision-maker's state of information, which constitutes his perception of the possible consequences of his actions. Similarly, every decision-maker has desires that are expressed as preferences (or values) over the possible outcomes of the decision. It is worth noting that decision-making would be completely meaningless if the decision-maker were indifferent among all possible outcomes of his actions. In representing the decision-maker's preferences, it is important to quantify and measure together (i.e., **commensurate**) the various attributes that describe an outcome. For instance, it is often useful to distinguish the decision-maker's **time preference** (i.e., his desire to receive good outcomes sooner rather than later and bad outcomes later rather than sooner) from the rest of his preference structure.

Referring to our car purchase example, the decision-maker's circumstances might include that he has a wife and four small children, that he and his family like to go camping with a small sailboat that needs to be towed, and that he lives in an area that gets heavy winter snows. His preferences might include his willingness to trade fuel efficiency for power or safety, his desire for a stick shift as opposed to an automatic transmission, and, of course, his willingness to pay for the car and for its various features.

In Chapter 8, we will discuss the decisions faced by infertile couples seeking medical help. There, a couple's circumstances might be, for instance, that they are urban, middle class, with a male partner whose sperm count[2] is low, or that they are rural, of modest means, with the female partner having had an ectopic (tubal) pregnancy and the male partner having a left scrotal varicocele. In turn, their preferences might involve trade-offs among financial cost, pain and discomfort, and a successful pregnancy. Whether we are seeking medical treatments or purchasing automobiles, the decision situation denotes the aspects of that decision unique to the decision-maker—those that pertain to the decisions faced by few other, if any, individuals.

We will refer to the union of the decision domain and the decision situation as the **decision context**. Hence, the decision context includes both generic and unique elements, as illustrated in Fig. 2.1.

The domain and the circumstances of a decision often include a set of **constraints**. A **hard constraint** is inviolable. For instance, in a scheduling problem, there are exactly 24 hours in a day. A hard constraint can be introduced into a decision problem through a formal definition (e.g., 24 hours

---

[2]Medical and other technical terms used in the book are defined in the Glossary.

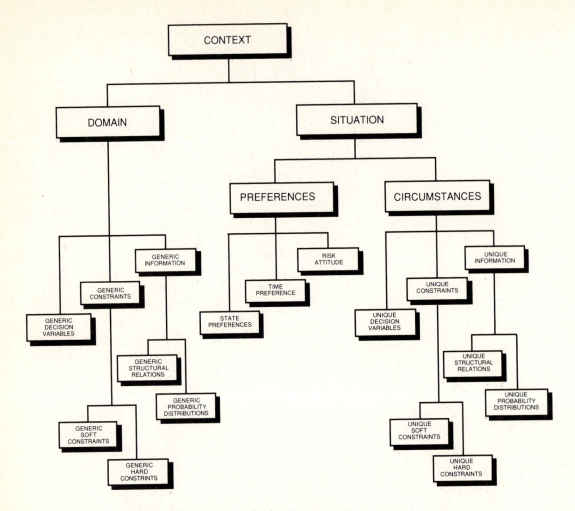

FIGURE 2.1   Structure of a decision context.

per day), or it can be imposed by the decision-maker as a matter of principle (e.g., a moral belief that precludes considering certain alternatives, such as murder). In general, few constraints are truly hard. In many cases, hard constraints are merely simplified representations of soft constraints. A **soft constraint** reflects a cost in using a resource. For instance, although a standard workday is 8 hours long, many individuals may be willing to work considerably longer if they are compensated with overtime wages.

In our car purchase example, the decision-maker may want to impose the hard constraint that for comfort and safety reasons, he will not consider cars with only two doors. This hard constraint is clearly a simplification of a more complex soft constraint—for instance, it would be hard to imagine he would not accept a two-door car for free. However, stating it as a hard constraint makes sense for all realistic possibilities and greatly simplifies his decision problem.

Another essential feature of any decision is the **alternatives** from which the decision-maker must choose. Strictly speaking, without alternatives, there would be no decision. As we will discuss in more detail in Chapter 3, alternatives can be designed from a set of **decision variables**. In turn, decision variables may be either generic—part of the decision domain—or unique—part of the decision circumstances. In our car purchase example, selecting a brand and model of car from those available in the market would be a decision variable that is generic to the domain of car purchase decisions and not specific to any given decision-maker. In contrast, the possibility of taking a loan offered by a family member exclusively for this purchase would be a decision variable unique to this particular decision and, thus, part of its circumstances.

When a decision has been followed by a corresponding allocation of resources—the action—the decision-maker is subject to a corresponding **outcome**. That is, after all uncertainties have been resolved, he or she will observe a state of the world. When the decision context includes uncertain elements, it is important to distinguish between decisions and outcomes. As we will discuss in more detail in Chapter 3, a good decision can lead to an unwanted outcome, and vice versa. This concept is illustrated in Fig. 2.2.

For instance, our car purchaser could make a fantastic deal where he buys a car from a highly reputable manufacturer at a very low price—a good decision—and ends up with a lemon that gives him nothing but trouble—a bad outcome. In contrast, he may be suckered into paying a great deal of money for a car that does not meet his needs—a bad decision—and end up selling the car at a profit because of a totally unexpected change in currency exchange rates—a good outcome.

Similarly, consider purchasing for $1 a 1-in-100 chance of getting $100 million. For most people, this would be a fantastic decision despite leaving the decision-maker with a 99-out-of-100 chance of a bad outcome (i.e., of losing $1). Alternatively, consider paying $1000 for a 99-out-of-100 chance of getting $1001 and a corresponding 1-in-100 chance of losing $100 million. Most individuals would see this as a very bad decision despite its near certainty (99-out-of-100 chance) of resulting in a good outcome.

For decisions involving uncertainty, we will extend our description of a decision situation along two additional dimensions. First, we must measure the decision-maker's **information** about the possible ways in which the uncertainty could be resolved. Second, we must establish the decision-maker's **risk attitude**, that is, his or her willingness to be exposed to risk.

A decision-maker's information is an important part of the decision circumstances. Besides codifying deterministic relationships among decision elements, measuring the information of a decision-maker means

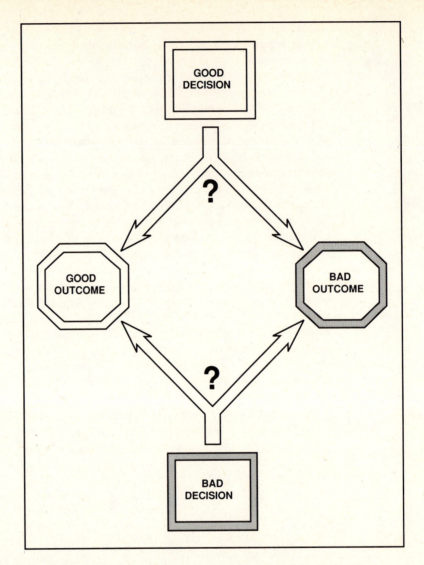

FIGURE 2.2   Good (bad) decisions do not guarantee good (bad) outcomes.

that we must both determine the possible values, or **range**, of each
uncertain element in the decision as perceived by the decision-maker or his
or her appointed experts and measure the likeliness of each value (also
according to the beliefs of the decision-maker or his or her appointed
experts), including any dependencies among uncertainties. Powerful
arguments can be made indicating that in decision-making a measure of
uncertainty must obey the axioms of a probability measure [Kolmogoroff,
1933, 1950]. In essence, measuring uncertainty in a way that violates the

axioms of probability would be equivalent to stating that the decision-maker is willing to accept deals where he or she would lose for sure—a statement that few individuals would make. While the details of this argument are beyond the scope of this book, Chapters 3 and 6 develop this point further. (Interested readers should refer to the literature [Cox, 1946; Tribus, 1969; Lindley, 1982] for a full discussion.) Hence, in addition to determining the range of every uncertain element of a decision problem, we need to assess a corresponding **probability distribution**.

It is important to be aware of the subjective nature of the decision-maker's perception of his or her decision problem and, in particular, of his or her information. Despite attempts by some misguided statisticians to lure us into a false sense of security through claims of impartiality and objectivity based on vast quantities of data, we need to avoid the illusion of certainty and recognize that *everything* we know is subject to interpretation. Regardless of how much data are available on a subject, we must interpret what we know in terms of the specific situation at hand. (This point is illustrated by the epigraph at the beginning of Chapter.3.) The quality of this interpretation is a critical ingredient of wise decision-making, since it is easy to abuse and misuse data [Huff, 1954; Jaffe and Spirer, 1987]. We will come back to the issue of interpretation and objectivity later in this chapter.

Finally, a decision-maker's risk attitude is a part of his or her preferences. Establishing it implies determining an unambiguous procedure for evaluating risky propositions that enables these risky propositions to be compared with riskless (i.e., certain) propositions. The topic of decisions involving uncertainty is addressed in more detail in Chapter 3.

The Nature of Formal Decision Methods

In the terms we have defined, a **formal decision method** is a *conditional statement*. Its antecedent is the context of a decision (i.e., a formal description of the decision domain and the decision situation, including a description of the decision-maker's preferences, information, and alternatives). Its consequent is a recommendation for action.

Formal decision methods are a special class of formal deductive methods because they reach **prescriptive** conclusions; that is, they yield recommendations for action. By construction, nothing in the decision method's antecedent (i.e., in the description of the decision problem) is prescriptive. Hence, the definition of a formal decision method must contain at least one prescriptive axiom [McCarthy, 1984], which we will refer to as an **action axiom**. An action axiom defines a set of sufficient conditions for action. Since these axioms embody the philosophical belief that underlies the method's prescriptions, their validity is central to the success of a formal decision method.

It is important to realize that because an action axiom is a statement about real actions in the terms of a formal system, it constitutes an explicit *leap of faith*. For instance, the principle of maximizing expected utility (discussed in Chapter 3) prescribes specific action strategies given a formal model of a decision problem in the language of decision theory. Although we can quite effectively argue for the validity of this principle, we cannot prove it. In fact, the concept of a proof of validity does not apply to any axiomatic statement, and, in particular, it does not apply to an action axiom.

More specifically, inferential statements that "jump out of a [formal] system" [Hofstadter, 1979] cannot be studied solely within their own formal context. In other words, to discuss the action axiom, we must argue in terms of its effect on real actions. However, regardless of how much we analyze an action axiom, it must retain an element of faithful trust. For although we can strive to show that a given action axiom is reasonable (i.e., that it "makes sense"), we cannot prove the correctness of the axiom unless it is embedded in a larger axiomatic system that itself contains an action axiom.

Validity Conditions for Formal Decision Methods

Having defined formal decision methods, we can now turn to discussing the conditions under which they are valid as tools for making decisions— conditions that must be necessarily informal. Specifically, a formal decision method is valid when it can be trusted as a tool for developing insight to deal with difficult decisions. For this discussion, it is useful to think of a formal decision method as a procedure that embodies an action axiom and, hence, in a very fundamental sense, as a procedural implementation of a leap of faith. Thus, the validity of a formal decision method can only be established informally.

The validity of a formal decision method is highly dependent on the specific domain to which it is applied. In particular, to help develop insight, a formal decision method must satisfy two domain-specific conditions— **local correctness** and **extrapolability**. This requirement becomes increasingly important as the domain departs from the class of decision problems familiar to the decision-maker.

To be locally correct in a given domain, a formal decision method must yield intuitively correct solutions to a representative class of **toy problems**—simple situations that are solvable "by inspection" and to which the formal technique is applicable. Toy problems can be used to test the correctness of a formal method because they are small enough to enable us to compare the method's solutions to those obtained intuitively. If there is an agreement between formal and intuitive solutions and if the class of toy problems used in this test is representative of the more general class of problems to which the formal method is to be applied, then the test strongly indicates that the method may be valid in the given domain.

However, local correctness is not enough to validate a formal method. In addition, the structure of decision problems in the given domain must exhibit a certain amount of regularity, such that the method is extrapolable with respect to that domain. Otherwise, the method would be quite useless since it would only apply to problems that are already addressable by intuition. Specifically, a formal method is extrapolable if an increase in the size and complexity of decision problems within its domain of discourse does not change their nature, thereby making the formal decision method inapplicable.[3] When the extrapolability condition is satisfied, it enables us to assume that within the given problem domain, solutions to toy problems (which can be intuitively verified) can be extrapolated to large problems (which cannot be checked, at least with as much accuracy). Note that when a method is extrapolable only for a restricted class of problems (e.g., for problems that are "not too complex or too large"), then the application of the corresponding formal method to problems in the domain is valid only when these problems belong to the restricted class.

When a formal decision method is both locally correct and extrapolable with respect to a decision domain, the method's solutions to large, unintuitive problems can be considered superior to intuitive (and, possibly, conflicting) solution alternatives, although this superiority can never be formally proved. In particular, formally derived solutions are superior because there is typically nothing in a sound formal method (aside from computational limitations) that is adversely affected by the complexity and size of the problem. This cannot be said of intuitive methods, which are subject to our bounded rationality [Simon, 1976, 1982].

Conversely, if either local correctness, extrapolability, or both conditions do not hold, then there is little reason to rely on the results of the formal method because intuitive methods tend to be much less sensitive to their assumptions than formal methods. Specifically, because they are general, intuitive decision methods typically work well even when the simplifying assumptions needed to formulate the decision problem in a manageable manner are somewhat inaccurate. We will refer to the ability of a solution method to remain valid in the presence of problem formulation inaccuracies as its **robustness**. Intuitive methods are generally much more robust than formal methods.

––––––––––––––

[3] In some cases, a formal method could be effective only for "large" (or "complex") problems and not for "small" (or "simple") ones. For example, statistical methods that require large sample sizes are inappropriate with small sample sizes.

To illustrate the concepts of local correctness and extrapolability, let us consider two well-known applications of formal models to real problems. The successful application of the formal techniques known collectively as linear programming to various problems—including the design of optimal chemical mixtures, the development of transportation algorithms, and the design of strategies for dealing with dynamic resource allocation—is an example where the two conditions can be intuitively justified [Hillier and Lieberman, 1967; Luenberger, 1973]. In contrast, many applications of nonlinear optimization theory to macroeconomics are questionable because they fail to satisfy one condition or the other, and sometimes even both [Holtzman, 1983a].

EFFECTIVE PROBLEM-SOLVING STRATEGIES

So far we have talked about a formal decision method in terms of its ability to yield an answer to a problem. In addition, the algorithm that usually embodies the formal technique can also contribute to the solution process by imposing, either implicitly or explicitly, an effective problem-solving strategy. Although not essential to understanding the nature of formal decision methods, problem-solving strategies can greatly affect their practical applicability. The effectiveness of these strategies often results from the guidance they provide for focusing the decision-maker's attention. In some important cases, it is this procedural contribution, rather than the specific answers it provides, that gives a formal method its power.

For example, the need to specify an objective function for an optimization algorithm guides the participants in the decision process to reason in a goal-directed fashion. While the concept of goal-directed, or backward, reasoning is well known as a powerful problem-solving heuristic in academic circles, particularly in mathematics and computer science [Polya, 1945; Nilsson, 1980], most decision-makers find the idea of reasoning in a backward fashion both unusual and refreshing. In fact, goal-directed decision-making directly addresses the need to focus attention in an information-rich environment. In the business community, this process is often called the **top-down** approach, and, correspondingly, managers refer to forward reasoning as the **bottom-up** approach. Chapters 3 and 4 will discuss the procedural benefits of backward reasoning using influence diagrams—a language for representing uncertain decision problems.

Other useful problem-solving heuristics have yet to be introduced outside the academic environment [Simon, 1977]. The introduction of such heuristics is likely to be an indirect consequence of the use of formal methods to provide answers to unfamiliar problems.

USING FORMAL DECISION METHODS IN PRACTICE

This section discusses the practical application of formal decision methods. The discussion begins by developing a taxonomy of ignorance and examining the relevance of current decision techniques to the various types of ignorance. It then explores the central role of distinction in decision-making, highlighting the limitations inherent in making distinctions and arguing that distinctions can always be modified to increase their usefulness because they are designed by people. Finally, the section develops in two steps a methodology for using decision methods. First, formal decision methods are discussed as a means for developing insight into a decision by using them to obtain answers to a sequence of increasingly refined formulations of the decision problem. Second, these methods are viewed as a means for focusing the attention of the decision participants, ultimately leading to a recommendation for action that is both intuitively appealing and defensible.

A Taxonomy of Ignorance

To determine how we can effectively use formal decision methods, it is useful to discuss the kind of difficulties we might encounter when dealing with unfamiliar decision problems. This issue can be thought of as a special case of the following more general question: What does it mean to "not know something?"

When asked about an unfamiliar topic, people often say "I know nothing about that." However, ignorance never occurs in a vacuum. The mere fact that one knows that one does not know something implies the availability of sufficient knowledge to at least recognize the ignorance. Hence, to describe ignorance, we need to describe the corresponding knowledge within which it occurs. This section proposes a taxonomy of ignorance that, in an admittedly speculative manner, classifies ignorance into seven levels according to the extent of an individual's knowledge about a given domain of discourse. In order of roughly increasing depth, the seven levels of ignorance are the following: combinatorial, Watsonian, Gordian, Ptolemaic, magical, dark, and fundamental.

The simplest type of ignorance—referred to as **combinatorial** ignorance—arises when we know how to find the desired answer in principle (i.e., we have a good model—a clear formal representation—of the problem and a theoretically effective solution method), but we cannot compute the answer in practice. For example, think of a linear programming problem with 10^{20} variables.

Watsonian ignorance refers to the situation where we have a complete model of the problem but where we lack an effective solution method. The canonical example of this type of ignorance, and the source of its name, is the well-known relation between Sherlock Holmes and Dr. Watson [Doyle, 1982]. Near the end of many of their adventures, Holmes and Watson have been exposed to essentially the same information, yet only Holmes can solve the case in question. Both characters share a set of facts and applicable inference rules; however, they have different solution methods. In other words, even though Watson has all the clues available to Holmes, his solution method does not enable him to distinguish the important from the unimportant information. The logical and literary power of the phrase "Elementary, my dear Watson" is that there is no discernible reason for Watson, or for most readers, not to have arrived at the same conclusion as Holmes.

The next level of ignorance is called **Gordian**, in reference to the knot that Gordius, king of Phrygia, tied for the future ruler of Asia to untie. At this level, we no longer have a complete model of the problem at hand. Hence, the problem is insolvable in its own terms, because we have explicitly excluded elements that, for some reason, we thought negligible or inappropriate. Therefore, regardless of the availability of an effective solution method, a solution is unattainable. In this case, then, answering the problem requires that we restate it. As for the Gordian knot itself, Alexander the Great reframed the problem of untying it, enabling him to solve the problem by cutting the knot with his sword. By the way, whether the knot had anything to do with history we shall never know, but Alexander did become the ruler of most of Asia.

As another illustration, consider the legend that claims that toward the end of his voyage to the new continent Christopher Columbus was faced with a possible mutiny because of a scarcity of drinking water. To calm his crew, Columbus allegedly challenged everyone to stand an egg on either end, with the successful egg stander to receive double water rations. It is easy to determine empirically that the task is next to impossible, particularly on the deck of a small ship in the middle of the ocean. According to the legend, after no one else had succeeded, Columbus slightly tapped the egg on one end and stood it on the small but relatively flat surface he had created. This action apparently reassured everyone that he was smart enough to be trusted to lead a venture as risky as theirs, which, rather than potable water, was the real question troubling the crew, who were beginning to doubt Columbus' sanity. Like Alexander the Great, Columbus solved an apparently insolvable problem by reframing it.

The question remains, of course, whether Alexander really untied the Gordian knot and whether Columbus really stood the egg on its end. For instance, in the case of Columbus, our answer would depend on our willingness to accept deforming the egg as a valid part of the solution. However, we must recognize the ambiguity of the problem statement, which neither allows nor prohibits such deformation. In any case, it seems much easier to accept Columbus' tapping procedure than to accept a solution to the famous "cannibals and missionaries" problem[4] [Nilsson, 1980] that assumes the existence of a bridge across the river. The "intelligent cheating" needed to deal with Gordian ignorance is, thus, only sometimes acceptable.

It is important to realize that Gordian ignorance (which is closely related to the concept of circumscription [McCarthy, 1980]) transcends simple puzzles and, in fact, pervades human thought. Regardless of the accuracy of our descriptions, we can never capture the full reality of a situation. It can even be argued that our uncanny ability to assume more than we are told has a strong evolutionary justification, because it allows us to deal with complex situations in a simple manner [Minsky, 1975, 1980]. However, despite its survival value, Gordian (or **circumscriptive**) ignorance is often a major reason for our inability to solve problems. The methodology discussed in this book is particularly relevant to the problem of Gordian ignorance as a barrier to effective decision-making. As we will see later in this section and in Chapter 3, decision analysis helps decision-makers deal with Gordian ignorance by facilitating the generation of new alternative courses of action.

Ptolemaic ignorance denotes a situation where despite having a model of the problem at hand and, perhaps, also a solution method, the model is highly inadequate for the problem at hand, and developing an actual solution is at best extremely awkward. This level of ignorance derives its name from the events that led to the paradigm shift from a Ptolemaic to a Copernican model of the solar system [Kuhn, 1962]. Although phenomena such as retrograde planetary motion (the fact that planets periodically appear to reverse the direction of their motion across the sky) could be described using epicyclic geocentric orbits (a hierarchical system of orbits where the primary orbit is centered on the earth—assumed to be stationary—and subsequent orbits are centered on a point rotating along the previous orbit), the physics necessary to explain such behavior would consist essentially of a collection of exceptions. In contrast, in a heliocentric (sun-centered) planetary system, most of the observed phenomena could be explained in a simple manner in terms of general principles. Kepler, and later Newton, would have had a much harder time developing a simple theory of celestial mechanics with the Ptolemaic framework than with the Copernican model. In general, we can argue that Ptolemaic ignorance is deeper than Gordian ignorance, since the latter can be overcome by augmenting the existing model whereas the former requires formulating a completely new model.

The ubiquitous nature of Gordian and Ptolemaic ignorance in human thought has motivated much research in the representation of knowledge. The fields of mathematics, decision analysis, and artificial intelligence, in

---

[4] The cannibals and missionaries problem consists of devising an algorithm for three cannibals and three missionaries to cross a river using a two-person boat such that there are never more cannibals than missionaries in any place at the same time.

particular, have addressed this type of ignorance very successfully by producing effective representation languages that make explicit important aspects of their domains of discourse.

Sometimes our models of reality contain an essential element for which we have no effective formalization. We refer to these as magical elements and to this lack of knowledge as **magical** ignorance. Two simple examples of such a situation are the behavior of a Stradivarius violin and the pain-relieving effect of aspirin. In either case, although our current understanding can account for much of the observed phenomena, our descriptions need to explicitly include unexplained elements. As an old advertisement for Alka-Seltzer® (which contains aspirin) states, "no one knows *how* it works, but everyone knows *that* it works."

An interesting class of instances of magical ignorance can be illustrated by the thought experiment of giving a box of matches (with instructions) to a caveman. The matches would be a mixed blessing for the individual who receives them. On the one hand, he would gain power from his ability to start a fire at will. On the other hand, he would become dependent (probably unknowingly) on the success of a process he does not understand. Consider, for instance, the consequences of getting the matches wet. One could easily compare this dependence with some people's reliance on a skilled auto mechanic. Magical ignorance also has profound implications on the relationship between patients and their physicians, particularly in the presence of modern-day technology.

When we simply do not have any model of a given situation, we suffer from **dark** ignorance. The quintessential example of dark ignorance we all must deal with is embodied in the question "What is life?" For most of us, the only way to model life is as a single magical element, which is no model at all.

The deepest level of ignorance occurs when we are not even aware of a given situation, let alone have a model for it. We can refer to this as **fundamental** ignorance, and, obviously, we cannot give any current examples to illustrate this concept. It is possible, however, to imagine the plight of avid sunbathers prior to the discovery of ultraviolet light and its relation to skin cancer. Our extensive perceptual limitations are but one major source of fundamental ignorance.

Having defined these seven levels of ignorance, summarized in Fig. 2.3, we can immediately notice that they are not mutually exclusive. In fact, one could argue that all are always present in everything we do and think about. However, our ignorance does not become apparent (one might say it does not actually exist) until it stands in the way of something we want to accomplish. In more technical terms, our ignorance comes into being when we have a break (or a discontinuity) in existence [Winograd and Flores, 1986]. For example, someone's magical ignorance about how a car operates does not exist for that person until the car stops working. This perspective helps us illustrate what we mean by providing a decision-maker with the

Type of Ignorance	Characteristics	Example(s)
• Combinatorial	Appropriate Model and Solution Method Are Available, but Cannot Compute Answer	Very Large Linear Program
• Watsonian	Appropriate Model Is Available, but Solution Method Is Incomplete	Sherlock Holmes and Dr. Watson
• Gordian	Model Is Incomplete	Gordian Knot; Columbus' Egg
• Ptolemaic	Model May Be Complete, but Is Awkward	Ptolemy Versus Copernicus
• Magical	Model Contains One or More Unexplained Elements	Alka-Seltzer
• Dark	Aware of Issue, but No Model Is Available	Life
• Fundamental	Unaware of Issue	- ? -

FIGURE 2.3 Seven-level taxonomy of ignorance.

insight necessary for action. Specifically, providing insight can be viewed as removing all ignorance impinging on the decision at hand—that is, assisting the decision-maker to negotiate the break in existence that led to his or her need to make a decision.

Extensions to the Taxonomy of Ignorance

This seven-level taxonomy of ignorance suffices for our discussion. Nonetheless, it is interesting to explore two directions in which the classification could be extended. A clear limitation of the current taxonomy is that it is deterministic. Thus, a first extension would be to add the dimension of uncertainty. This addition would make our classification of ignorance considerably richer by allowing it to account for disjunctive knowledge, that is, knowledge about many possible scenarios. A second interesting extension would account for the dynamic—or time-dependent—nature of knowledge. To illustrate the need for explicit time dependence, consider the type of ignorance faced by the receiver of a telegram from an unknown source just prior to reading the message.

An important problem for decision-makers is the need to plan for unanticipated (as opposed to uncertain) situations. Commonly referred to as unknown unknowns—or **unkunks**, for short—these situations have received little attention in the literature, perhaps because we have not had a good language to describe them. The taxonomy of ignorance developed here may provide a useful starting point for designing such a language. For instance, distinguishing between the different levels of ignorance where an unkunk occurs might simplify its analysis. Such a distinction would allow us to realize that not all unkunks are fundamental, which is a likely misperception. In fact, it may be feasible to devise ways to deal with shallower cases of ignorance where unkunks might occur (such as Ptolemaic and magical) but where the possibility of expert advice exists. Also, one person's fundamental ignorance may well be another's knowledge. In this case, extending our taxonomy to address uncertainty and time dependence would be particularly useful.

Relevance of Current Decision Techniques to the Taxonomy of Ignorance

It is interesting to comment on the current status of decision techniques in terms of their effect on ignorance. Of particular importance are the products of research in mathematical optimization and knowledge engineering, for which decision-making is a central concern. As is usually the case with the birth of a scientific research area, the founding works in both fields provided effective representations for problems for which previous descriptions were, at best, awkward. For mathematical optimization and knowledge engineering, the representational change was sufficiently drastic to be considered a paradigm shift [Kuhn, 1962] and, hence, to deal with Ptolemaic ignorance. However, once mathematical optimization concepts (such as objective functions, optimality conditions, lotteries, and shadow prices) and knowledge engineering concepts (such as inference engines, rules, frames, semantic networks, and means-ends analysis) were established, most of the research effort in these fields moved away from Ptolemaic concerns.[5]

---

[5] Designing representation languages has remained an important concern in knowledge engineering. However, although logic programs and object-oriented languages are examples of significant contributions, current research is concerned more with improving the existing paradigm than with replacing it.

The major concern in mathematical optimization has been to improve the efficiency of solution algorithms and, thus, to deal with combinatorial ignorance. Although strict efficiency has also received some attention in knowledge engineering, the most important contributions of this field, from the point of view of decision-making, have dealt with Watsonian and, to a lesser extent, Gordian ignorance.

The Role of Distinction in Decision-Making

As we have just noted, most normative decision research has focused on developing algorithmic approaches to solving already formalized decision problems. Formal decision methods, such as mathematical programming and decision theory, are solution techniques and, as such, do not explicitly address the issue of problem formulation. These algorithms need to be complemented with a methodology primarily concerned with *formulating* decisions rather than with *solving* them.

As we mentioned in our discussion of ignorance, the need to decide always arises in the context of a break in the continuity of the decision-maker's existence. To provide the insight necessary for the decision-maker to act, we must assist him or her in acquiring or developing whatever knowledge is necessary to either remove or sufficiently mitigate any ignorance arising in the context of the decision at hand.

Formulating a decision and solving the formulated problem concern different levels of ignorance. Whereas developing new solution methods is largely concerned with combinatorial and Watsonian ignorance, developing new ways to formulate problems must address Gordian, Ptolemaic, and sometimes even deeper levels of ignorance. Solving a formulated problem is essentially a computational task; formulating it, on the other hand, is primarily a conceptual and representational issue.

To better appreciate the task of formulating a decision, consider the meaning of the verb *to decide*. In its original latin meaning, *to decide* means *to cut off* [Gove, 1971]. Interpreting decision-making as an act of separation has profound implications for using formal decision methods. In particular, a decision-maker must "carve out" a definition of his decision problem by *making distinctions* that reflect his view of reality.

Consider the job of a surgeon as an analogy. At first glance, the surgeon's task seems to consist of opening the patient's body as cleanly as possible, removing (or modifying) the afflicted parts, and neatly closing when the operation is complete. However, almost anyone who has seen an open human body would, to some extent, disagree with this view, because the human body is a closely knit continuum of live tissue, not just an assemblage of crisply defined parts. Distinguishing parts such as the heart, veins, brain, cells, or bones constitutes a highly simplified view of reality.

More accurately, a large part of a surgeon's skill is focused on defining (i.e., deciding) what to remove. In other words, he is constantly designing distinctions that define his task.

Like surgeons, decision-makers also rely heavily on making distinctions. For example, before a decision-maker can make a choice, he must have a set of alternatives from which to choose. Alternatives are by definition the result of distinction and, thus, the product p human design. Therefore, an essential task for a decision-maker, perhaps his most important task, is to design his perception of the world as a set of distinctions. Consequently, effective decision assistance must consist largely of managing the decision-maker's distinctions.

Inherent Limitations of Distinctions

When dealing with a set of conceptual distinctions (such as representations of the human body or alternative courses of action), we must recognize that *all* distinctions are limited. For example, having a preconceived breakdown of the anatomy and physiology of something as complex as the human body is valuable because it vastly reduces the burden of designing specific distinctions when time is short (e.g., in the operating room). However, we must remember that the map is not the territory and, in fact, that the map is a necessarily **incomplete** (and hence, ultimately, incorrect) model of the territory. Any model of reality becomes increasingly inappropriate the closer it is scrutinized. No one, for instance, could give a general rule to determine whether a given cell belongs to what we refer to as the heart. This notion has been exploited by Zadeh [1978] in his definition of a fuzzy set.

An additional weakness inherent in all distinctions is that they must be based on a **stationarity** assumption. That is, making a distinction requires that we assume that, at some level, the world as we perceive it stays the same. Such permanence must be assumed for a model, which is a collection of distinctions, to exist at all; however, it may well occur at a level of abstraction far removed from the domain of discourse of the model (e.g., at a high-order derivative for a system of differential equations). As a result, distinctions can break down when a stationarity assumption is violated.

For example, a common model of the human voice views the vocal tract as a resonant cavity excited by the vocal folds as air passes through them [Rabiner and Schafer, 1978; Holtzman, 1980]. Although both the resonator and the excitation vary in time, the model assumes that the former varies much more slowly than the latter and that the relation between these rates of change remains nearly constant. However, while this assumption is very good for modeling vowels, it is well known that the model breaks down during certain consonants (such as plosives—e.g., "p" and "b"), which are made by rapid changes in the shape of the vocal tract. The point to notice is that although this excitation/resonator model is highly effective, it is based on an assumption of permanence, which, in turn, is the source of important model limitations.

Incompleteness and stationarity are two crucial limitations of all distinctions. Therefore, distinctions are always in some sense incorrect and can become highly inappropriate when used outside the specific context for which they were developed. This fact has major implications, because the idea of distinction is the essence of Western thought [Kapleau, 1967; Capra, 1975; Howard, 1980b]. For instance, an extended form of Boolean algebra (a mathematical representation of logic) can be constructed directly from the notion of distinction, which is equivalent to the notion of form [Spencer-Brown, 1972].

Distinctions as Manufactured Objects

That distinction is a part of our everyday life is evident from the fact that the consequences of our ability and willingness to distinguish, such as the modus ponens syllogism,[6] are so intuitively obvious that most of us find it difficult to imagine a world where they do not hold. However, as in the surgeon's case, distinctions are artificial (i.e., the product of design) and, hence, modifiable [Simon, 1982].

Generally, this design effort is performed quite effortlessly and often goes unnoticed because it draws heavily on the set of distinctions we have inherited through culture. Without this heritage, we would be unable to perform many of the complex tasks we accomplish daily. In particular, most of our decision problems are greatly simplified by having access to a vast collection of distinctions about such matters as personal relations, objects, timing, goals, and feelings.

However, it is crucial to realize that although these distinctions are very convenient artifacts, they are the product of human design and, therefore, are neither absolute nor unique and, ultimately, neither correct nor incorrect. As a result, making a decision can be difficult because it is based on a set of distinctions that render it awkward. Since these distinctions are implicit in the decision problem to be solved, a likely source of difficulty in decision-making occurs because the problem itself is inappropriately presented. This is an important case of Ptolemaic and Gordian ignorance.

The fact that the difficulty of a decision problem often lies not in the method used to solve it but in the question about the decision itself is, as we have seen, central to this book. An important consequence of this point of view is that to help decision-makers with difficult problems, we must often concentrate not on *solving* their problems but on *formulating* them.

---

[6] The modus ponens syllogism states that if A is known to be true and we know that A implies B, then B is also known to be true. See the Glossary for a more rigorous definition.

A Methodology for Using Formal Decision Methods

Developing Insight by Obtaining Answers

As defined earlier in this chapter, a formal decision method is a conditional statement whose antecedent is a formalized decision problem (a system of axioms) and whose consequent is a prescription for action. Strictly speaking, a conclusion reached by applying the method to the problem description is a tautology. In other words, the purpose of a formal decision method is to tell the decision-maker something that, in principle, he or she already knows. Simply stated, the method is saying the following: "If you believe your model represents your decision problem, then you should act as my conclusion recommends." The conditional nature of a formal decision method is illustrated in Fig. 2.4.

It is important to note that a formal method makes no statement about the correctness of its input and does not deal with the validity of the prescription that constitutes its output; it merely deduces the logical implications for action from the decision-maker's assumptions, as stated in the formal description of his or her problem.

In practice, using formal decision methods requires that we formally capture the decision context in question as a decision model and that we interpret the formal recommendations resulting from applying the decision method to the model. Hence, we can view the practical use of formal decision methods as a three-stage process (illustrated in Fig. 2.5) whose three stages are **formulation** (i.e., development of the formal decision model), **evaluation** (i.e., computation of a recommendation from the model), and **appraisal** (i.e., interpretation of the formal recommendation).

However, this strictly sequential approach to using formal decision methods has a major shortcoming—it does not account for the likely disagreement between the decision-maker and the method's prescription. In fact, such disagreement is almost certain to occur. Given that he requires

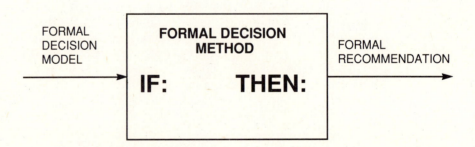

FIGURE 2.4   A formal decision method is a conditional statement.

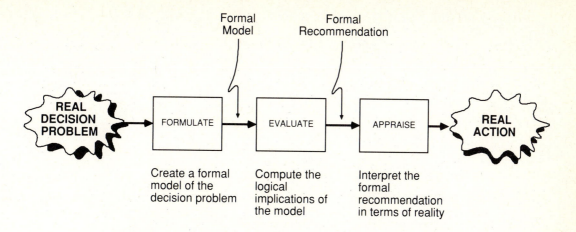

FIGURE 2.5   The three formal decision stages: formulate, evaluate, and appraise.

assistance to gain new insight into his problem, we can assume the deci-sion-maker is having difficulty dealing with his decision. Therefore, a for-mal analysis of the decision is likely to expose many of the inconsistencies and lack of focus that made the decision difficult in the first place. More-over, such disagreement is very beneficial, because it exposes important flaws in either the decision-maker's understanding of his decision (i.e., how he perceives and interprets it) or his logic. This is so because (as we have discussed) given the axioms and theorems that constitute the problem de-scription and the formal decision method, the prescription is a tautology.

A simple way to deal with the possible unacceptability of a formally obtained prescription—in fact to take advantage of it—is to extend the se-quential process by explicitly adding a **feedback** path, as shown in Fig. 2.6. Such a closed-loop decision process allows the decision-maker to react to any surprising element of the formal prescription by reevaluating and pos-sibly modifying his formulation. Alternatively, if after developing enough insight he agrees with the suggested strategy or if he determines that his disagreement results solely from logical error, he may choose to follow the formal prescription. Hence, by producing a sequence of increasingly re-fined decision models, we can help the decision-maker develop the insight necessary for action [Tani, 1975; Holtzman, 1981].

The main value of this three-stage, closed-loop decision process is that it constitutes a framework for developing insight by obtaining answers to a sequence of increasingly accurate descriptions of a real decision problem. For the process to do this, the decision-maker must be actively involved in the formulation and appraisal stages, an involvement that yields insight by exposing flaws in his assumptions and logic.

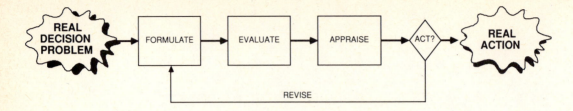

FIGURE 2.6   Closed-loop decision process.

Focusing Attention

The closed-loop decision process described in Fig. 2.6 can be viewed as a blueprint for a conversation. This conversation can focus both on developing new possibilities for action and on generating actual commitments for action [Winograd and Flores, 1986]. This conversation is illustrated in Fig. 2.7. It involves two key participants: the decision-maker (and his or her team of domain experts) and a decision-facilitator (e.g., a decision analyst). During the formulation stage of the process, the decision-maker teaches the details of the decision at hand (e.g., available resources, deadlines, attitude toward taking risks) to the decision-facilitator, who learns by building an appropriate decision model. These activities are reversed during the appraisal stage, where the decision-facilitator teaches the decision-maker the implications of the formal recommendation for action obtained during the evaluation stage. Most of the insight developed in the closed-loop decision process shown in Fig. 2.6 results from this interchange of information and new knowledge between the decision-maker and the decision-facilitator. Moreover, this interchange is effectively guided and focused by the formal machinery embodied in the evaluation stage (e.g., through sensitivity analysis). This attention-focusing effect assists the decision participants in producing an increasingly simple, yet representative, model of the decision as the process progresses.

From the perspective of this conversation, it is useful to view a formal decision method as a closed inferential procedure whose input is an axiomatic description of a decision process and whose output is a prescription for action. The efficiency of the three-stage decision process can be improved by considering the input/output, or *black box*, behavior of this procedure.

Experience in using formal decision methods and, particularly, in using decision analysis (which we will discuss in Chapter 3) shows that when people confront a difficult decision problem, they have an uncanny ability to list the factors **relevant** to their problem, that is, to circumscribe their problem. Formal techniques, on the other hand, are poor at accomplishing this circumscriptive task [McCarthy, 1980].

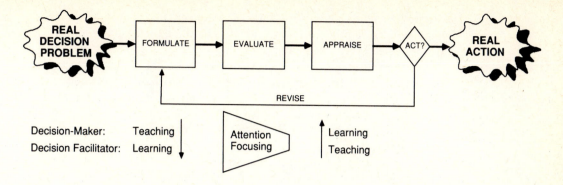

FIGURE 2.7   The closed-loop decision process is a carefully engineered conversation.

The situation is reversed when the task involves sorting, in order of importance, the elements of a list of factors relevant to a decision. In this case, formal techniques tend to significantly outperform common sense. This latter claim requires that we more precisely define the term *important*. For the present discussion, we will define the **importance** of a factor as its ability to change the recommended action strategy given the factor's range of possible values. We will elaborate on this definition in Chapter 3, when we have introduced the concept of sensitivity.

The efficiency of a formal decision method is often mistaken for the computational efficiency of the inference procedure that lies within the decision process. However, given the previous discussion, we can argue that a more complete view should include the efficiency of the formulation and appraisal stages as well. Given the current availability of powerful algorithms and computational facilities, it is often the efficiency of these two outer stages of the decision process—and, particularly, the formulation stage—that imposes the most constraining limits on the applicability of formal methods.

The efficiency of the formulation stage is directly related to how effective the target formal language is as a means of representing the decision problem. If the decision-maker can easily produce a simple formal statement (i.e., one that is close to his or her view of the problem), then the formulation effort needed is likely to be small. This effort will be further reduced if, in addition, the resulting representation is succinct. As an added benefit, making the representation succinct may make it easier to evaluate the problem in the inference stage and to perform the appraisal effort that follows.

Unfortunately, because decision-makers are generally unable to distinguish what is important from what is relevant, they tend to construct very large representations. By necessity, then, a formal decision method must be designed to contend with a trade-off between how much the decision-maker will be required to adapt to the language of the method and how much the method fits his or her thought processes.

One way to deal with this trade-off is to realize that the formulation task can be performed gradually through a formal **attention-focusing method**. An attention-focusing method is a formal technique that contains an **attention-focusing axiom**, which is like an action axiom, except that instead of making a statement about action strategies, it yields a sorting function for the elements of the formal model that constitute its input. Like an action axiom, an attention-focusing axiom is a leap of faith (and, thus, subject to local correctness and extrapolability criteria). Such axioms are best viewed as heuristics and are usually developed with respect to an associated decision method or to another attention-focusing method.

Usually, the sorting function produced by an attention-focusing method orders the elements of its input model by their importance in the terms of an associated decision method. Hence, we can use an attention-focusing method as a *preprocessor* for its associated decision method, thus allowing the latter to be applicable to a considerably wider class of inputs. Clearly, for an attention-focusing method to be useful, its input language and its computational needs should be, respectively, simpler and less extensive than those of its associated method. In decision analysis, the concept of a formal attention-focusing method is used to justify the widespread use of deterministic sensitivity analysis (as well as other more advanced methods, including time and risk sensitivity, probabilistic sensitivity, value of information, and value of control). More generally, the concept of an attention-focusing method is a formalization of the idea of heuristic problem solving as applied to decision problems [Simon, 1977].

Figure 2.8 illustrates the use of attention-focusing methods. This figure shows a progressive formulation process that ends in a final decision method, which, ultimately, recommends an action strategy. This framework

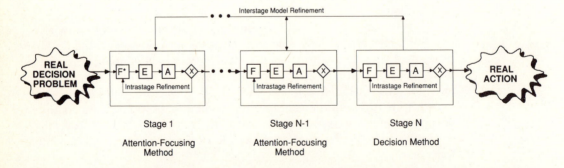

FIGURE 2.8 Progressive formulation using attention-focusing methods as preprocessors for the final decision method.

for formal decision-making has several desirable features. First, and foremost, the framework encourages the decision-maker to actively participate in the decision process. In particular, formulation, appraisal, and action tasks (respectively labeled F, A, and X throughout the figure) explicitly require the decision-maker's participation. In general, evaluation—labeled E—requires little or no participation.

Second, the most onerous formulation effort (labeled F* in the figure) in this framework occurs at the beginning of the process. Thus, most of the formulation effort occurs in terms of the input language of the first attention-focusing method, which, by design, should be the simplest input language of all the methods in the sequence. Formulation in the other stages should be much simpler, because a well-designed collection of methods would be constructed so that the result of each attention-focusing method would directly yield an input for the next (associated) method.

A final feature of this decision framework is that it can maintain a fairly constant level of computational effort throughout the decision process. This feature can be explained by noting that each successive phase receives an increasingly succinct input and, correspondingly, can depend on an inference procedure that requires increasingly greater computational resources. Maintaining a constant level of computational burden is desirable if we apply the **wince factor** heuristic for engineering designs, which states that "If a designer can easily tell where to invest an extra unit of effort to improve the design, then the design is not properly balanced" [Howard, 1968]—that is, some areas are overdeveloped, while others are underdeveloped.

Designing the process to have a constant wince factor can be justified by acknowledging the generally reasonable belief that the original model has many unimportant elements that can be safely removed by simple procedures. As successive attention-focusing heuristics are applied to the model (to yield the needed sequence of input models for each successive method), it becomes increasingly difficult to distinguish important from unimportant model elements. Hence, we need an increasingly complex process to compute the desired sorting function.

3

Decision Analysis

In the days when the student was a novice, the teacher once came to him as he sat working on a decision problem.
"What are you doing?" asked the teacher.
"I am trying to solve this problem without using a prior distribution."
"Why are you avoiding the use of a 'prior'?" asked the teacher.
"I do not want the solution to reflect any of my personal biases. You see, I am trying to be objective."
The teacher shut his eyes.
"Why do you close your eyes?" the student asked his teacher.
"So the room will be empty."
At that moment, the student was enlightened.

Decision analysis is a discipline for assisting decision-makers facing difficult decisions that involves applying decision theory—a formal decision method—to real decisions. This chapter discusses decision analysis in terms of the general framework for using formal decision methods developed in Chapter 2. A primary role of decision analysis is to focus the decision-maker's attention on important aspects of the decision and away from unimportant ones, which guides the decision-maker toward a simpler and more effective formulation of the decision at hand and, hence, toward a clear course of action. Viewing decision analysis in this light is a first step toward a methodology for automating it in the form of intelligent decision systems.

DECISION THEORY

The desire for a normative theory of decision-making has led to the postulation, during the last half century, of several reasonable action axioms. Some particularly successful examples are the minimax rule, the various forms of mathematical programming (e.g., linear, integer, convex), and the maximization of expected utility. Of these axiomatic statements, only **maximum expected utility (MEU)** is specifically designed to deal with uncertainty and constitutes the foundation of the discipline of decision analysis.

Based on ideas that date back to Bernoulli [1738] and Laplace [1812], Savage [1972] defended the wisdom of basing decisions on the principle of MEU, using the concept of a utility function [von Neumann and Morgenstern, 1947] to represent the decision-maker's preferences and the concept of probability [de Finetti, 1937, 1968] to measure his or her uncertainty. These efforts led to what is known today as decision theory.

In a nutshell, decision theory is a mathematical framework for determining a best action from a description of a decision problem. In addition to providing optimal recommendations, decision theory defines many important decision-related concepts, such as the value of information and the value of control.

Decision theory is built on the formal definition of mathematical logic [Carnap, 1958; Tarski, 1965] and probability measure [Kolmogoroff, 1933, 1950]. For this discussion, we will consider these formalisms as sufficiently well accepted to make it unnecessary to explicitly analyze them here. However, we are implicitly assuming that the decision-maker chooses to view the world with a Western perspective. In many Eastern philosophies, the concepts of logic and, more importantly, of decision-making are moot [Kapleau, 1967; Capra, 1975; Howard, 1980b]. It is with respect to Western thought that logic and probability are assumed to be self-evident.

Five Axioms of Decision Theory and Their Local Correctness

In addition to logic and probability, decision theory requires that the decision-maker accept a set of five axioms of utility theory, which together imply the MEU action axiom. Thus, MEU is not really an axiom but rather a theorem within utility theory. However, to be consistent with previously defined terminology, we will refer to it as an action axiom. Given our previous discussion on the validity of formal methods for real decision-making, we need to verify that the MEU action axiom satisfies the conditions of local correctness and extrapolability in terms of personal decision-making. In the following discussion, we assume the reader is familiar with the fundamentals of decision theory as presented by North [1968], Raiffa [1970], or McNamee and Celona [1987]. In particular, the concepts of preference, outcome, lottery (or gamble), and certain equivalent are used without explanation.[1]

The five axioms that define utility theory are developed by Savage [1972, Sections 5.2 and 5.3] and presented by Howard [1970] in a simplified form. We now list these five axioms and, subsequently, explain them and discuss the local correctness of each. We then consider the extrapolability of the full set of axioms with respect to the area of personal decisions.

- U1.   ORDERABILITY AXIOM

  The decision-maker's preferences impose a complete transitive ordering on the outcomes pertinent to his or her decision.

- U2.   MONOTONICITY AXIOM

  Let $\succ$ denote strict preference and $\{ X_1, p_1; X_2, p_2; ...; X_N, p_N \}$ denote a lottery with N outcomes, X_i, and corresponding probabilities, p_i.

  If A and B are outcomes such that $A \succ B$ and if $1 \geq p > q \geq 0$, then: $\{ A, p; B, (1 - p) \} \succ \{ A, q; B, (1 - q) \}$.

- U3.   DECOMPOSABILITY AXIOM

  Compound lotteries (i.e., lotteries whose outcomes are themselves lotteries) can be simplified using the laws of probability without affecting preferences.

- U4.   CONTINUITY AXIOM

  Let $\succ$ denote strict preference, $\sim$ denote indifference, and $\{X_1, p_1; X_2, p_2; ...; X_N, p_N\}$ denote a lottery with N outcomes, X_i, and corresponding probabilities, p_i.

  If A, B, and C are outcomes such that $A \succ B \succ C$, then there exists a unique number $p \in (0, 1)$ such that $\{A, p; C, (1 - p) \} \sim \{B, 1\}$.

- U5.   SUBSTITUTABILITY AXIOM

  The decision-maker is indifferent between any lottery and its certain equivalent.

While the MEU axiom is not explicitly contained in the above set, Savage [1972, Section 5.3] proves that a utility function can be constructed for a decision-maker wishing to abide by all five axioms so that he will always want to act to maximize this function. Savage's proof restates and simplifies a similar one developed by von Neumann and Morgenstern [1947]. Hence,

---

[1]Technical terms are defined in the Glossary.

although the MEU action axiom is not explicitly included in this formulation of decision theory, it is implicitly stated within it.

The orderability axiom (U1) states that the decision-maker can consistently and completely rank all possible outcomes he could receive as a result of his decision. This axiom implicitly requires the decision-maker have a well-defined set of outcomes to consider. By *well defined*, we mean the decision-maker has successfully circumscribed his decision context to make the definition of each outcome clear. The problem of circumscribing a real context has received some attention in the literature [McCarthy, 1980] and has been characterized operationally by Howard [1981b] in terms of a hypothetical "clarity" (or "clairvoyant") test. Still, no real decision problem can be defined completely without ambiguity. Outcomes must be defined so they are clear to the decision-maker in the particular context of the decision at hand. Given our previous discussion of Gordian ignorance, we can see that our ability to circumscribe real decision problems is a mixed blessing.

To analyze the local correctness of an axiom, we use the criterion offered by Savage [1972, p. 7]:

> So, when certain maxims are presented for your consideration, you must ask yourself whether you try to behave in accordance with them, or, to put it differently, how you would react if you noticed yourself violating them.

We can argue for the local correctness of axiom U1 by recognizing that a transitive ordering of the decision-maker's preferences over the outcome set is a direct consequence of the reasonable desire of most decision-makers not to voluntarily engage in sure-loss actions. A sure-loss action is defined as an act guaranteed to leave the decision-maker worse off than he or she was prior to acting. The metaphor of a **money pump** is often used to illustrate this concept [Raiffa, 1970; Howard, 1970].

For example, consider three teams: A, B, and C. When matched against each other, A always beats B, B always beats C, and C always beats A. A naïve gambler could become a money pump (i.e., could be made to give all his money away) if he preferred betting on team A over team B, on B over C, and on C over A to win the championship. If it is not obvious why this is undesirable, suppose you give him a free ticket—an A ticket—that pays him money if team A wins the championship. Since he would rather bet on C than on A, you could sell him a C ticket for some money and his A ticket. Similarly, you could sell him a B ticket for some money and his C ticket. Now, you could sell him back is original A ticket for some money and his B ticket. This cycle could continue indefinitely until the unfortunate gambler—a money pump—would have given all his money away. Because no one would deliberately want to be a money pump, axiom U1 makes intuitive sense.

We can therefore argue that the orderability axiom (U1) is locally correct. In fact, defining a transitively ordered outcome set is an integral part of the formulation stage described in Chapter 2 and, by itself, can contribute significantly to developing insight.

The monotonicity axiom (U2) should be self-evident. It simply states that given two outcomes, one of which is strictly preferred to the other, and two lotteries, both involving exactly these two outcomes but having different probability assignments, the decision-maker will prefer the lottery with a higher probability of getting the more desired outcome. Since there is no reason for a decision-maker to explicitly violate this axiom, we can claim that it is locally correct.

The decomposability axiom (U3) is informally referred to as the "no-fun-in-gambling" (or "no-pain-in-gambling") axiom [Howard, 1970], because it implies that the decision-maker derives no pleasure (or displeasure) from "decomposing" (breaking down) an uncertain event into a set of components that, together, yield a compound event with a probability of occurring equal to that of the original. This is clearly a normative statement, since it opposes the observed behavior of most clients of a gambling casino. From a normative perspective, however, the decomposability axiom requires that for the purpose of decision-making, no distinction be made between compound and simple lotteries describing the same sample space (i.e., the same outcome set with the same probability measure). In this sense, axiom U3 states that the decision-maker is willing either to ignore the benefit that results solely from decomposing uncertain events related to his decision or to include this benefit explicitly in describing his outcome set. Again, since the decomposability axiom seems to be a reasonable assertion to make about desirable decision-making behavior, it satisfies the local correctness condition.

The continuity axiom (U4) is the only utility theory axiom subject to controversy. According to U4, given three outcomes A, B, and C, such that the decision-maker prefers A to B and B to C, he is always able to find a number, p, between zero and one such that he is indifferent between outcome B and a lottery that gives him outcome A with probability p and outcome C with probability $1 - p$. Furthermore, U4 states that p is unique.

Much of the axiom's controversy focuses on people's inability to visualize uncertainty effectively [Kahneman et al., 1982]. Given this limitation, the requirement imposed by U4 seems unrealistic. This difficulty is emphasized by the fact that the indifference probability, p, is, as the name of the axiom implies, assumed to be obtainable with an arbitrary degree of precision.

Several areas of research have arisen in response to the difficulty of assessing probabilities in practice. An important contribution has been made by psychological research that describes important biases and heuristics usually involved in people's perceptions of uncertainty [Tversky and Kahneman, 1974]. This work has defined important biases, such as anchoring, availability, and representativeness, that tend to distort intuitive perceptions of the probability of uncertain events. Motivational biases are also important in this regard. Another element affecting the way people deal with uncertainty is the way decisions are framed. To deal with this problem, prospect theory [Kahneman and Tversky, 1979; Tversky and Kahneman, 1981] has been proposed.

Attempts to counteract human misinterpretations of uncertainty in practice have contributed many techniques for encoding probabilities. Excellent reviews of these techniques can be found in the literature [Wallsten and Budescu, 1983; Merkhofer, 1987]. Generally, encoding techniques attempt to ensure that the events over which probabilities are being assessed are clearly defined and to balance the natural biases of the individual providing the information. Another important feature of an encoding technique is that it reduces the need to explicitly use the language of probability, which is often misunderstood [Staël von Holstein and Spetzler, 1973; Spetzler and Staël von Holstein, 1975].

Current encoding techniques are quite successful in assessing personal probabilities [Wallsten and Budescu, 1983]. Given this success, much of the controversy of axiom U4 can be resolved, and we can claim that the continuity axiom is locally correct.

A final comment should be made about the continuity axiom in terms of future research. Several researchers have explored the possibility of replacing a person's single probability measure with a set of such measures or with alternative representations of uncertainty [Smith, 1961; Good, 1962; Dempster, 1968; Shafer, 1976; Zadeh, 1981]. There are two major problems with these alternatives to probability as a measure of uncertainty. First, recent results [Lindley, 1982] show that under very reasonable, weak assumptions, an admissible measure of uncertainty for decision-making must obey the axioms of probability. Nonprobabilistic measures of uncertainty are inadmissible because any action axiom based on them can be shown to allow money pump behavior. Thus, an admissible action axiom based on these measures cannot be developed (although these measures may be useful in developing attention-focusing methods).

Second, interpreting the parameters of nonprobabilistic measures of uncertainty with respect to reality has received much less attention than the interpretation of probabilities [de Finetti, 1968]. These parameters are, at best, poorly defined and essentially unassessable with any degree of reliability. Therefore, although they cannot be completely ruled out, nonprobabilistic measures of uncertainty are highly inferior to probability measures for decision-making.

The fifth and final axiom of utility theory is the substitutability axiom, U5. This is a simple, yet fundamental, element of the decision-theoretic methodology. Also known as the "do-you-really-mean-it" axiom [Howard, 1970], U5 states that lotteries with the same certain equivalent are interchangeable without affecting preferences. In particular, this interchangeability applies to degenerate lotteries where all the probability mass is applied to a single outcome. Since this last axiom seems intuitively appealing, we can claim it is locally correct.

The Extrapolability of the MEU Action Axiom

Having argued that all five axioms of utility theory are locally correct, we now consider the extrapolability of the overall MEU action axiom with respect to the area of individual decisions. A claim of extrapolability amounts to accepting that decision problems can be represented by a set of well-defined variables (controllable as well as uncertain), by an explicit set of dependence relations between these variables, and by a comprehensive utility function. The MEU action axiom can be extrapolated to any decision problem that can be formulated in terms of this representation.

Whenever we can abide by this representation, and given that we accept the MEU action axiom, we can show that decision theory can formally solve choice problems, at least in principle [von Neumann and Morgenstern, 1947; Savage, 1972].

A clear practical limitation of decision-theoretic calculations is the computational burden inherent in the methodology. With only rare exceptions (one of which will be explored in Chapter 5), probabilistic descriptions grow exponentially with the number of variables in a problem. Given such rapid growth in problem complexity, useful techniques such as coalescence [Matheson and Roths, 1967; Rousseau and Matheson, 1967] and efficient search algorithms [Chen and Patton 1967; Nilsson, 1980] can only have a limited effect on efficiency. Experience with highly optimized decision-theoretic evaluation systems shows that the expense of solving problems with even a few dozen variables can be prohibitive [Olmsted, 1982]. Even future advances in computer technology can do little to alleviate this burden, and, hence, decision-theoretic solutions must be reserved for relatively small problems (e.g., those with fewer than 100 variables).

However, what seems to be a major limitation of the MEU paradigm can, in fact, be seen as evidence of the generality of decision theory. Specifically, because uncertainty can be interpreted as implying many possible scenarios, solving decision problems in an uncertain environment is an inherently complex problem, regardless of the methodology used. This means, in turn, that unless strong relations exist between the elements used to describe the decision problem, the need to consider the spectrum of possible combinations of these elements will inevitably produce exponentially large models. Therefore, the computational burden of decision-theoretic calculations is a consequence of the nature of the discourse domain and the generality of the methodology, not an artifact of decision theory. An appealing way to reduce this computational burden is to introduce domain-specific knowledge into the methodology in return for a loss of generality. We will consider an application of this idea in Chapter 5.

Furthermore, given our previous discussion about using formal methods to solve real decision problems, we can see that the need to limit the size of problems to be solved in terms of decision theory is an advantage, because it helps decision-makers develop insight by forcing them to think in simple terms. This is particularly true given the availability of compatible attention-focusing methods. The last section in this chapter describes some important techniques, such as sensitivity analysis, that serve precisely this purpose.

Beyond problems of efficiency, decision theory is also not well suited to some puzzle-related decision problems. This issue can best be illustrated with a simple example. Consider a situation where you are offered a reward for solving a crossword puzzle. Successfully solving a complex puzzle is partly controllable and partly uncertain. While it is possible to model puzzles as a sequence of decisions and uncertainties, such representations can be very awkward if done carelessly and may not properly account for the possibilities the solver has for learning and discovery.[2] Therefore, we need to be careful when using the MEU paradigm for puzzle-related decisions.

Aside from these two qualifications, extensive professional experience applying decision analysis provides powerful reasons to believe that algorithms based on maximizing expected utility can be used to solve complex, real decision problems [Matheson, 1970; Howard, 1980b, 1983, 1987b]. This confidence is particularly strong given the closed-loop framework we discussed, and even more so given the existence of related attention-focusing methods allowing the input to a final MEU decision method to be obtained in stages. (See Fig. 2.8.)

HEURISTIC DISTINCTIONS IN DECISION ANALYSIS

Much of the power of decision analysis lies in its ability to effectively integrate the many factors that commonly affect a decision. In industry, for instance, decisions often involve financial, legal, technological, and labor issues that are difficult to address simultaneously because of their diverse nature and their lack of a common language. Similarly, medical decisions usually combine physiological, therapeutic, financial, and morbidity-related factors with legal and, possibly, ethical and moral concerns. Such an integrating capacity makes decision analysis a very successful means of facilitating the decision-making process.

---

[2] This is an important difficulty in R&D decision analysis [Menke *et al.*, 1981].

This integrating capacity primarily results from a set of conceptual distinctions at the core of decision analysis methodology. As was true for the surgeon discussed in Chapter 2, these concepts serve to guide the problem formulation task. Their value is primarily heuristic, and they may require a substantial amount of validation and customization when applied to specific situations. Furthermore, it is important to remember that such conceptual distinctions are not necessarily useful in all contexts.

In Chapter 2, we mentioned several concepts, such as objective functions and resource constraints, that pertain to normative decision-making. These notions primarily concern the formal model to be used as an input to a decision-theoretic evaluation method. Beyond these concepts, decision analysis involves a set of procedural distinctions that deal explicitly with the model formulation process. The intuitive appeal of these concepts is reinforced by their empirical success, as evidenced by over two decades of professional decision analysis practice [Howard, 1980b].

An interesting set of decision-analytic definitions concerns the roles various participants play in the decision process [Holtzman, 1981]. For instance, decision analysts distinguish the decision-maker (who controls the valuable resources to be allocated and who defines the situation within which the decision is to be made) from domain experts (who provide domain-specific knowledge).

The role domain experts play in decision analysis is different from the role they play in knowledge engineering for expert systems. In knowledge engineering, human experts are often seen as surrogate decision-makers, which blurs the distinction between the decision domain and the decision situation. Mixing these two elements of a decision makes it impossible to single out the source of the preference structure used for decision-making. In addition, when this distinction is not made, problem information (e.g., probability assessments and relations between variables) is difficult or impossible to change reliably. Beyond its technical implications, being so inexplicit in representing preferences and information can be criticized on ethical grounds, because recommendations could implicitly impose someone else's preferences and information on the decision-maker without his or her knowledge and approval.

Another useful role distinction can be made between the decision analyst and both the decision-maker and the set of experts. The legal maxim, "A lawyer who defends himself has a fool for a client," applies directly to decision analysts. Most people find it unproductive to be their own devil's advocate. Distinguishing the decision analyst from domain experts is mainly useful as an attempt to combat Gordian and Ptolemaic ignorance. Specifically, a decision analyst with little or no expertise in the decision domain is much more likely to ask embarrassing questions than an expert. And because good embarrassing questions challenge the way the problem is being posed, they are often the best way to bring insight to the decision process.

As with any other set of distinctions, it is important to remember that decision-analytic roles are in no sense absolute. For example, a given individual can play more than one role or several people can play the same role. The usefulness of role distinctions is particularly great, in fact, when the mapping from individuals to roles is many-to-many.

A particularly important class of decision-analytic distinctions concerns the structure of an **objective function**—a mathematical description of the decision-maker's preferences. So important is this class of distinctions that different opinions about how they should be designed have created a technical rivalry between practitioners of normative decision-making. Regardless of its specific breakdown, however, a decision-theoretic objective function must measure together—commensurate—a possibly large class of distinct attributes in a way that accounts for the decision-maker's risk attitude. Some researchers have argued that attribute commensuration should be modeled in conjunction with the decision-maker's attitude toward risk [Keeney and Raiffa, 1976]. The concept of a multiattribute utility function is central to this line of thought. A contrasting approach to designing decision-theoretic objective functions is to explicitly separate commensuration from risk-attitude modeling [Howard, 1973; Keelin, 1977, 1981], which allows all commensuration—except that for risk—to occur in deterministic terms. As we will see, we can use sensitivity analysis to exploit deterministic commensuration, which, within the framework illustrated in Fig. 2.8, can be effectively used as an attention-focusing method in conjunction with decision theory.

Another dimension of decision-theoretic objective functions is time preference. As in finance, it is useful to treat people's time-related values independently from their static preferences. The net present value (NPV) approach to dealing with dynamic outcome streams has been effective for modeling time preference in the not-too-distant future. Other methodologies have been proposed for handling, for instance, decisions that affect future generations [Owen, 1979]. However, distinguishing time preference from other value considerations can be quite awkward in some important contexts. As an example, consider the class of decisions where the decision-maker must trade length of life for such other attributes as quality of life or economic rewards. Since length of life is inherently linked to our notion of time, we must be careful in seperating commensuration and risk attitude from time preference. Moreover, in some important cases [Pollard, 1969; Howard, 1979, 1980a, 1984], this separation is quite meaningless.

The final decision-analytic distinction we will discuss is the one made between decisions and outcomes. The *quality of a decision* depends on the correctness of the action the decision-maker takes given a formal model and on the degree to which that model represents the decision-maker's perception of reality. The *quality of an outcome*, however, depends solely on the decision-maker's preferences and is therefore only probabilistically related to a given decision (unless, of course, there is no uncertainty in the decision problem). From this distinction, we can see that (as shown in Fig. 2.2) good decisions can lead to both good and bad outcomes and that bad decisions can also result in outcomes of varying quality.

This reveals an important philosophical issue about normative decision procedures—one can never really know if a better decision would have been made by using any given normative procedure than by not using it. Although we can compare a decision to similar ones to claim a procedure is reasonable, we can only possess a reasoned faith (as opposed to a dogmatic faith) that the decision method (or decision analysis, in particular) is useful, since the situations of any two decisions are *always* different [Howard, 1980b]. It is not any more feasible to determine whether decision analysis yields better decisions than to establish that abiding by the laws of logic improves decision-making quality. As the proverb says, "One cannot cross the same river twice." Similarly, one cannot make *exactly* the same decision twice.

THE DECISION ANALYSIS CYCLE

To implement decision analysis, we typically use an interactive process known as the **decision analysis cycle** (see Fig. 3.1), which has been shaped by extensive research and professional decision analysis practice [Howard and Matheson, 1983–1984]. Rather than seeing this cycle as an inviolable recipe, we should view it as a means of ensuring that essential steps in the decision process are taken. Our focus here is on the methodological issues that arise in applying decision analysis to real decision problems. A more detailed description of the cycle and its professional use can be found in the decision analysis literature [Matheson, and Howard, 1968; Howard 1968, 1981b, 1983].

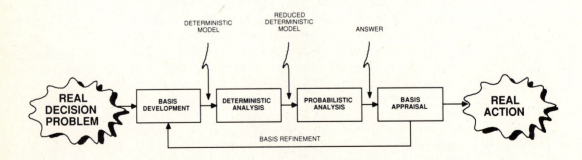

FIGURE 3.1   Decision analysis cycle.

Basis Development

The decision analysis cycle is divided into four distinct phases. The first phase, **basis development,** corresponds to the leftmost formulation stage shown in Fig. 2.8. The term **decision basis** refers to the formal model of a decision problem in its most comprehensive form. The decision basis encompasses the formal definition of the decision-maker's preferences and a quantitative description of that part of his reality that he considers relevant to his problem.

The quantitative description of reality in the basis contains variables of two types—controllable (decisions) and aleatory (uncertainties)—and a set of relationships among them. At this initial stage of the cycle, these two types of variables are treated differently. Controllable variables are fully modeled, including a clear specification of the alternatives they represent; aleatory variables, however, are only incompletely modeled. Usually, this incomplete description consists of asserting the values of a low fractile[3] (e.g., 10 percent), one or more base-case fractiles (e.g., the median), and a high fractile (e.g., 90 percent). By incompletely representing aleatory variables at this phase, we avoid building a probabilistic (and, hence, expensive) model of all the variables the decision-maker deems relevant. Such elaborate modeling is only worth its cost after the next phase in the cycle.

Deterministic Analysis

The incomplete basis developed in the first phase is used as the input to the **deterministic analysis** phase, whose purpose is to reduce the size of the original model by eliminating unimportant variables. This "weeding out" process is accomplished by deterministic sensitivity analysis. First-order (as well as second- and higher-order, i.e., joint) sensitivity analysis is performed in this phase.

First-order deterministic sensitivity analysis, which consists of measuring the sensitivity of individual variables in the basis, is largely a domain-independent task. It may, however, require some domain-specific knowledge to determine the ranges on some variables, to describe how the values of several aleatory variables are dependent on each other, or to specify that a set of possible decision settings is deemed to be either impossible or deterministically dominated by another decision setting. Measuring the sensitivity of a dependent set of aleatory variables also requires knowledge of their relations. Accounting for the effects of one decision on another, as well as for dominance, means that deterministic sensitivity measurements must be

---

[3] Fractiles are also commonly referred to as percentiles.

made in the specific context of the decision. It is generally possible to avoid using domain-specific knowledge to guide sensitivity measurements if all dependencies are included in the formal decision model. However, efficiency considerations often make it advantageous to keep some dependencies unaccounted for in the model. A detailed description of this procedure is given in the decision analysis literature [Matheson and Howard, 1968; Howard, 1973; Staël von Holstein, 1973].

Measuring second- and higher-order sensitivities is reserved for those sets of variables whose joint sensitivity is expected to differ significantly from the corresponding first-order sensitivities of the elements of the set. Hence, unlike first-order sensitivity analysis, multiple-order analysis is always a domain-dependent task, requiring significant knowledge of the decision context.

The deterministic analysis phase yields a complete ordering of the variables of the decision basis. A variable is ranked according to how sensitive the model is to variations in its value. When single and multiple sensitivities exist for a given variable, it is common to use the maximum of the two. A more elaborate, but more expensive, approach for dealing with widely different single and multiple deterministic sensitivities for a set of variables involves remodeling the set so the sensitivity is captured by newly designed individual variables.

The model variables are then ordered by their deterministic sensitivity to reduce the size of the original decision model. Without such analysis, the model would be too large to be the subject of probabilistic (decision-theoretic) analysis. Hence, we can view deterministic sensitivity analysis as an *attention-focusing method* associated with a decision-theoretic decision method. Its attention-focusing axiom states that a model variable will have a negligible effect on probabilistic analysis if it has a small deterministic sensitivity value.

Two important points must be made with respect to this axiom. First, there is no a priori threshold for sensitivity values. Thus, determining the size of the set of sensitive variables out of the set of relevant variables requires domain knowledge and engineering craftsmanship. Second, decision theory makes no formal claim about the validity of the attention-focusing axiom of deterministic sensitivity analysis. Claiming that deterministically insensitive variables are probabilistically negligible is, strictly speaking, a heuristic that, although widely applicable, should be validated in the specific decision context. Fortunately, when this heuristic fails, there is usually a context-dependent reason to foresee the failure. A common case of this foreseeable failure occurs with low-probability, high-consequence events. In general, these events should be deemed worthy of probabilistic modeling despite their possibly low deterministic sensitivity values.

It should be noted that the ability to perform deterministic analysis is a direct result of the distinction between commensuration and risk-attitude modeling discussed earlier. This distinction makes it possible for all commensuration to occur in deterministic terms. Thus, we can argue that multiattribute utility functions may be a poor means for modeling decision problems other than very small ones, since they require that probabilities be assessed for all relevant variables rather than solely for important ones.

Probabilistic Analysis

Probabilistic analysis, the third phase in the decision analysis cycle, consists of three tasks: (1) probabilistic and risk-attitude assessment, (2) calculation of the optimal policy, and (3) evaluation of probabilistic and risk sensitivities. In terms of the first task, we can assess probabilistic information using a variety of techniques described in the literature [Staël von Holstein and Spetzler, 1973; Spetzler and Staël von Holstein, 1975; Miller and Rice, 1983; Wallsten and Budescu, 1983; Merkhofer, 1987]. Except for very simple decisions, it is infeasible to do probabilistic assessment without first doing deterministic sensitivity analysis. Furthermore, assessing probability measures depends strongly on the context (i.e., the domain and the situation) of the specific decision-maker's problem.

Similarly, risk-attitude assessment is much more meaningful after the decision problem has been well defined. As in the case of deterministic sensitivity analysis, the ability to delay risk-attitude modeling until this late point in the cycle when the problem is much more clearly and succinctly defined is a direct consequence of the distinction made between commensuration and risk-attitude assessment discussed in the previous section.

The second task—computing the decision-maker's optimal policy given the current model of his decision problem—is the central task in the probabilistic analysis phase. It is here that we take explicit advantage of the MEU action axiom.

In addition to yielding the optimal policy and its certain equivalent, the probabilistic analysis phase can provide a wealth of useful information from straightforward decision-theoretic calculations. A particularly meaningful result of these calculations is the **profit lottery**—a probability distribution of possible decision outcomes—that corresponds to the optimal policy. In fact, it is quite useful to compute profit lotteries for a variety of nearly optimal policies to gain insight into their suboptimal features.

The final task of this phase involves assessing stochastic and risk sensitivities. For instance, one method used for stochastic sensitivity analysis (referred to as sensitivity to probabilities) resembles the one used for doing deterministic sensitivity analysis—model variables are swept through their range and their effect on the profit lottery and its certain equivalent are observed; however, the reason for doing it is different. Although it is possible for a variable in the probabilistic model to be so insensitive that it could be effectively removed from the model (e.g., by fixating it), the primary reason for measuring its sensitivity is to validate the model.

Specifically, since any model is an inaccurate representation of reality, it is important to know whether its conclusions are strongly dependent on the accuracy of its parameter values. If this is the case, it is wise to extend the model around the sensitive variables to reduce their sensitivity. Such additional modeling effort would introduce additional domain and situation knowledge into the decision basis and would remove some of the recommendation's sensitivity to the oversensitive variables.

Other forms of stochastic sensitivity include value-of-information and value-of-control calculations. These forms of analysis are typically considered to be part of the basis appraisal phase of the cycle and are discussed in the next section.

Risk sensitivity also serves both to focus attention and as a model-validation technique. If the recommendation is too sensitive to the decision-maker's risk attitude, we should perform further assessment and review the decision model. As in the case of deterministic analysis, stochastic sensitivity can be measured to first and higher orders. Most of the comments in this respect made about deterministic analysis also apply to the probabilistic phase.

Basis Appraisal

The last phase of the decision analysis cycle—**basis appraisal**—consists of reviewing the decision basis and the corresponding recommendation resulting from the probabilistic analysis phase. If the basis is deemed valid, then the recommendation should be heeded. Otherwise, it is necessary to return to a previous phase in the cycle (probably, but not necessarily, to the basis development phase) to modify the basis.

Basis appraisal can benefit from the machinery of decision theory. For example, **value-of-information** calculations can indicate the wisdom of resolving uncertainties (e.g., through research) prior to action. These calculations are directly related to the probabilistic sensitivities calculated in the probabilistic phase. In particular, computing the value of perfect information (i.e., clairvoyance) is a simple way to bound the value of such information-gathering efforts. In general, however, appraising a decision basis is a commonsense task. The traditional engineering practice of testing for the behavior of a model in extreme or degenerate situations is very helpful for this purpose.

A crucial objective of this final phase is to investigate the effect of unexplored alternatives. This exploration deals directly with the problem of Gordian ignorance discussed in Chapter 2. Fundamental ignorance is, of course, also important, but there is little we can do about it unless someone else is aware of it and points it out. The deliberate ignorance of pertinent alternatives through Gordian circumscription can be addressed by having the basis evaluated by domain experts and other decision-makers in similar situations. This approach can also yield Copernican insights (as opposed to Ptolemaic ignorance) that can considerably simplify the decision basis.

Beyond dealing with information and alternatives, the most important task in the basis appraisal phase is to validate the preference model used to represent the decision-maker's values. In this regard, we need to remember that decision analysis is a dynamic process whose aim is not to produce a somehow "correct" decision model and a corresponding answer but rather to produce insight where it is otherwise lacking. Much of the power of decision analysis lies in its ability to make explicit the logical consequences of the assumptions embodied in a model that encompasses domain, preference, risk, and other types of decision-related knowledge and to modify this model where inconsistencies or inappropriatenesses are discovered. Thus, decision analysis helps us deal with our limited cognitive abilities when making complex choices. To this end, the basis appraisal phase includes a review of the decision-maker's preferences given their implications for action.

PROGRESSIVE FORMULATION IN DECISION ANALYSIS

By simply restructuring the decision analysis cycle, we can view it as an instance of the closed-loop progressive-formulation framework shown in Fig. 2.8. In terms of this framework, the cycle can be broken down into six rather than four phases, as shown in Fig. 3.2.

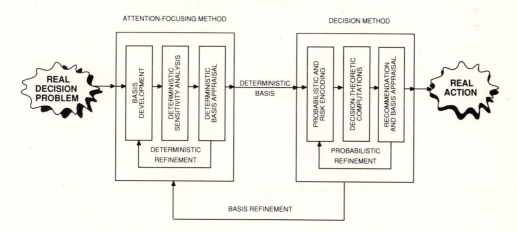

FIGURE 3.2 Decision analysis cycle as a closed-loop progressive-formulation scheme.

The attention-focusing method in this scheme comprises the first two phases of the traditional cycle. Here, however, the basis-development effort is aimed at designing a deterministic model from which a probabilistic problem description can eventually be developed. Thus, the initial basis design effort can allow a certain amount of overmodeling, which can be removed at a later point in the decision process.

The central task of the deterministic attention-focusing method consists of computing the first- and higher-order sensitivities of basis variables. These computations, which occur mostly without domain-specific knowledge, yield a ranking of model parameters that can be used to eliminate those deemed unimportant. Performing formal computations, however, does not suffice to produce the desired reduced basis—one without unimportant elements.

Eliminating basis parameters involves two additional creative tasks: selecting a sensitivity cutoff threshold and, more importantly, earmarking oversensitive portions of the basis that require remodeling. Thus, the deterministic attention-focusing method includes a final validation stage. If remodeling is necessary, the decision process must return to earlier basis-development tasks. Successive deterministic analyses, however, should be progressively easier to perform and should provide decision participants with considerable insight. Only after no further remodeling is required can model variables be selected for probabilistic modeling by comparing their sensitivity values with the cutoff threshold.

The reduced basis can then be given as input to the probabilistic decision method. Here, the formulation stage consists of enriching the basis with probability measures and with a utility function. Delaying probabilistic and risk attitude assessments until this point in the decision process has two important advantages. First, it concentrates the assessment effort on only those uncertain model parameters sensitive enough to warrant such detailed treatment. Second, it facilitates the assessment effort by allowing it to occur within the more restricted context of the reduced basis, which is simpler and more focused than the initial basis.

The decision-theoretic formalism at the center of the probabilistic decision method takes the fully assessed reduced basis as input. By maximizing expected utility, the decision method produces an optimal policy for the formulated decision problem, as well as profit lotteries and certain equivalents of nonoptimal policies for comparison. Value-of-information calculations can also be performed at this point.

Basis appraisal in our restructuring of the decision analysis cycle corresponds to the appraisal stage in the probabilistic decision method. Note that the basis being appraised is the fully assessed reduced basis completed after deterministic analysis, not the initial basis.

An important internal decision must occur at this stage of the process: whether to accept the reduced basis as a valid representation of the decision problem and, hence, to act according to the recommended policy or to reject the current decision model and return to an earlier point in the decision process for remodeling.

As depicted in Fig. 3.2, the decision analysis cycle does not differ in content from the standard structure shown in Fig. 3.1. The advantage of the revised cycle structure is that it emphasizes the existence of two distinct formal processes (a deterministic attention-focusing method followed by a probabilistic decision method) and their relation to one another. Possible extensions and modifications of the cycle can thus be envisioned as alternative attention-focusing methods, without sacrificing the power of decision theory as a formal decision method.

Throughout the decision analysis cycle, the participants in the decision process interact with one another and contribute to developing insight. Thus, the decision-maker, the decision analyst, and the various domain experts provide knowledge that is progressively incorporated into the decision basis. (A model of these interactions as a multiple-actor system is contained in [Holtzman, 1981].) Of all these participants, however, the most important is the decision-maker, for the success of the decision analysis methodology depends greatly on whether the decision-maker "owns" the eventual decision and the model on which it is based.

Owning a decision refers to the decision-maker's feeling that the decision follows directly from his or her own insight (much of which may have been developed throughout the decision analysis process) and implies a commitment to implement it. Many normative decision efforts fail because the decision-maker does not develop a feeling of ownership. A common mistake is to assume that such ownership will follow if a decision recommendation is made based on a logically correct argument. Many a manager has wondered why his or her recommendations and orders have not been followed by people who could not dispute their correctness. In medicine, the problem of patient noncompliance has similar roots. Ownership, however, has much more to do with active discovery than with logic. An effective decision analysis will, therefore, benefit from the decision-maker's intense involvement. Within economic considerations, such involvement should be greatly encouraged.

From an ethical standpoint, the decision analyst must also ascertain that the decision-maker fully endorses the preference model. The decision analyst and others with expertise in modeling preferences should, of course, contribute to designing the preference model, and the decision-maker may also elect to delegate certain portions of this part of the decision basis to others who, for instance, have a stake in his or her decision (e.g., family members). Ultimately, however, the decision-maker must own the preference model.

4

Using Influence Diagrams to Represent Decision Problems

It is seen in this essay that the theory of probabilities is at bottom only common sense reduced to calculus; it makes us appreciate with exactitude that which exact minds feel by a sort of instinct without being able ofttimes to give a reason for it. It leaves no arbitrariness in the choice of opinions and sides to be taken; and by its use can always be determined the most advantageous choice. Thereby it supplements most happily the ignorance and the weakness of the human mind.
—*A Philosophical Essay on Probabilities,*
Pierre Simon, Marquis de Laplace

Being able to clearly and concisely represent decision problems is essential for helping decision-makers. For many years, decision trees served this purpose well. However, while decision trees are still highly useful, a more recently developed representation for decision problems—influence diagrams— outperforms them in many respects. This chapter describes influence diagrams and discusses their use in decision analysis. In addition, it discusses how influence diagrams naturally lend themselves to being generated automatically, making them the representation of choice for intelligent decision systems.

ADVANTAGES OF INFLUENCE DIAGRAMS OVER DECISION TREES

To conduct a decision analysis, we need an effective means of representing decision problems. For this discussion, it is important to realize that formally representing a decision problem (or any other aspect of human experience) is a task that reflects someone's perception of the world. Thus, a decision model constitutes a declaration made by the decision-maker and other decision participants to assist them in analyzing a decision. Consequently, a decision model should not be labeled "correct" or "incorrect" except inasmuch as it is consistent with how the decision participants view the decision at hand.

The best-known representation language for decision problems is the **decision tree**. Representing a choice problem as a decision tree makes each controllable and uncertain variable explicit. Furthermore, decision trees directly tell the decision-maker the value of each possible outcome.

However, despite their widespread use, decision trees have several significant drawbacks as a representation language for decision problems. These drawbacks can be better appreciated by noting that formulating decision problems involving uncertainty is usually a combinatorially explosive task that, in addition, must account for complex and sometimes subtle relations between model elements.

From a technical standpoint, decision trees often do not allow independence relations to be exploited. In fact, in their most general form, decision trees are highly symmetric structures that take little or no advantage of independence among variables. Furthermore, if we want to extract information other than an optimal policy recommendation from a formal decision model (e.g., value of information), we will need to construct a fully symmetric tree, at least in principle. Thus, an already large decision problem will usually require a highly redundant tree representation. And introducing asymmetries to correct this inefficiency can lead to significant losses of information [Olmsted, 1983].

Beyond purely technical concerns, decision trees suffer from several practical disadvantages. Since trees grow exponentially with problem size, they can only be used to represent very small problems. Also, trees naturally lead the decision participants to think in a forward direction about the decision at hand. As we saw in Chapter 2, forward reasoning is not efficient for addressing decision problems; a backward reasoning approach is much more attractive. In addition, some practitioners using decision trees confuse chronology with the order of probabilistic expansions, giving decision-makers an erroneous idea of the structure of their problem.

For example, consider the tree in Fig. 4.1(a). Although aleatory (i.e., uncertain) variables A and B are independent—the distribution of the

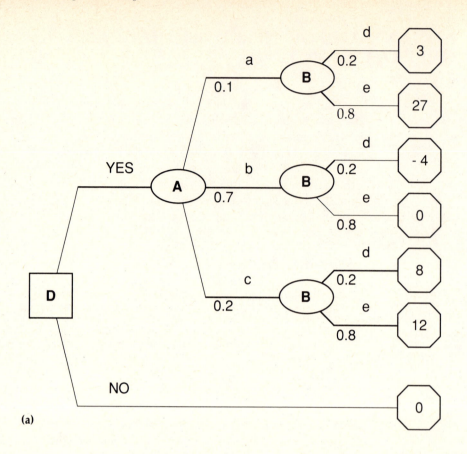

(a)

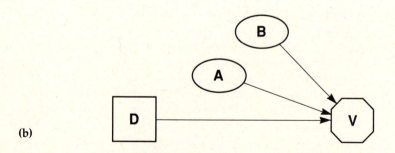

(b)

FIGURE 4.1   Comparing decision trees and influence diagrams. (a) Sample decision tree. (b) Equivalent influence diagram.

outcomes of *B* does not depend on the outcome of *A*—this independence is not apparent from the tree structure. It is necessary to examine the numerical distributions to discover it. Furthermore, the tree in Fig. 4.1(a) is asymmetric. Although it has enough information to compute an optimal policy, it is incomplete for use in value-of-information calculations, which generally require a fully assessed symmetric tree.

In contrast, consider the influence diagram in Fig. 4.1(b). Even without having defined influence diagrams mathematically (we will do so in the next section), it is clear that this diagram is much simpler than the equivalent tree in Fig. 4.1(a). As we will see, the absence of an arrow between chance nodes *A* and *B* explicitly indicates their (conditional) independence. Moreover, fully defining the diagram in Fig. 4.1(b) allows all valid value-of-information calculations to be performed.

In general, **influence diagrams** [Howard and Matheson, 1981] have significant theoretical and practical advantages over decision trees [Owen, 1978; Olmsted, 1982]. In addition to representing probabilistic independence effectively, enforcing a clear distinction between informational and probabilistic relationships, and preventing the loss of information from asymmetries, influence diagrams grow linearly (as opposed to exponentially) with the size of the problem they represent and, thus, can be used to model much larger decisions than trees can model. These technical advantages are enhanced by the fact that the mathematical concept of influence, conditional as well as informational, is very close to its intuitive counterpart.

MATHEMATICAL DEFINITION OF AN INFLUENCE DIAGRAM

As defined by Howard and Matheson [1981], an influence diagram is a singly connected, acyclic, directed graph with two types of nodes—*decision* and *chance*—two types of arrows or arcs—*conditioning* and *informational*—and, typically (although not necessarily), a single sink node of type *chance*. The acyclic, singly connected nature of influence diagrams implies that sets such as predecessors, successors, direct (or immediate) predecessors, and direct (or immediate) successors of a node are defined in the usual manner. Furthermore, for an influence diagram to represent a decision problem for a single decision-maker who does not intentionally forget information (known as the *no-forgetting* condition), the set of decision nodes in the diagram must be fully ordered, and the direct predecessors of any decision must be direct predecessors of all subsequent decisions.

The two types of nodes in an influence diagram closely resemble those in decision trees. **Decision nodes**—usually represented by a rectangle or a square—denote variables under the decision-maker's control. **Chance** nodes—usually represented by an oval or a circle—denote probabilistic variables. However, arrows in influence diagrams have a different meaning and do not represent the same relation as branches in a decision tree. **Conditioning arrows** are always directed toward a chance node and denote probabilistic dependence. The aleatory variable represented by a chance node is modeled as being probabilistically dependent on the variables (controllable or aleatory) represented by its set of direct predecessors. **Informational arrows**, however, are always directed toward a decision node and denote available information. A decision is assumed to be made with knowledge of the outcomes of its direct predecessors. Furthermore, the no-forgetting condition mentioned above implies that the direct predecessors of a decision that is itself a predecessor (direct or not) of another decision must also be direct predecessors of the latter decision.

Nodes that lack either successors or predecessors play a special role in influence diagrams. (A node that lacks both types of neighbors, however, is quite uninteresting.) As we have already stated, an influence diagram typically has a single chance node with no successors (i.e., a sink node), which is called its **value node**.[1] Chance nodes without direct chance predecessors (i.e., chance source nodes) are called **border nodes**. As we will see later in this chapter, border nodes play an important role in constructing an influence diagram.

Figure 4.2 shows a simple influence diagram. Despite its simplicity, this influence diagram captures the essence of many important decision problems in business, medicine, and many other decision arenas. For example, a decision to have surgery performed (S) is preceded by a decision (T) to perform a medical test on the pertinent medical condition (e.g., a possibly malignant tumor). The result (R) of the test depends on an unobservable actual condition (A) and is known when the surgery decision (S) is made. The outcome (O) of the surgical intervention is, of course, dependent on the actual condition being treated and on the decision to have surgery. Finally, the decision-maker's value (V) on the overall decision outcome depends on the specific choices made (T and S), the actual condition (A), and the surgical outcome (O). Although it is unnecessary to make this distinction for mathematical purposes, it is often convenient to depict the value node somewhat differently from other chance nodes in the diagram. Thus, the value node in Fig. 4.2 is shown as an octagon. For completeness, note that node A is the only border node in the diagram.

---

[1]Labeling an influence diagram node as a value node is a statement about preferences in a decision problem and not strictly within the formal definition of the diagram. In general, an influence diagram may have more than one sink node, and it need not have a value node. Furthermore, a value node need not be a sink node. However, for describing decision problems, influence diagrams must have a value node influenced (directly or indirectly) by at least one decision node to enable the computation of an optimal policy.

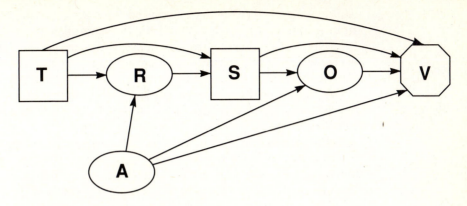

FIGURE 4.2   Simple influence diagram.

It is useful to discuss the different meanings of informational and conditioning arrows in Fig. 4.2. The informational arrows from T to S and from R to S indicate that the surgery decision (S) is made with knowledge of the test result (R) and, trivially, with knowledge of the outcome of the decision (T) whether or not to test. In contrast, the lack of an informational arrow from A to S means that the surgery decision is made without direct knowledge of the actual condition affecting the patient. Similarly, the conditioning arrows from S to O and from A to O imply that the outcome of surgery is probabilistically dependent on the outcomes of the surgery decision and the actual condition of the patient. There is no conditioning arrow from R to O, because given the actual condition (A), the outcome of surgery is independent of the test result (R).

Several important features of an influence diagram are noteworthy. For instance, informational arrows imply a chronological order, whereas conditioning ones do not. Thus, decision T is made before decision S, whereas aleatory variables A and O have no chronological relation. Another important feature of an influence diagram arises from the definition of a conditioning arrow. Since there are several possible expansions for a set of two or more aleatory variables, the influence diagram representation of a fully specified formal decision problem is generally not unique. For instance, the diagram in Fig. 4.2 could have been assessed with the arrow from A to R in the opposite direction.

A more mundane, but nonetheless significant, feature is that influence diagrams may have a large number of arrows whose existence is deducible from the structure of the diagram. These logically redundant arrows result from the no-forgetting condition, and, while necessary to formally solve the decision problem [Olmsted, 1983; Shachter, 1986a], they can often be omitted from explicit graphical representations of the diagram without loss of generality. For example, the arrow from decision T to decision S in Fig. 4.2

could be deduced from other arrows in the diagram and could be omitted from graphical representation. If all these implicit arrows are omitted, the resulting set of arrows is known as the diagram's minimal set of influences, which is unique for each diagram (up to possible arrow reversals) [Shachter, 1986a].

An influence diagram can represent a decision problem completely, not just in terms of its structure. A full description of a decision problem requires that the diagram contain at least one decision node directly or indirectly influencing a value node and that consistent, detailed specifications exist for each node in the diagram. For decision nodes, the set of possible outcomes corresponds to the set of decision alternatives; for chance nodes, this set of outcomes corresponds to the sample space of the variable being represented. Furthermore, for chance nodes, a detailed description should also include a probability measure over the set of possible outcomes. An important, yet subtle, fact about probabilistic specifications of chance nodes is that they must be consistent with the set of direct predecessors of the node and their respective outcomes. In addition to containing a list of its direct predecessors (or successors), a node's description should include its name and a label for each of its possible outcomes. Furthermore, because influence diagrams are likely to be implemented in a computer-based environment, it is useful to include a short statement describing each variable being represented.

A structurally complete influence diagram whose nodes and relations have not been specified in detail is said to be defined at the level of **structure**. A diagram developed in all the necessary detail is defined at the levels of **function** and **number**. An influence diagram is well formed only when it has been consistently defined at all levels: structure, function, and number.

MANIPULATING AND EVALUATING INFLUENCE DIAGRAMS

Once we have a **well-formed influence diagram** (WFID), we can manipulate it by performing four key elementary operations—reversing an influence, merging two nodes, splitting a node, and removing a node [Olmsted, 1983]—and still preserve the state of information embodied in the original WFID. Operations that preserve this state of information are very useful, particularly when the WFID includes at least one decision node directly or indirectly influencing a value node; such a diagram is referred to as a **well-formed decision influence diagram** (WFDID). Since a WFDID fully defines a decision problem in the language of decision theory, the diagram logically entails a recommendation for action. Thus, two diagrams that imply the same recommendation for action are similar, regardless of their internal structure. Specifically, two influence diagrams are considered **decision-equivalent** if they lead to the same recommendation for action and yield the same certain equivalent. Such operations as influence reversal, node merger, node splitting, and node removal produce diagrams that are decision-equivalent to the original. By generating a sequence of decision-equivalent diagrams, these operations can be used to evaluate a WFDID to yield a recommendation for action. In particular, influence reversal—which corresponds to the application of Bayes' theorem—and node removal—which for decision variables corresponds to maximization and for chance variables corresponds to expectation (and, if a profit lottery is desired, integration)—are sufficient to define an evaluation algorithm for WFDIDs [Olmsted, 1982, 1983; Shachter, 1986a].[2] (These two operations are described in some detail in the Glossary.)

We will now outline an algorithm for evaluating a WFID to solve a decision problem. A detailed description of this evaluation algorithm for influence diagrams is beyond the scope of this book and can be found in the literature [Olmsted, 1983; Shachter, 1986a].

To understand the evaluation procedure for an influence diagram, it is useful to consider a simple data structure, which we will call the **partial recommendation** associated with the diagram. When a diagram is originally specified, its associated partial recommendation does not contain any information. Whenever a decision node is removed as the evaluation procedure progresses, the node's optimal decision policy is appended to the partial recommendation so that the latter will contain a recommended decision policy for each and every decision node considered. This recommended decision is a conditional statement that indicates the best choice for that decision variable given every specific combination of the outcomes of its direct predecessors. When the evaluation procedure terminates, the partial recommendation associated with the diagram becomes a **complete recommendation** (or, simply, a **recommendation**) and contains a recommended decision for all decision variables in the diagram. Given the notion of an associated (partial) recommendation, we can extend the concept of decision-equivalence between diagrams to include the explicit choices embodied by the recommendation.

The basic idea behind the procedure for evaluating an influence diagram is that by successively removing each node other than the value node from the diagram, we can derive a decision-equivalent diagram with an associated complete recommendation and a single (value) node that describes the diagram's certain equivalent and, possibly, its overall distribution over outcomes (i.e., its profit lottery). Whenever a decision node is removed, its

---

[2]More general and efficient influence diagram solution algorithms use other operations besides node removal.

recommended decision becomes part of the partial recommendation; whenever a chance node is removed, its information is incorporated into the overall certain equivalent (and profit lottery) by expectation (and integration) calculations.

However, evaluating an influence diagram in general is not merely a straightforward series of node removals. Since the removal of a node is subject to strict structural conditions on the diagram, a WFDID may have no removable nodes. Fortunately, we can always use a series of influence reversals to transform a WFDID with no removable nodes into one with at least one removable node. Shachter [1986a] has constructively proven that any WFDID can be evaluated by a finite number of reversals and removals. Based on this proof, Breese and Holtzman [1984], Shachter [1986b], and Breese [1987] have implemented several computer-based influence diagram processing systems. More recent systems [Holtzman, 1986] use a more general and efficient algorithm based on similar elementary operations.

Besides manipulations that transform a WFDID into another decision-equivalent WFDID, there are several other interesting manipulations that do alter a diagram's state of information. Many of these manipulations can be viewed as a form of sensitivity analysis. For instance, the **value of perfect information** on a variable can be measured by adding an arrow from its associated chance node to the decision node where such value is being measured (provided no cycles are created). Similarly, the **value of control** on a border node in the diagram (i.e., the value of being able to impose a state of nature) can be measured, roughly speaking, by converting the node's associated chance node into a decision node. The **value of imperfect information** (or the **value of imperfect control**) can also be measured by adding nodes representing the results of appropriate experiments and a corresponding set of arrows.[3] Notice that the acyclic nature of an influence diagram imposes certain restrictions on the validity of value-of-information and value-of-control questions. Because these restrictions are not present in decision trees, an analyst using trees can easily be misled into asking ill-posed questions. These pitfalls of trees are discussed in detail in the literature [Miller et al., 1976; Olmsted, 1983]. In influence diagrams, the values of **clairvoyance** (perfect information) and **wizardry** (control) are measured by manipulating the diagram at the level of structure. Lower-level (i.e., functional and numerical) changes can be used to measure the value of imperfect information and the probabilistic sensitivity of aleatory variables.

---

[3] Correctly computing the value of information and the value of control on a variable is subject to important, albeit subtle, restrictions concerning the nature of free will and the meaning of counterfactual statements. A discussion of these restrictions is beyond the scope of this book.

GOAL-DIRECTED GENERATION OF INFLUENCE DIAGRAMS

In Chapter 2, we argued that the process by which a real problem is formulated plays a crucial role in using formal decision methods. Specifically, we discussed how a goal-directed (backward) approach to formulation helps us deal effectively with the need to allocate attention efficiently in our information-rich world. An important feature of influence diagrams—one that decision trees do not possess—is that they strongly promote goal-directed formulation. Of course, influence diagrams need not be generated in a purely goal-directed fashion (in fact, they rarely are), but the fact that their structure naturally lends itself to this mode of development makes them very attractive.

Before describing a goal-directed approach to influence diagram generation, it is essential to emphasize that this generation effort should occur within a progressive formulation framework, such as the one shown previously in Fig. 2.8. The purpose of such a framework is not to produce a somehow "correct" model but rather to help the decision-maker and his or her team of experts develop insight about their decision. To accomplish this task, we want to expose the decision participants to their assumptions (and to the logical consequences of these assumptions) by explicitly representing them. Thus, generating an influence diagram should be viewed as an attempt to formally represent a real decision in a progressive manner. As the development proceeds, the diagram should become an increasingly accurate statement about the decision-maker's perception of reality.

An important feature of the progressive nature of influence diagram generation is that the diagram is often generated first at the level of structure. Once the structure is reasonably stable, the diagram is further defined in more detail. We will find it useful to refer to nodes that have been fully specified at all levels as **assessed** nodes and to nodes not fully specified as **unassessed** nodes. In particular, unassessed border nodes are referred to as **frontier** nodes because, as discussed below, they mark the frontier of the fully assessed diagram being constructed in goal-directed fashion. Unassessed nodes are judged as being or not being **assessable**. An unassessed node is assessable if the decision-maker or any of his or her experts feel that an actual assessment of a corresponding probability distribution is obtainable with reasonable effort, even though it may not yet have been obtained.

If an outcome space and, in the case of a chance node, an *unconditional* probability distribution are specified, then the node is said to be **directly assessed**. It is also possible for a node to be **indirectly assessed** if, instead of directly specifying an outcome space (and for a chance node, an

FIGURE 4.3   Minimal influence diagram for a surgical decision.

unconditional probability distribution), a conditional **assessment function** is given that maps every possible combination of outcomes of its set of direct predecessor variables to a unique outcome space (and for a chance node, a corresponding *conditional* probability measure) for the node.

An important case of indirect assessment occurs when the assessment function is deterministic. **Deterministic assessment functions** map sets of direct predecessor values to outcome spaces with a single element that bears the full mass of the associated probability measure (i.e., it occurs with unit probability). Deterministic assessment functions are discussed later in more detail. Whether the assessment function is deterministic or probabilistic, an **indirectly assessable** node is one for which an assessment function is deemed to be obtainable.

To design an influence diagram for a real decision, we will use the example of a patient considering surgery. For this discussion, we assume that the patient has three mutually exclusive choices: (1) to have the surgery done at a state-run hospital, (2) to have it done at a costlier private institution with better facilities and a better reputation, or (3) to forgo the surgical treatment. Furthermore, we assume the patient wants to make a choice so as to reduce his financial cost ($) and his discomfort (D), while simultaneously increasing his life expectancy (LE).

Figure 4.3 shows a concise statement of the decision problem. The only predecessor of the value node, V, is the decision node, S, which represents the choice among the three possible alternatives: state-run surgery, private surgery, or no surgery.

We will refer to an influence diagram with exactly a single decision node influencing a single value node as a **minimal influence diagram** for the decision problem.[4] Philosophically, to have a decision, the decision-maker must have alternatives from which to choose (represented by the decision node), must have distinct preferences over possible outcomes (represented by the value node), and his actions must in some way affect his welfare (represented by the influence from the decision to the value node). Removing any element of this diagram—the decision node, the value node,

---

[4] Figure 4.3 shows a minimal influence diagram for a single-decision problem. The concept of a minimal influence diagram can be extended to the case where multiple decisions must be made. A discussion of this extension is beyond the scope of the book.

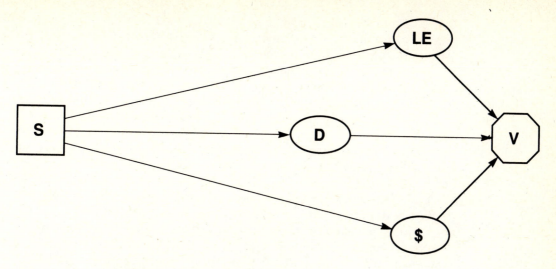

FIGURE 4.4   Decomposing the value node.

or the influence from the former to the latter—would no longer represent a decision (although the remaining elements would still constitute a valid influence diagram).

If the diagram in Fig. 4.3 were fully specified at the levels of function and number, the formulation process would be complete. However, such specification requires that both nodes—and V in particular—be directly assessed, which is extremely unrealistic given the multiattribute nature of the outcome space valued by the patient. Since a full assessment of the value node is necessary to complete the specification of the diagram, we must indirectly assess V. This is a straightforward task given that a value function, $v = v(\$, D, LE)$, has been defined. For this discussion, we will assume that the function, v, exists. However, as we will see later, assessing effective value functions (particularly in a medical context) is a very challenging task. (Chapter 8 and the Appendix discuss medical value functions in some detail.) Thus, we consider v to be a (deterministic) assessment function for the value node, V. A direct consequence of this assignment is that the node V has acquired three direct predecessor nodes—$\$$, D, and LE—as shown in Fig. 4.4.

This more detailed representation of the patient's decision has apparently made the task of fully specifying the diagram more complex. We must now assess three frontier nodes—LE, D, and $\$$—instead of just one, V. However, the ease with which the newly added nodes can be assessed should more than offset the increase in the number of entities to be assessed. Goal-directed generation of an influence diagram is, thus, a divide-and-conquer strategy.

A minimal influence diagram whose value node has been indirectly assessed by means of a value function, such as the one in Fig. 4.4, is the first step in the process that will eventually yield a fully assessed influence diagram for the decision at hand. We distinguish such diagrams from other more extensively developed, nonminimal diagrams, because constructing a value function is a major assessment task, quite unlike all other indirect assessments. This distinction is particularly important for medical decisions, where value functions tend to be more difficult to access than in business decisions. Thus, it is useful to think of such influence diagrams (as opposed to minimal influence diagrams) as the inception of the goal-directed generation of an influence diagram. Hence, we refer to a minimal influence diagram whose value node has been indirectly assessed as an **incipient influence diagram**,[5] that is, a diagram beginning to come into being.

Adding predecessors to a node as a result of an indirect assessment is a basic operation in developing an influence diagram, which we will call **decomposing** a node into a set of inputs (i.e., its new direct predecessors). An important task in decomposing a node is reassigning influences from its original direct predecessors (if any exist) to its new inputs. In general, every original direct predecessor will influence every input and, possibly, the decomposed node itself.[6] Usually, however, we can take advantage of pertinent domain-specific knowledge that indicates that some inputs are independent of some or all the original direct predecessors. Since adding arrows increases the complexity of a diagram, we should use such knowledge as much as possible to reduce the number of arrows added in decomposing a node.

To construct an influence diagram, we need to determine whether each and every frontier node is directly assessable. Recall that a frontier node is an unassessed chance node with no direct chance predecessors. By construction, nodes that are not frontier nodes must have been either directly or indirectly assessed. If every frontier node is directly assessable, then the diagram generation task is essentially complete, although actual outcome spaces and distributions may still need to be developed.

Any frontier node not considered to be directly assessable must be indirectly assessed. Failure to develop the necessary assessment function should be seen as an indication that previous node decompositions were

---

[5] Strictly speaking, an incipient influence diagram (or any other diagram with frontier nodes) is not well formed even at the level of structure, because the predecessors of frontier nodes have not been established.

[6] More generally, new nodes are commonly added to an influence diagram as part of a disjoint knowledge map [Howard, 1987a], and every arrow missing from a new node to already existing nodes in the diagram denotes a statement of conditional independence that may or may not be valid. The decision participants should explicitly verify or modify these statements. However, as we will discuss in Chapter 5, domain knowledge can often be used to greatly reduce the need to explicitly review these statements of conditional independence.

not realistic and, hence, should be redone. Also, a node's decomposition may require an input node that already exists. This can be done as long as the corresponding arrow does not create a cycle in the resulting diagram and as long as the outcome space of the existing input node is consistent with the assessment function.

Given the diagram shown in Fig. 4.4, we must ask whether nodes *LE*, *D*, and *$* are directly assessable. Figure. 4.5 illustrates the decomposition of node *$*. For this example, the financial cost of the operation depends on the advent of surgical or postsurgical complications (and, hence, on the level of discomfort suffered as a result of these complications), on the patient's insurance coverage, and on the surgeon's skill. Thus, node *$* is modeled as being probabilistically dependent on node *D*, which was already present in the incipient influence diagram, and on two new nodes: *SK*—surgeon's skill—and *MI*—medical insurance. We will assume that the only surgeon being considered is the patient's personal physician and, hence, that surgical skill does not depend on the surgery decision, *S*. Thus, the diagram in Fig. 4.5 has no arrow from node *S* to node *SK*.

The diagram generation process terminates when every frontier node is assessable or, of course, assessed. Figure 4.6 shows a plausible termination diagram for the surgical example. After decomposing nodes *LE* and *D* (and introducing a new variable, *R*, which represents the ability of the patient to recover from surgery), the frontier nodes in the diagram (*MI*, *SK*, and *R*) are considered to be assessable. In the resulting diagram, discomfort (*D*) is considered to be dependent on the surgery decision (*S*), the surgeon's skill

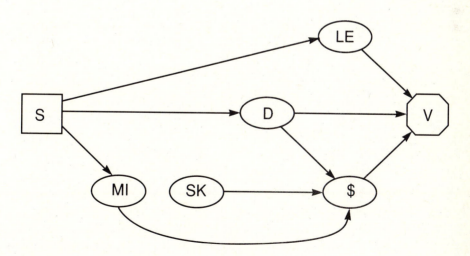

FIGURE 4.5   Decomposing the financial cost node.

(SK), and the patient's ability to recover (R). Similarly, the patient's life expectancy (LE) is considered to be dependent on the surgery decision (S), the surgeon's skill (SK), and the level of discomfort (D) from medical complications.

In summary, the goal-directed influence diagram generation process consists of a recursive sequence of attempts to develop a fully assessable diagram. If every node is assessable, the remaining nodes are assessed, and the generation process terminates. Otherwise, an unassessable node in the diagram is selected for decomposition.

An important question about this influence diagram generation process is whether it will terminate. Formally, it cannot be shown that termination will occur. However, realizing that humans have an uncanny ability to circumscribe problems and noting that every decomposition is aimed at disaggregating the uncertainty behind the value node, we can see that generally the goal-directed process will lead to a diagram with frontier nodes representing decision elements so elementary that direct assessment is feasible in every case. Furthermore, since professional decision analysis experience shows that decomposition is highly modular (decomposing a node affects very few other nodes in the diagram), it is usually possible to categorize the frontier nodes in a diagram by areas of expertise. Such modularity means that the diagram generation process can rely on the knowledge of an appropriate set of specialized domain experts. Using specialists is likely to reduce the depth of the decomposition process, because domain expertise allows individuals to reason at higher (more aggregate) levels within their domain and, hence, to feel comfortable making direct assessments sooner than a nonexpert would.

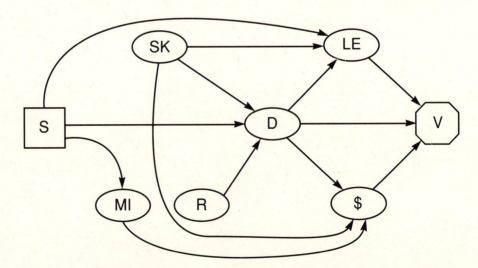

FIGURE 4.6   Fully assessable influence diagram for the surgical decision problem.

Developing an influence diagram in a goal-directed manner is valuable because it provides an important communication tool for promoting the interaction of experts from many different fields. As a result of specialization, experts from different fields often develop conceptual frameworks and a resulting jargon that, while simplifying their immediate task, create significant interfield communication barriers. These barriers prevent them from contributing their knowledge and from incorporating the knowledge of others into their reasoning. What often prevents the participants in a decision from successfully communicating is the absence of a common language. Influence diagrams provide the needed language in a concise and intuitive form [Owen, 1978].

Before concluding our description of goal-directed (i.e., backward) influence diagram generation, we must recognize that there is nothing wrong with forward generation if it used sparingly and judiciously. In fact, it is often quite convenient to reason in this direction when formulating some aspects of a problem. Consider, for example, the task of adding a diagnostic test decision (T) to the diagram in Fig. 4.6, which would typically be performed prior to making the final surgical decision. This task is not motivated by our need to satisfy the original goal of constructing a fully assessable diagram but rather, for example, by the fact that the décision-maker became aware of the availability of the test after having formulated his or her problem without it. Thus, the addition of the test decision is a data-driven (i.e., forward) extension of the diagram.

Figure 4.7 shows the updated influence diagram. In addition to the test decision node (T), the diagram now includes variables for the test result (TR) and the actual condition (AC) being tested. Notice that updating the

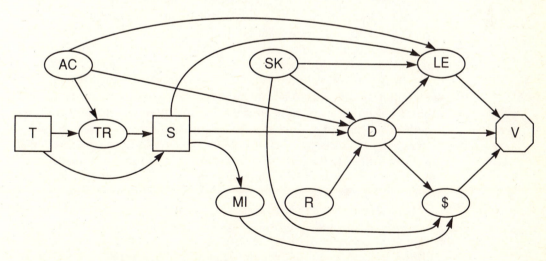

FIGURE 4.7 Adding a decision node and related uncertainties.

diagram after a data-driven addition must include a reassessment of the existing nodes to account for the possible dependence of existing variables upon newly added ones. In the surgical example, node *AC* was included as a direct predecessor of nodes *LE* and *D*, in addition to being a direct predecessor of node *TR*.

DETERMINISTIC RELATIONS

Goal-directed influence diagram generation depends on the availability of effective decompositions for frontier nodes. These decompositions, in turn, rely on the existence of an associated assessment function, which can be of two types: probabilistic and deterministic. Mathematically, the latter type is merely a special case of the former one, since a deterministic function can generally be seen as a mapping onto the space of probability distributions whose total mass happens to be concentrated on a single point. But, as Chapter 6 shows, deterministic assessment functions can greatly facilitate the formulation of influence diagrams. Here, we briefly discuss what effect deterministic assessment functions have on evaluating influence diagrams.

When an indirectly assessed node has a deterministic function associated with it, we call it a **deterministic node**. For example, the value node is very often deterministic. Other deterministic nodes are sometimes marked by depicting them with double bordered ovals or double bordered circles. Figure 4.8 shows the diagram from Fig. 4.6, where node *D* is explicitly shown to be deterministic.

A useful way to think of a node's determinism parallels the concept of independence between two nodes (strictly speaking, between the variables represented by the nodes). In an important sense, independence is merely a numerical feature resulting from our beliefs about the joint distribution of a set of variables. However, we usually choose to announce the independence between two nodes at the level of structure by omitting the arrow between them. This explicit omission conveys important information and can yield important insights. Also, an omitted arrow allows the evaluation algorithm to be significantly more efficient. The ability to omit arrows is a direct benefit of representing a decision problem as an influence diagram rather than as a decision tree. Mathematically, however, adding a conditioning arrow to an influence diagram without modifying its functional and numerical definition always leads to an equivalent diagram (albeit with less information), as long as no cycles are created.

Similarly, a node's determinism can be viewed as a numerical feature. However, as with independence, explicitly representing the deterministic nature of the node at the level of structure can yield important insights. In addition, it is efficient to inform the evaluation procedure that a node is deterministic. The evaluation procedure can then take advantage of the special features of deterministic nodes for computational efficiency. A more

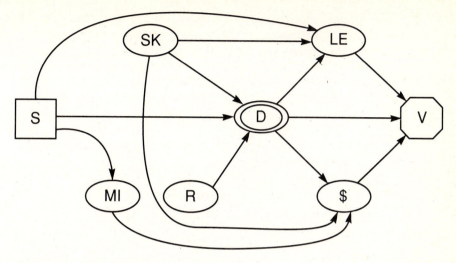

FIGURE 4.8   Marking a deterministic node.

nodes—would lead to either the same or to an equivalent recommended strategy, but it would take longer to compute. A close analogy could be made between informing the influence diagram evaluator that some nodes are deterministic and informing a linear programming package that a given problem qualifies as a "transportation" problem [Hillier and Lieberman, 1967; Luenberger, 1973]. This special type of problem can be treated more efficiently than a general linear program, but the answer given by the specific and the general algorithms should be equivalent (i.e., equally optimal and, possibly, even identical).

Let us consider more specifically the operations of node removal and influence reversal when these involve one or more deterministic nodes. In evaluating a decision problem represented as an influence diagram, removing a chance node is subject to several restrictions [Olmsted, 1983; Shachter, 1986a]. All but one of these restrictions prevent the creation of cycles, and they apply to deterministic nodes as well. An additional constraint on removing a chance node, N, and usually the most binding one, is that N must have the value node, V, as its one and only successor. This precondition on chance node removal is necessary to guarantee that the information required to calculate the conditional expectation of V with respect to N (which underlies chance node removal) is available.[7]

Since a deterministic node has a single possible outcome given a full specification of the outcomes of its immediate predecessors, calculating

---

[7]The potential generalization of influence diagrams from the propositional calculus to the predicate calculus would remove this restriction, except, perhaps, for reasons of efficiency. This is an interesting topic for research [Breese, 1987].

conditional expectation associated with removal becomes trivial, because the expected value of a constant is itself. Hence, deterministic nodes can be removed anywhere in the diagram without disturbing the calculation of the certain equivalent, as long as their removal does not create cycles.

This relaxation of the removal restrictions for deterministic nodes in an influence diagram can have a significant impact on the efficiency of an evaluation algorithm. A deterministic node can be eliminated by incorporating the effect of its deterministic assessment function into its immediate successors. Because this operation is a one-to-many version of node merger [Olmsted, 1983], it can be done with little storage or computational expense. Thus, evaluating an influence diagram with deterministic nodes can be thought of as a two-step operation. The first step eliminates all deterministic nodes from the diagram; the second step removes the remaining decision and chance nodes to complete the evaluation.

An evaluation procedure that eliminates deterministic nodes prior to any removals would never need to reverse an arrow that touches a deterministic node. However, reversing an arrow into or out of a deterministic node is a useful operation in formulating the diagram, because such a reversal can exhibit important features of the probabilistic structure of the decision problem at hand. An important sense in which the deterministic nature of a node affects arrow reversal is that the node may cease to be deterministic as a result of the operation. (Also, a stochastic node may become deterministic as the result of a reversal. This latter conversion is, of course, much less likely to be encountered, but it is nonetheless possible.) Moreover, note that reversing an arrow from a deterministic node would make the arrow disappear (Why?).

As we have seen, recognizing deterministic nodes in evaluating an influence diagram may noticeably affect efficiency. However, most of the usefulness of these nodes occurs because of their role in formulating a decision problem, a point discussed in more detail in Chapter 6.

INTERACTIVE DIAGRAM FORMULATION

Goal-directed generation of an influence diagram does not guarantee that the resulting decision model will be a good representation of the real decision problem. The decision-maker must ultimately determine the quality of the model intuitively. No amount of formal analysis can eliminate the need for final approval from the individual committing the resources at stake.

It is interesting to consider an influence diagram development environment that promotes a convergence of the decision problem formulation process toward a model deemed a valid representation of reality. As we will discuss in Chapter 6, a computer-based implementation of such an environment is an important element of an intelligent decision system. Such an environment would promote the active involvement of each of the individuals whose authority and knowledge make them a participant in the decision process. A plausible architecture for this environment might distinguish between six tasks: expansion, reduction, checking, evaluating, mining, and justifying. The nature of these tasks is explained below.

An influence diagram is a formalization of a decision problem given a certain state of information. Thus, an influence diagram is an evolving model whose progress reflects changes in how the decision-maker and appointed experts perceive the world. Like the evolution of a biological system, the development of an influence diagram is governed by the interplay of creative and destructive processes. On one hand, we desire to **expand** the diagram to increase the accuracy and comprehensiveness of the representation it embodies. On the other hand, we wish to **reduce** the diagram to make it more intuitively appealing and more computationally manageable.

In addition to expanding and reducing the diagram, we must account for the possibility of construction errors within the diagram development process. Therefore, we must **check** the diagram for mathematical correctness as the development effort proceeds. This combination of expansion, reduction, and checking constitutes a useful basis for designing the formulation aspects of intelligent decision systems [Holtzman, 1981].

Another important element of the diagram development task is the ability to **evaluate** the influence diagram as it progresses. In fact, from this perspective, the practical distinction between the formulation and evaluation stages of a formal decision method can become quite blurred. Conceptually, these two tasks remain distinct, but incorporating the ability to evaluate formal decision models into the formulation effort greatly demystifies the evaluation task and exhibits its fallibility.

Having a formal decision model and a corresponding evaluation algorithm is sufficient to enable a recommended strategy to be computed. However, as discussed in Chapter 2, such a strategy needs to be appraised (i.e., interpreted in terms of reality). To appraise a strategy, we need to ask two types of questions: about features of the model and about how the model was developed. First, many features of the decision model can be exhibited to support the formal recommendation it entails. An important example of these features is the sensitivity of model variables. Other interesting model characteristics that bear on the intuitive appeal of that model's recommendation are profit lotteries and value-of-information measurements on its uncertain variables. Obtaining information about these features is referred to as **mining** the model because, as in a gold mine, what we want is already there, but it takes work to get it out.

The second type of question one might ask to clarify a formal recommendation pertains to the reasoning that led to the specific model being used. To develop an intuitive understanding of a model's recommendation, a decision-maker needs to **justify** that model. Justifying a model differs from mining it in that the desired information is extralogical (i.e., not contained within the model itself). The information needed to justify a model lies primarily in the methodological decisions and trade-offs made to construct it and in the theory (if any) that underlies the methodology.

Thus, the development environment proposed to promote the construction of a valid decision model consists of an interactive composition of the six tasks described above: expansion (*Ex*), reduction (*R*), checking (*C*), evaluation (*Ev*), mining (*M*), and justification (*J*). For this development environment to be successful, *no rigid order* should be imposed on applying these tasks within the formulation process (except, of course, for such prerequisites as the fact that one cannot evaluate a model that has not been expanded at all). Rather, like a painting created by experimenting with different forms and colors and with no overall guiding principle other than a general feeling the artist is trying to create, a decision model should be developed as the successive, ad hoc application of each of these six activities

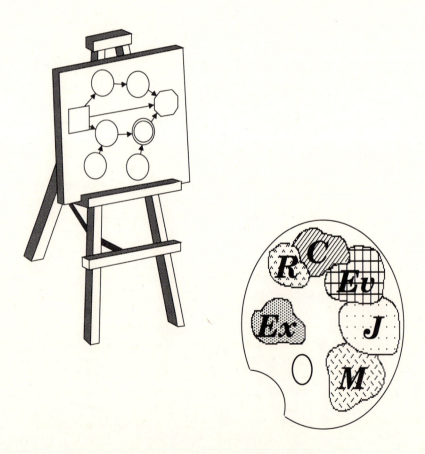

FIGURE 4.9 Building a decision model is like painting a picture.

toward the final objective of having an intuitively appealing, well-formed decision model. (See Fig. 4.9.) From this perspective—and as discussed in Chapter 3—the decision analysis cycle (Figs. 3.1 and 3.2) should serve as a guide to ensure that essential steps in the decision analysis process are taken.

5

Analyzing Classes
of Decisions

Abstraction is a crucial feature of. . .knowledge, because in order to compare and to classify the immense variety of shapes, structures, and phenomena around us we cannot take all their features into account, but have to select a few significant ones. Thus, we construct an intellectual map of reality. . . . Because our representation of reality is so much easier to grasp than reality itself, we tend to confuse the two and to take our concepts and symbols for reality.

—*The Tao of Physics,*
Fritjof Capra

Because the decision analysis process relies on the participation of the decision-maker whose specific preferences and circumstances must be addressed, the decision-maker must be identified early in the analysis. In contrast, providing automated decision analysis assistance requires the decisions in question be primarily analyzed without the benefit of knowing exactly who the decision-maker will eventually be. This chapter develops a methodology for analyzing classes of decisions in which the decision-maker's identity and characteristics are, at best, only partially known. Analyzing classes of similar decisions as a single unit can greatly reduce the overall expense and time typically associated with professional decision analysis. Moreover, the methodology for analyzing classes of decisions developed in this chapter sets the stage for introducing the concept of intelligent decision systems.

COST CONSIDERATIONS IN DECISION ANALYSIS

Many years of professional experience have clearly shown that decision analysis is a powerful aid in helping individuals face difficult decisions [Howard, 1980b, 1987b]. However, for personal decision-making, the professional application of decision analysis has remained far beyond the financial reach of most individuals. Therefore, industry and government have been the primary users of decision analysis.

In general, conducting a decision analysis entails two major costly activities—designing a model of the decision and constructing a preference function representing the decision-maker's desires. Evaluating the formal models represents only a small portion of this cost. Modeling the decision domain is similar to building a simulation model, except that for a decision, the simulation does not have to be as detailed as it would have to be in a more general context. Constructing a preference function is basically a task of quantifying and jointly weighing many distinct attributes that depend on the specific nature of the decision context.

To reduce the cost of decision analysis, it is useful to recall our discussion in Chapter 3 where we viewed decision analysis as an integrator of decision knowledge. Designing a strategy for action requires that domain-specific and situation-specific knowledge be effectively combined to yield a formal model from which a recommendation can be inferred. Typically, domain experts provide domain-specific knowledge, while the decision-maker furnishes information about his or her circumstances and preferences (i.e., situation-specific knowledge). In many difficult decisions, each knowledge source is ignorant of the other's knowledge. This ignorance is typically Gordian or magical but is also often dark and fundamental.

Furthermore, it is unrealistic to expect the decision participants to become fluent in each other's expertise. In fact, such fluency is quite unnecessary, because only a small portion of each participant's knowledge is needed for any specific decision. In its integrator role, decision analysis focuses on acquiring knowledge from the decision participants, thus facilitating the development of a consistent decision model that properly represents the decision's domain and situation. As we have seen, influence diagrams play a major part in this integrator role because they provide an effective communication language that promotes efficient, goal-directed generation of decision models. In addition, decision-theoretic computations can be used directly on a WFDID to recommend a strategy for action.

Based on this view of decision analysis, we can consider reducing its cost and increasing its speed, thus making it available to a much wider population of decision-makers by treating a set of decisions having some degree of similarity among them as a single unit. We will refer to this unit as a **class of decisions** and to the corresponding collective analysis as a **decision class analysis**. More specifically, the decisions in a class should share a common domain and, perhaps, also some common situation features.

Once we have defined a class of decisions and developed a corresponding decision class analysis, we can inexpensively analyze individual decisions within the class by simply creating an instance of the collective analysis given the specific situation of an individual decision-maker. This procedure can greatly reduce the cost of individual analyses, because if the class is properly defined, all the decisions that fall within it should share a substantial amount of structure. And since we only have to analyze this shared structure once (albeit in a much more general form than would be needed for an individual analysis), we can save large amounts of duplicate effort.

Furthermore, viewing a class of decisions as a unit may lead to unique formulation approaches that may not have resulted from analyzing decisions individually. We will see an example of this in Chapter 8, when we discuss the Rachel system. Thus, not only can the cost of analysis be considerably reduced by a collective approach that exploits available economies of scale, but the eventual individual analyses may be qualitatively improved.

To analyze a class of decisions, we need to understand two concepts of technical and philosophical importance—the nature of a decision class analysis and the task of designing a class of decisions.

ANALYZING A CLASS OF DECISIONS

When a single decision is analyzed, both the domain and the situation of the decision are known. While it is necessary to actively elicit much of the knowledge needed to develop a decision model, by the time a decision analysis is complete, there remains no deliberate ignorance of the decision context in which resources are to be allocated.

By contrast, analyzing a class of decisions implies deliberately omitting knowledge pertaining to the decision situation. If this omission did not occur, then the class of decisions being analyzed would have a single element. Hence, analyzing a class of decisions occurs at a higher level of abstraction than analyzing a single decision.

An interesting way to think about analyzing a class of decisions is to view the collective analysis as a *set of instructions* for performing individual decision analyses. Thus, whereas the end result of an individual decision analysis is a decision, the end result of a decision class analysis is an individual decision analysis. In other words, analyzing a class of decisions is an operational statement about how to perform a decision analysis on the single decision of each individual decision-maker to which the class analysis is applicable. Given as input the specific decision situation of an individual, the output of a class analysis is the process of an individual decision analysis.

Being able to successfully implement a decision class analysis requires a considerable capacity for processing information. In fact, the viability of this approach to decision-making heavily relies on the assumption that a decision class analysis will be implemented as a computer program. Moreover, to properly represent the analysis of a class of decisions at a sufficiently high level of abstraction, we must take advantage of the relatively sophisticated techniques that have come to be collectively known as **knowledge engineering** [Barr *et al.*, 1981–1983; Hayes-Roth *et al.*, 1983]. In particular, the concept of analyzing a class of decisions can be naturally described in terms of a rule-based[1] system.

A rule-based system, which is described in detail in the computer science literature [Nilsson, 1980; Buchanan and Shortliffe, 1984; Harmon and King, 1985; Genesereth and Nilsson, 1987], is a computer-based implementation of a theorem prover. In essence, a rule-based system consists of a set of formal axioms (generally referred to as its **knowledge base**) and a set of programs (known as its **inference engine**) that implement one or more inferential syllogisms (generally referred to as inference algorithms). The inference engine can act on the axioms to deduce theorems.

Although at first glance a rule-based system might seem to pertain exclusively to the domain of mathematics, many important practical problems can be stated in terms of a theorem-proving task, making the methodology of rule-based systems applicable far beyond mathematical problems. In fact, the applicability of this methodology is so great that several computer programs that perform significant tasks (such as diagnosing human disease or interpreting petrochemical data) at the level of a human expert have been recently developed as rule-based systems [Barr *et al.*, 1981–1983; Hayes-Roth *et al.*, 1983].

For our purposes, a rule-based system is an excellent way of implementing the analysis of a class of decisions. The goal of this particular system is to constructively prove the existence of a formal decision model that represents the decision being analyzed. The necessary domain-specific knowledge can be composed of a set of assertions in the system's knowledge base. If we wish to restrict the population of decision-makers for whom the decision class analysis is appropriate, we may also want to include some situation-specific assertions into that knowledge base. In general, however, we should obtain situation-specific knowledge from the decision-maker, or his or her appointed experts, when a particular decision analysis is carried out.

Therefore, analyzing a class of decisions consists of developing a domain-specific knowledge base for a rule-based system that contains a set of assertions designed to guide the analysis of <u>specific</u> decisions in a way that reflects the decision-maker's unique situation. Figure 5.1 illustrates the view of a decision class analysis as a rule-based system.

---

[1] We are using the term rule-based in a generic sense. Actual implementations may use such other knowledge engineering techniques as frames, scripts, and semantic networks.

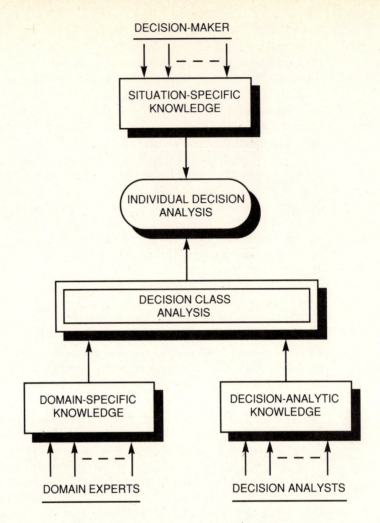

FIGURE 5.1   Analyzing a class of decisions consists of designing a set of rules to guide individual decision analyses.

We can more clearly describe the nature of a decision class analysis if we commit ourselves to a specific representation language for the desired formal decision model. From our previous discussion, influence diagrams are the language of choice. Not only do they represent decision problems in a simple and mathematically correct way, but their natural appropriateness for goal-directed development makes them ideally suited for use in conjunction with a rule-based system.

In terms of influence diagrams, the goal of the rule-based system that embodies a decision class analysis is to generate a fully assessed WFDID that represents the decision-maker's problem. As discussed earlier, the desired constructive proof of the existence of an appropriate WFDID begins by developing a minimal influence diagram (i.e., by determining a set of decisions and a value function whose probability distribution must be assessed for every possible decision policy). Since these distributions are generally not directly assessable, we must provide the theorem prover with rules that allow indirect assessment by means of assessment functions. As these indirect assessments create frontier nodes in the diagram, we must either directly assess the distribution of those nodes (which can be aided by the rule-based system) or continue the indirect assessment process. As argued previously, this process of goal-directed diagram generation should end when all remaining frontier nodes in the decision model are directly assessed. In addition to suggesting assessment functions and guiding the direct assessment of frontier nodes, the rules in a decision class analysis can propose decision alternatives that decision participants had not previously considered.

It is precisely these assessment functions, possible decision alternatives, and plausible frontier node distributions, together with their corresponding antecedents, that constitute most of the rules within the rule-based system's domain-dependent knowledge base. Another important component of the decision class analysis knowledge base consists of a set of rules to guide the assessment of probability distributions and the elicitation of a value function. A particularly attractive means of representing value function knowledge is as a set of plausible parametric preference models. In this case, eliciting an appropriate value function would consist of selecting a parametric model, followed by assessing the specific values of its parameters.

In addition to proposing plausible expansions to the decision model, the rules in a decision class analysis can propose model reductions. Domain-specific rules, as well as more general ones (e.g., those based on sensitivity calculations), can be useful for this purpose. An important class of domain-specific reduction rules concerns the possible similarity between two or more nodes in the diagram. While recognizing such similarities must necessarily result from domain knowledge, it may be aided, for instance, by discovering close probabilistic dependencies. Domain-independent reduction rules might embody various forms of sensitivity analysis, including probabilistic sensitivity and value-of-information calculations. In addition, it may be useful to include rules that recognize near-independence between nodes, as well as near-determinism of chance nodes. In all these cases, we can make simplifying assumptions to reduce the model's complexity. Figure 5.2 illustrates the process of expanding and reducing the decision model through a set of rules.

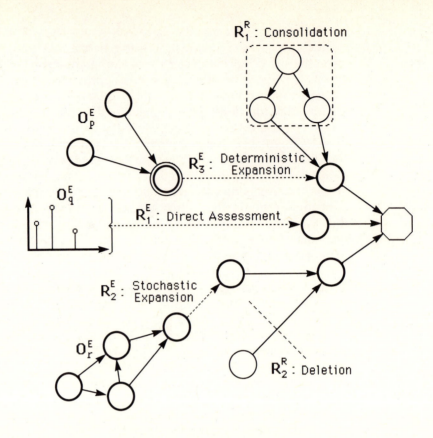

O_p^E

R_1^R : Consolidation

R_3^E : Deterministic Expansion

O_q^E

R_1^E : Direct Assessment

R_2^E : Stochastic Expansion

O_r^E

R_2^R : Deletion

O_i^E : i^{th} Expansion Object

R_j^E : j^{th} Expansion Rule

R_k^R : k^{th} Reduction Rule

FIGURE 5.2   The rules in a decision class analysis can either expand or reduce the decision model.

DESIGNING A CLASS OF DECISIONS

Throughout our discussion on analyzing a class of decisions, we have assumed that the class of decisions had been previously defined. Although the notion of a decision class should be quite intuitive, the effect of its definition on the eventual success of a decision class analysis is significant and, thus, requires more detailed discussion.

In a very fundamental sense, no two decisions are the same. A diametrically opposed argument can also be made stating that all decisions are essentially the same problem. More specifically, at a sufficiently high level of abstraction, every decision consists of the design of a strategy for action (i.e., a strategy for the irreversible allocation of valuable resources).

This apparent inconsistency implies that we must review what we mean when we say that two decisions are similar. A crucial point in this regard is that the similarity between decisions is not a feature of nature but rather a characteristic of the way we perceive reality. Since the notion of a decision is itself an abstraction, any relation among decisions is necessarily a manufactured concept. In particular, we can view a class of decisions as a distinction resulting from the definition of a similarity criterion over the set of all decisions. Hence, as discussed in Chapter 2, defining a class of decisions is the product of design.

When designing a class of decisions, we must remember that it is being constructed as the foundation for a collective analysis. Losing track of this fact would remove the criteria needed to guide the design effort, thus making it a futile exercise. It is useful to think about the design of a decision class and of its corresponding analysis as a "yin-yang" pair. One cannot exist without the other, yet they are different. The interconnectedness between a decision class and its corresponding decision class analysis is an important instance of the interaction between representation and reasoning, which has received considerable attention in the field of artificial intelligence [Winston, 1977; Nilsson, 1980; Webber and Nilsson, 1981; Genesereth and Nilsson, 1987].

Like any engineering endeavor, designing a decision class involves many trade-offs. In general, these trade-offs are specific forms of the following dichotomy: If the decision class is too narrowly defined, it will represent too few individual analyses; if it is defined in an overly general manner, its corresponding class analysis will lose the benefits of domain specificity and may be prohibitively expensive. At either extreme, the economic value of an aggregate analysis is lost (although it may still be attractive to perform the analysis for academic reasons). We can only design a decision class that is neither too restrictive nor too comprehensive if we have a clear notion of its corresponding decision class analysis and of the general features of the situations (circumstances and preferences) to which the analysis must apply.

Another crucial issue in designing a class of decisions is that creating distinctions invariably carries with it many extralogical implications—implications that are not explicitly stated yet that can profoundly affect the behavior of individuals basing their decisions on the corresponding decision class analysis. In particular, the specific nature of a class of decisions can mold the way individuals frame their decision problems and can greatly affect what aspects of the problem are made explicit and how pertinent information and preferences are brought to bear on the decision [Tversky and Kahneman, 1981]. As discussed in Chapter 2, the need for formal decision methods is primarily related to their power in helping individuals formulate decision problems. Hence, designing a class of decisions is likely to have profound consequences on the success of the overall class analysis.

Much of the definition of a class of decisions depends on the specific decision context it is designed to represent. However, since certain design criteria are relatively context-independent, we will propose several guidelines for designing a decision class that are, to a large extent, generally applicable. We can begin by noting that differences between decisions occur both in terms of their domain and their situation. As defined in Chapter 2, we should expect the situation of a decision to have many more unique characteristics than its domain. Consider, for instance, the relative stationarity of prevailing real estate regulations (an important part of the domain of home purchase decisions) versus the volatility of home purchasers' financial situations, residential needs, and geographical preferences (all likely elements of a corresponding decision situation). Therefore, we usually associate a class of decisions with a specific decision domain. Including decision features of foreseeable decision situations in designing a decision class is useful only when these features are expected to be generally relevant to the set of decisions being considered and when their relevance is expected to endure.

In designing a class of decisions, we can often exploit culturally predetermined decision domains. For instance, we can distinguish financial, medical, and legal decisions. Within medicine, to carry the example further, we might want to separate pediatric from geriatric decisions. The main advantage of following such a culturally established breakdown is that we can benefit from the wealth of terminology (itself a set of distinctions) associated with the categories such a breakdown implies.

However, accepting previously defined decision domains also has an important disadvantage—it can be precisely this definition that leads to the failure of intuition in decision-making. Consider, as we will do in Chapter 8, the decision problem an infertile couple faces when seeking medical help. Many erroneous infertility decisions are made because of the traditional medical distinction between the fields of gynecology and urology[2] [Silber, 1980; Steinberger and Rodriquez-Rigau, 1981; Steinberger *et al.*, 1981]. In business, the common distinction among sales, marketing, financial, engineering, legal, and other departments in a corporation is operationally effective, but it can impair the quality of decisions by creating communication and motivational barriers that prevent important factors from being considered. As discussed in Chapter 3, an important role of decision analysis is to cut through these barriers.

In cases where this problem does not arise, designing a decision class based on culturally established distinctions is particularly attractive when

---

[2]It is interesting to notice that as of the writing of this book, the field of andrology—the male counterpart of gynecology—is not widely recognized within the medical profession.

domain experts are available to help in the design effort. An even better situation occurs when the expertise within the decision domain is well codified and is explicitly taught on a regular basis. In this case, we can be reasonably assured of the relative reliability and stability of the domain knowledge used to design the desired class of decisions.

THE ECONOMIC VALUE OF ANALYZING A CLASS OF DECISIONS

The general guidelines discussed so far are primarily concerned with some of the implicit effects of imposing artificial boundaries on decision-making behavior. We now turn our attention to the issue of economic value, which, as we saw earlier, is a central motivation for analyzing classes of decisions.

The economic value of a class of decisions is directly related to the stakes involved in the individual decisions it addresses. Similarly, this value grows in direct proportion to the number of individual decisions for which it is an appropriate means of analysis. Thus, a rough measure of the value of a decision class analysis is the product of the average stakes under consideration in the individual decisions it addresses and the number of these decisions.

The primary context in which a class decision analysis has economic value is one where a large population of individuals is regularly making less-than-satisfactory intuitive decisions. In addition, if relatively satisfactory decision-making is already prevalent in some context, a class analysis can be very useful when further improvement in decision quality is desirable, for example, to gain competitive advantage. Therefore, to help us identify decision contexts that would make worthy candidates for class decision analyses, we need to review some of the reasons that make decision-making challenging.

An important feature of a decision context that challenges and often undermines intuitive decision-making is the presence of major uncertainties. However, saying that something is a "major uncertainty" is essentially a matter of declaration. The important question is not whether a given decision context involves uncertainty (in a sense they all do), but whether we should bother recognizing any given uncertainty explicitly. Clearly, this depends on the value of the resources at stake. Thus, what makes uncertainty "major" (that is, worthy of explicit attention) is the magnitude of the stakes in a decision together with the lack of perfect information, rather than a feature of nature. Therefore, uncertainty in a decision model should be viewed as a direct consequence of the decision-maker's values and information.

We can make a similar argument about the complexity of models of decision-makers' preferences. The higher the stakes involved in a given decision, the more it becomes useful to add detail to the description of preferences. In principle, one can always build a highly complex preference model, regardless of how trivial the stakes in a decision are. However, we do not typically build such a complex model for low-stakes decisions, because it would be a waste of effort. Thus, we can argue that the need to explicitly develop complex preference models for major decision problems is motivated by economic considerations.

A third argument along the same lines can be made about the inferential complexity of a particular decision task. The higher the stakes involved, the greater the amount of detail worth modeling explicitly. Even the least important decision domain could be formulated in a highly complex manner. However, it is only worthwhile to do so for decision problems where the resources to be allocated are sufficiently valuable.

Of course, the effect of a decision-maker's values on uncertainty, preference structure, and inferential complexity can be mitigated by having individuals with enough decision-making experience to have developed powerful, high-level heuristics to guide their decisions. To a large extent, this type of expertise is what makes top business executives, experienced physicians, and senior airplane pilots, for instance, so valuable to society. The purpose of a decision analysis (either individual or collective) is to improve the making of decisions where this expertise is not available or is too expensive. Moreover, by integrating the knowledge of decision-making experts within a consistent and general framework, decision analysis can be aimed at improving decision-making behavior where the quality of such behavior is already high.

In designing a class of decisions, we should avoid decision contexts where it is common to find **dominating alternatives**. A dominating alternative is a course of action that would be recommended to nearly all decision-makers in a given situation. For example, given a diagnosis of appendicitis, very few people would prefer not to undergo an appendectomy. The prevalence of dominating alternatives in a decision context greatly diminishes the value of decision analysis and makes that context a poor candidate for designing a decision class analysis.

A good way to identify the presence of dominating alternatives in a decision context under consideration is to ask the following question: "Does describing the generic aspects of a decision typically suffice to indicate a best course of action?" An affirmative answer would imply that dominating alternatives are common. In contrast, answering that a course of action cannot typically be recommended until the specific preferences and circumstances of the decision-maker are considered would imply that dominating alternatives are rare.

Within an organization, decision quality can be challenged by factors other than uncertainty, preferences, and inferential complexity. In particular, decisions throughout an organization need to be made consistently. Much time, effort, and money can be wasted when distinct parts of an organization follow contradictory courses of action. To remedy this kind of situation, executives establish organization-wide policies. Often, however, these policies

- A class of decisions is a manufactured object, not a feature of nature.

- While the design of a class of decisions should take advantage of culturally established distinctions, it may have to depart from tradition when established distinctions impair the decision-making process.

- Codified domain expertise and recognized domain experts will facilitate the design of a class of decisions.

- A decision class analysis is likely to be valuable in domains where uncertainty, complexity, dynamics, and conflicting preferences are major sources of decision diffiiculty. In contrast, a decision class analysis is likely to be of little value in domains where dominating alternatives are pervasive.

- Analyzing a class decision analysis can be aimed at enhancing good decision-making as well as at improving poor decision-making.

- A class of decisions should comprise a domain where analysis can have a significant overall impact. This impact is related to the product of average stakes and decision-maker population size.

FIGURE 5.3   Guidelines for designing a class of decisions.

tend to be rigid and insensitive to the specific circumstances of individual decision-makers. A decision class analysis can be a very effective tool for developing and implementing policies that guide decision-making throughout an organization in a way that is responsive to the local situations where day-to-day decisions are made.

Thus, the economic value of analyzing a class of decisions is inversely related to the prevalent decision-making quality in the decision context being modeled. Furthermore, the analysis of a class of decisions can give competitive advantage if the quality of decision-making is raised above accepted standards. Therefore, not surprisingly, analyzing a class of decisions collectively is economically justified when the analysis addresses an unfamiliar decision context involving high stakes and where difficult decisions are made relatively often. Figure 5.3 summarizes the guidelines for designing a decision class discussed in this chapter.

6

Intelligent Decision Systems

Science promised man power. But, as so often happens when people are seduced by promises of power, the price extracted in advance and all along the path, and the price actually paid, is servitude and impotence. Power is nothing if it is not a power to choose. Instrumental reason can make decisions, but there is all the difference between deciding and choosing. . . . Perhaps every human act involves a chain of calculations of what a systems engineer would call decision nodes. But the difference between a mechanical act and an authentically human one is that the latter terminates at a node whose decisive parameter is not "Because you told me to," but "Because I chose to."

—*Computer Power and Human Reason,*
Joseph Weizenbaum

This chapter presents the concept of an intelligent decision system as a means for providing automated decision analysis assistance. An intelligent decision system implements the analysis of a class of decisions using the technology of expert systems to give decision analysis guidance to the user and to deliver domain knowledge.

A DECISION CLASS ANALYSIS AS AN EXPERT SYSTEM

In Chapter 1, we argued that the conspicuous lack of interaction between decision analysts and knowledge engineers was a major reason for the lack of a comprehensive methodology for designing and implementing effective decision systems. However, the concept of analyzing a class of decisions, developed in Chapter 5, is an attractive and natural way to merge decision analysis and knowledge engineering. It is particularly interesting to envision the situation where the rules that constitute a decision class analysis are so developed that they represent the knowledge of expert decision analysts and one or more experts in the decision domain. In this case, the rule-based system that implements the decision class analysis is an expert system. This expert system, together with a powerful facility for manipulating and evaluating decision-theoretic models (such as influence diagrams), constitutes an **intelligent decision system**.

An intelligent decision system provides its users with a substantial amount of domain-specific knowledge—knowledge specifically designed to guide the formulation and the appraisal of an influence diagram for the problem of a given decision-maker. Therefore, an intelligent decision system enables individuals to exploit the normative power of decision analysis in a relatively simple, fast, and inexpensive way.

ADVANTAGES OF INTELLIGENT DECISION SYSTEMS OVER EXPERT SYSTEMS

In contrast to more traditional expert systems designed to aid the decision-making process (that is, expert systems that make recommendations for the irreversible allocation of valuable resources), intelligent decision systems have three distinct advantages: normative power, ease of representation and use of uncertainty, and clarity in the acquisition of knowledge.

Normative Power

When a strictly rule-based decision system issues a recommendation, it is difficult to make a defensible claim that what it recommends is a better course of action than some other alternative. Of course, when the recommended action constitutes a dominating alternative—an action superior to others given any set of reasonable circumstances and preferences—this claim can be safely made. However, when dominating alternatives do not exist (as is the case with most interesting decision problems), rule-based reasoning cannot be a reliable source of decision recommendations.

In general, expert systems prescribe action based on recommendations obtained from one or more individuals, recommendations that must either be of the following form or be interpretable as such: "If some condition is known to be true, then perform some action." We will refer to rules of this form as **condition-recommendation rules**.

Typically, domain experts provide these rules based on their behavior as decision-makers. Thus, rule-based recommendations embody the explicit and implicit heuristics [Lenat, 1981; Lenat *et al.*, 1981; Pearl, 1984] used by these experts in performing their job and, hence, do not typically reflect any kind of general norm for making good decisions. Furthermore, these recommendations reflect an interpretation of the problem at hand that may differ markedly from how the decision-maker interprets it. Expert rules are included in the system's knowledge base simply because they appear to be effective. However, the lack of norms underlying most recommendation-action rules and their possibly inappropriate semantics imply that rule-based systems have little normative power and may leave a decision-maker with considerable magical ignorance about the reasoning behind the system's prescriptions.

More importantly, the expert or experts who provide these recommendations are, by necessity, removed from the actual situation where the decisions occur. Therefore, for the expert system to be useful, these recommendations must have anticipated (and be applicable in) all or most of the decision situations where the system will be used. This requirement places a considerable burden on designing these recommendations. In particular, the set of conditions under which these recommendations will apply must include all (or at least most of) the possible decision circumstances and preferences the system might encounter. Clearly, this will be feasible only when the range of these possible decision circumstances and preferences is both static and either small or very well structured. This strong limitation greatly restricts the use of expert systems for decision-making to very stable decision contexts where preference structures are simple and where uncertainty is not a major issue.

In contrast, intelligent decision systems can perform superbly in decision contexts where preferences and circumstances are complex, dynamic, and uncertain [Holtzman and Breese, 1986]. The absence of condition-recommendation rules that directly prescribe action (other than the MEU action axiom, which embodies the full normative power of decision theory) eliminates the need for the system designers to fully anticipate the range of decision situations that could be encountered. Guided by the methodology of decision analysis and within the scope of its underlying decision class analysis, an intelligent decision system can elicit important unanticipated features of the given situation from the decision-maker and other decision participants and can then incorporate these features into a decision model specifically developed to address the decision at hand as interpreted by the decision participants. Of course, anticipating and addressing such features will greatly facilitate and expedite the elicitation of the decision situation. However, whenever these features are new or otherwise unanticipated, an intelligent decision system can apply decision analysis techniques to obtain the needed knowledge directly from the decision participants.

An interesting way to view intelligent decision systems is as *expert systems for when there are no experts*. To illustrate this view, consider the point in an intelligent decision system consultation when a decision model is completed and a corresponding decision strategy is presented to the decision-maker. In a sense, this strategy is precisely a condition-recommendation rule that has been custom-made for the specific decision being analyzed and for the specific decision-maker. However, unlike the rules used in traditional expert systems, this condition-recommendation rule is very defensible, since it incorporates expert domain knowledge, an accurate description of the decision's circumstances, and a direct representation of the decision-maker's knowledge and preferences. Furthermore, the reasoning behind this rule is explicit and can—in fact, should—be reviewed and endorsed by the decision-maker and other appropriate decision participants.

The previous argument about the lack of normative power in traditional expert systems can also be made from a more technical standpoint. Our discussion in Chapter 2 implies that rule-based reasoning lacks normative power because of the lack of a valid action axiom. Specifically, recall that an action axiom is intuitively valid only if it meets two conditions: local correctness and extrapolability. These two validity conditions must be met by rule-based decision systems, because such systems constitute a formal statement (any computer program is a formal statement) that produces recommendations for action. Consequently, rule-based decision systems must contain (either explicitly or implicitly) one or more action axioms. Therefore, for a rule-based decision system to have normative power, these action axioms must be both locally correct and extrapolable with respect to the system's domain.

While we may be able to successfully argue that a purely rule-based system is locally correct because its condition-recommendation rules are usually designed to deal successfully with a representative set of toy problems, we are hard-pressed to make a strong argument that a rule-based decision system is extrapolable with respect to its domain. The main difficulty in making such an argument is the lack of an underlying normative theory for integrating the knowledge embodied in the system's condition-recommendation rules with the decision-maker's knowledge of his or her particular preferences and circumstances.[1] As discussed in Chapters 3 and 5, being able to

---

[1] We are assuming, of course, that these rules do not embody a statement of the axioms of decision theory or of another normative action axiom.

integrate knowledge about the decision situation into a recommendation is essential for the success of any decision system. Therefore, the usefulness of a purely rule-based decision system as a normative agent is limited either to decision problems very close to the decision-maker's intuition or to problems where dominating alternatives exist. As we have defined them, intelligent decision systems have neither of these limitations.

Representation and Use of Uncertainty

A second area where traditional rule-based decision systems are severely restricted is in their handling of uncertain knowledge. As discussed in Chapters 2 and 3, Lindley [1982] showed that under very weak and highly desirable assumptions of normative decision-making behavior, the representation of uncertain knowledge for decision-making must obey the axioms that define a probability measure [Kolmogoroff, 1933, 1950]. Otherwise, it would be possible to construct a situation where the decision-maker would willingly, and with certainty, give away valuable resources (e.g., money or lifetime). Technically, this possibility—described earlier as a money pump—makes nonprobabilistic measures **inadmissible**. Besides Lindley, Cox [1946] and Tribus [1969] have argued similarly and powerfully. However, despite its admissibility, the calculus of probability has only rarely been used in knowledge engineering.

Nonprobabilistic measures of uncertainty have important technical shortcomings. Without exception, these measures [Shortliffe and Buchanan, 1975; Shafer, 1976; Zadeh, 1981, 1983] are theoretically inadmissible [Lindley, 1982]. In addition, they are not clearly defined (e.g., what does it mean for a statement to have a certainty factor of, say, -0.63?), which adds unnecessary difficulty to the task of knowledge engineering. Furthermore, this lack of clarity greatly reduces the credibility and defensibility of recommendations issued by expert systems based on these measures.

Most nonprobabilistic uncertainty measures used in knowledge engineering have been developed for either or both of the following two purposes: (1) to avoid the computational burden often associated with probabilistic calculations and (2) as an attempt to automate the way humans perceive and reason with uncertainty (which is demonstrably *not* according to the laws of probability). Based on our discussions in Chapters 3 and 4, we can argue that there is little need for these measures. First, decision analysis provides effective tools for creating tractable probabilistic decision models without forgoing the normative power of probability theory. Second, given the ample evidence showing that humans reason very poorly with uncertain knowledge [Kahneman *et al.*, 1982; Kong *et al.*, 1986; Kolata, 1986], there is little sense in automating this *lack* of ability. Moreover, it is worth noting that for those situations where it is desirable to model human reasoning in the presence of uncertainty (e.g., for psychological research), there is little evidence that currently available nonprobabilistic measures are appropriate models of human cognition.

The absence of probabilistic reasoning within most existing expert systems can be traced to a common major misconception that probabilities reflect a state of nature. This interpretation attaches a notion of "objectivity" to probabilistic measures, which (as discussed in Chapter 3) can be very misleading and which has been severely criticized on profound philosophical grounds [Heidegger, 1962; Kapleau, 1967; Rota, 1973; Capra, 1975; Howard, 1980b]. In fact, this criticism refers to the concept of objectivity itself and significantly transcends our immediate concern with measuring uncertainty. A more useful interpretation of probabilities views them as a representation of a state of information and, hence, as being inherently subjective [de Finetti, 1937, 1968; Savage, 1972].

The practical implications of the objective view of probabilities are quite significant [Huff, 1954; Jaffe and Spirer, 1987]. In the context of a decision system, this view has led some researchers to attempt to construct a priori probabilistic descriptions of the decision domain without regard to the identity of the decision-maker. These attempts have failed for three simple reasons. First, every individual has a unique state of information and may have a different probability assessment for any given event. Second, probabilistically modeling a nontrivial decision domain requires assessing a joint distribution for an unimaginably large outcome space. The few cases where such modeling has been done for realistic decisions have relied on a large set of questionable probabilistic independence assumptions to make the task manageable [Duda *et al.*, 1976; Duda *et al.*, 1978; Duda *et al.*, 1979; Duda and Reboh, 1984; Duda *et al.*, 1987]. Third, even if they were feasible, a priori probabilistic models of nontrivial decision domains would be of limited practical use for decision-making.

The uselessness of such a priori probabilistic assessment is a direct consequence of our discussion in Chapter 2. Specifically, since the task of helping a decision-maker consists primarily of facilitating the formulation of his or her problem, it is unreasonable to suppose that the eventual decision model could be known in advance [Holtzman and Breese, 1986]. Even the fact that a decision system can usually benefit from substantial domain knowledge is insufficient to justify making such a supposition. Furthermore, even if some portions of the eventual model could be anticipated, there is no general reason to assume that a corresponding prior probabilistic assessment could be carried out with any degree of validity, without accounting for the situation-specific knowledge of the decision-maker and his or her appointed experts. Only for uncertain variables for which there is a widely accepted definition and plenty of stable data can such assessments be made without direct input from the decision participants, and, even then, a priori probabilistic statements can be quite controversial [Henrion and Fischhoff, 1986]. However, such a priori assessments will usually be applicable solely under very specific circumstances and should be explicitly reviewed and endorsed by the decision participants.

Intelligent decision systems address both the feasibility and the validity of probabilistic assessments for specific decision problems. Feasibility is achieved by using attention-focusing methods, such as deterministic sensitivity analysis, which we discussed in Chapters 2 and 3. When we assess a joint probability distribution, we do so solely over the highly restricted sample space that represents the sensitive part of the decision context. As discussed in Chapters 3 and 5, selecting uncertain variables should directly reflect the preferences of each individual decision-maker and, hence, cannot be determined without the decision-maker's input.

The validity of probabilistic measurements in an intelligent decision system is addressed by delaying the assessment process until a succinct decision model has been constructed. At that point, the number of necessary measurements should be small enough that each can be made using the probability encoding methods discussed in Chapters 2 and 3 and with the explicit involvement of the decision-maker and his or her appointed experts. In fact, such active participation in the probabilistic assessment process is likely to be a powerful source of valuable insight, since it directly elicits the knowledge of decision participants and greatly demystifies the treatment of uncertainty. Of course, in cases where data are plentiful, where there are clearly identified domain experts, where information is stable, and where we foresee a stable decision situation structure, the a priori assessment of probability distributions for specific variables may be extremely useful. This special case of a priori probability assessment will be discussed later in this chapter and in Chapter 8.

Furthermore, it is critical that probabilistic assessments be explicitly recognized as someone's assertion and not as some "computer-generated" number. Thus, it is essential that each assessment have an associated **pedigree** [i.e., the name(s) of the individual(s) asserting it and a time when the assertion was made]. In addition, the pedigrees of different assessments must be appropriately combined as a probabilistic model (e.g., an influence diagram) is manipulated. Intelligent decision systems can take advantage of knowledge-based techniques [de Kleer, 1986] to carry out this task efficiently.

Knowledge Acquisition

A third area where the methodology of intelligent decision systems should prove superior to strictly rule-based approaches is in acquiring knowledge. Because an intelligent decision system is based on decision analysis, the acquisition process can benefit from the painstakingly clear definition of terminology within this discipline. For example, we can compare the interpretation of an ambiguous term such as "certainty factor" [Shortliffe and Buchanan, 1975] or that of a "fuzzy probability" [Zadeh, 1981] with the clear and well-defined concept of a probability [de Finetti, 1937, 1968] or that of an influence diagram [Howard and Matheson, 1981]. The success of obtaining knowledge from expert individuals depends greatly on the clarity of the terms used in the acquisition process. Having a carefully defined language to describe decision problems promises to make knowledge acquisition for an intelligent decision system a much simpler and more reliable process than it is for expert systems that do not benefit from as powerful an underlying theory.[2]

The claim that knowledge acquisition is relatively straightforward from a decision-analytic standpoint is substantiated by noting that the task of a decision analyst can be viewed almost completely as one of acquiring domain- and situation-specific knowledge. Thus, acquiring expert knowledge for an intelligent decision system can benefit from the many pertinent techniques developed for decision analysis [Matheson, 1970].

DELIVERING DECISION ANALYSIS THROUGH INTELLIGENT DECISION SYSTEMS

While intelligent decision systems were explicitly conceived to deliver automated decision analysis assistance, they go beyond this original objective. Besides reducing the cost and increasing the speed of the decision analysis process, intelligent decision systems effectively change its nature.

Decision analysis can be understood at a minimum of three different levels of abstraction: philosophy, process, and tools [Matheson, 1986]. At its core lies a philosophical foundation that defines the meaning of a good decision. (We discussed this philosophy in Chapters 2 and 3.) Based on this foundation, professional decision analysts have developed a rich set of processes and methods (covered in Chapters 3 and 4) to facilitate the application of this philosophy to real decision situations. In turn, these processes and methods rely on specific tools (e.g., computer programs, probability wheels,[3] strategy

---

[2]A direct benefit of this theory is embodied in the concept of a knowledge map [Howard, 1987a]—a strictly probabilistic influence diagram that represents the knowledge of one or more individuals. Distinguishing between evocative and substantive knowledge maps can greatly clarify the knowledge acquisition process. Similarly, using disjoint and redundant maps can significantly simplify knowledge acquisition.

[3]A probability wheel is a reference device similar to a wheel of fortune used to assess probability distributions. It consists of a disk divided into two different-colored sectors. The relative proportion of these sectors can be physically varied to represent events with different probabilities of occurrence [Staël von Holstein and Spetzler, 1973; Spetzler and Staël von Holstein, 1975].

tables[4]); some of these tools are standard practice, while others are continually being developed to enhance and simplify the interaction between decision participants.

To respect the philosophical underpinnings of decision analysis, intelligent decision systems will exploit their computer-based nature by following a process that will probably depart—to a greater or lesser degree—from the processes traditionally used in professional decision analysis. Similarly, the specific tools (e.g., probability assessment tools) used in intelligent decision systems may be quite different from those used in a more traditional setting.

Besides the obvious impact of automation on speed and interaction style, much of the effect of intelligent decision systems on the delivery of decision analysis assistance will be a direct consequence of the knowledge-based capabilities that these systems inherit from expert system technology. One important effect of these capabilities is the ability to provide an unprecedented level of automated guidance on how to analyze a decision in a particular class, thereby enabling individuals without professional training in the discipline of decision analysis to be effective decision analysts in that domain. Another important effect of the knowledge-based capabilities of intelligent decision systems is the possibility of delivering substantial domain-specific knowledge. Thus, the intelligent decision system could serve both as an analyst and an expert—an arrangement that would usually be inadvisable if the analyst were a human being.

There are several key implications of the differences between professional decision analysis and intelligent decision systems. First, as originally intended, the cost of analyzing individual decisions in well-chosen classes of decisions (including the prorated cost of developing the system) should be hundreds or even thousands of times lower than an equivalent set of decision analyses. Second, the possibility of carrying out much of the analysis prior to individual consultations and the potential for developing automated special-purpose tools could greatly streamline the analysis process, making it significantly simpler and faster than would be possible with more traditional means.

By substantially lowering the cost and speeding up the delivery of decision analysis assistance, intelligent decision systems open a wide new range of possibilities for assisting decision-makers. Thus, such arenas as personal decisions, small-business decisions, tactical and operational decisions in industry, and decisions performed by autonomous systems—all of which are well outside the current economic scope of professional decision analysis—can now be addressed with intelligent decision systems. Chapter 9 discusses the potential applications of intelligent decision systems in more detail.

---

[4]A strategy table is a matrix-like graphical representation used to elicit new alternatives for a given decision. It is particularly useful for concisely depicting the large number of dimensions typically needed to describe an alternative. A similar representation, called an outcome table, is used to elicit possible outcome scenarios for a decision.

KNOWLEDGE REQUIREMENTS FOR AN INTELLIGENT DECISION SYSTEM

We can divide the knowledge base of an intelligent decision system into at least five categories: domain knowledge, preference knowledge, probabilistic knowledge, user data (knowledge of the circumstances and information of the individual decision-maker), and process knowledge. The knowledge in each of these five categories has important special features that can affect the way it is represented.

Domain Knowledge

Most domain knowledge in an intelligent decision system concerns the indirect assessment of chance nodes in the evolving, partially defined decision model. As discussed in Chapter 4, indirectly assessing a chance node in an influence diagram requires that an assessment function be specified. This function can be either deterministic or stochastic, and its purpose is to break down the assessment of a single node into simpler assessments of one or more relatively less aggregate nodes. Therefore, domain-specific knowledge is largely coded in the form of indirect assessment functions, with the inputs to these functions exhibiting the variables that describe the domain and the form of these functions representing the relations between domain variables.

The role of deterministic nodes (i.e., nodes with an associated deterministic assessment function) within the domain knowledge base is particularly important for successfully implementing an intelligent decision system. In general, assessing a deterministic relation is considerably faster and less costly than assessing a more detailed stochastic version of the same relation. Consequently, it is much easier to obtain deterministic assessment functions than stochastic assessment functions from domain experts.

Attempting to construct a stochastic assessment function for every rule that proposes the indirect assessment of a chance node would be prohibitively expensive for nontrivial decision domains. Fortunately, the natural human tendency to think deterministically leads to the formation of many nearly deterministic relations in most conceivable decision domains. These relations can be exploited to design deterministic assessment functions. Otherwise, if representing a decision element as a deterministic node oversimplifies the problem, the cost of a stochastic assessment can be limited by judiciously selecting a low level of resolution for the distributions to be assessed.

It is important to recall that indirectly assessing a chance node in an influence diagram by using a deterministic assessment function does not imply that the node being assessed is deterministically specified. Given stochastic inputs, a deterministic node has a probability distribution over its sample space that can be computed from its assessment function and the distribution of its inputs by standard probabilistic techniques [Howard, 1981a]. Therefore, a variable represented by a deterministic node is only conditionally deterministic. Consequently, a useful way to think of deterministic assessment functions is as an effective means of describing complex stochastic relations.

In addition to indirect assessment knowledge, an intelligent decision system can have domain knowledge to help the decision participants deal with domain questions that arise while indirectly assessing influence diagram nodes. This knowledge is much like that found in traditional expert systems, since it is aimed at facilitating the task of establishing the conditions under which particular indirect assessments are applicable. Furthermore, some of this knowledge can be targeted at responding (either directly or indirectly) to user queries related to constructing a decision model, thereby extending the usefulness of an intelligent decision system to an arena where expert systems excel. However, to guarantee the normative power of the system's recommendations, neither this nor any other knowledge base must contain any condition-recommendation rules.

The domain knowledge in an intelligent decision system can also be designed to propose promising decision alternatives that decision participants have not yet considered. Another function for the domain-specific portion of the knowledge base is to suggest model reductions based on heuristic arguments. The proposal of alternatives and the suggestion of model reductions depend greatly on the specific decision domain and cannot be addressed properly here in a general discussion.

Preference Knowledge

Preference knowledge in an intelligent decision system is used to elicit a preference model from the decision-maker. As discussed in Chapter 5, a promising approach to structuring this knowledge involves developing a class of parametric functions representative of the preferences that could be encountered in the population of decision-makers for which the system is designed [Keelin, 1977, 1981; Holtzman, 1985a]. Consequently, preference knowledge can be divided into two subcategories: (1) knowledge about parametric functions and the conditions under which each particular function is applicable and (2) knowledge for eliciting parameter values once a parametric function has been selected. For each consultation, this knowledge can be used interactively with the decision-maker to yield a fully specified preference structure to be included in the overall analysis.

Probabilistic Knowledge

A third category of knowledge in an intelligent decision system—probabilistic knowledge—guides the assessment of probability distributions for chance nodes. This process can take advantage of the assessment protocols evolved from interactions among decision analysts, psychologists, and domain experts [Wallsten and Budescu, 1983; Merkhofer, 1987]. These protocols help compensate for the many biases that distort an individual's perception of uncertainty. In addition, since the process of encoding a decision-maker's risk attitude closely resembles that of assessing probability distributions, directing risk attitude assessment can be another function for probabilistic knowledge in an intelligent decision system, although, strictly speaking, risk attitude is actually an element of the decision-maker's preferences.

Another important role of probabilistic knowledge is suggesting actual probability distributions for chance nodes in the decision model. Such distributions do not constitute general a priori assessments (which were criticized earlier in discussing traditional expert systems). Rather, these distributions have a very limited scope within areas where the system's designers believe there may be consensus, and they should always be reviewed by the decision participants. Moreover, a priori distributions should always be conditioned by the antecedents of the rules that propose them, which may be quite restrictive. Furthermore, very different possible distributions for a variable may be proposed under even slightly different circumstances. The main purpose of having actual probability distributions in the knowledge base is to simplify the assessment process when the appropriate special conditions are discovered. For example, storing actual distributions resulting from the specific structure of the human reproductive system in the probabilistic knowledge base of an intelligent decision system has been particularly useful for dealing with infertility decisions. (See the discussion in Chapter 8.)

User Data

A fourth category of knowledge in an intelligent decision system is specific to each individual decision-maker who uses the system. Commonly referred to as user data, this category encompasses the set of facts that define the circumstances of the individual user. User data also include any information and alternatives that may be available to the specific decision-maker and that are not part of the system's domain knowledge. Clearly, all these data must be obtained at the time of consultation and should generally be requested when the more general knowledge in the system's knowledge base is used for the specific decision at hand.

Process Knowledge

A fifth category of knowledge—process knowledge—guides the user of an intelligent decision system through the process of decision analysis. Process knowledge gives advice on what to do next, warns of possible pitfalls in the analysis, and directs the analysis process with effective analytical guidelines. In addition, two other important functions of process knowledge are to help the decision participants understand the rationale behind the analysis and to support the decision-maker (should the need arise) in documenting his or her decision to defend it.

Process knowledge plays a central role in intelligent decision systems developed for classes of decisions where many unanticipated decision elements typically arise in the course of a consultation. Guiding an untrained user in the task of capturing these elements and incorporating them into the decision model can be quite challenging and should rely on the techniques discussed in Chapters 3 and 4.

AN ARCHITECTURE FOR INTELLIGENT DECISION SYSTEMS

Figure 6.1 shows a plausible architecture for an intelligent decision system [Holtzman, 1985c]. This architecture, which implements the interactive environment described in Chapters 3 and 4, consists of four interconnected parts: a general-purpose inference engine, a set of data structures, a corresponding set of specialized procedures, and a user interface (or front end).

The general-purpose inference engine (illustrated on the top left corner of Fig. 6.1 viewed from the side) interprets the knowledge bases throughout the system. Its function is to efficiently implement a useful portion of the first-order predicate calculus and associated syllogisms. Furthermore, to ensure that the overall system operates transparently and in a focused manner, it would be a good idea for the engine to exhibit search behavior that emphasizes a depth-first-like control strategy (which tends to focus the consultation on the current topic under consideration) with variable "askability" and "tellability."[5] Besides having a rule-based inference engine, an intelligent decision system would benefit from having the ability to reason with comparable structures, such as frames and semantic nets.

---

[5] Askability is the feature that enables the inference engine to query its user, in a customized manner, for unknown facts. Tellability is a similar feature that allows the inference engine to dynamically report the progress of a line of reasoning.

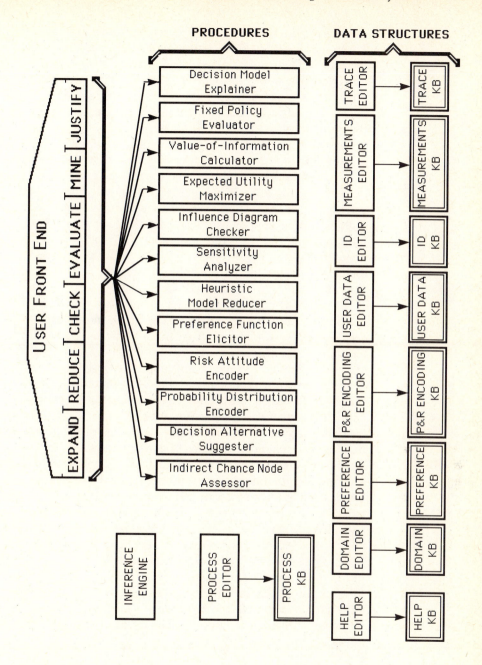

FIGURE 6.1   Architecture for an intelligent decision system.

The operation of the system revolves around a set of nine data structures. These structures, depicted as double-lined boxes along the left and bottom margins of Fig. 6.1, can be accessed through structure-specific editors. Editors allow all interactions with the data to occur with consistent syntax and semantics at a high level, which allows the rest of the system to be independent of the physical implementation of the data structures and helps ensure their reliability and integrity.

In the order drawn (skipping, for the moment, the HELP and PROCESS facilities), the leftmost four data structures (shown at the bottom of the figure) correspond to the knowledge base (KB) categories discussed earlier: domain-specific knowledge, preference knowledge, probability- and risk-encoding knowledge, and individual user data. The next three data structures represent various aspects of the evolving formal decision model: the influence diagram (ID) that embodies the model, a set of measurements about the current model (useful for mining the model), and a trace of the interaction between the system and the user that has led to the current model (useful for justifying the model).

It is worth noting that the set of measurements contained within the MEASUREMENTS knowledge base is by no means exhaustive. In fact, the set of possible model measurements is infinite. The contents of this data structure consist of the results of previous calculations (e.g., from sensitivity analyses) relevant to the current model—calculations that may have been performed either automatically by the system or explicitly at the request of the user and whose results may be useful later in the analysis.

The remaining two data structures are specifically designed to help the user through the analysis process. The HELP data structure is a source of helpful information for the user. Together with its editor, it can be a source of facts about system operation, general knowledge about the decision domain, theoretical foundations of the system, and external sources of information. The PROCESS data structure, which consists of a set of rules that describe and enforce the logical operation of the overall system, guides inexperienced users by, for instance, preventing a nonexistent model from being checked and an unchecked model from being evaluated. In addition, process knowledge might issue user warnings such as not to begin encoding probabilities until after deterministic sensitivity analysis has been performed. Including this last knowledge base in the system has two primary advantages. First, it allows the system to follow the logic of the user rather than imposing a rigid interaction protocol, and, second, it enables the rules that control the system's operation to be explicitly stated and, hence, to be modifiable and usable for explanatory purposes.

The data structures in the proposed architecture are manipulated by a set of specialized procedures. Figure 6.1 depicts a set of twelve such procedures, which are representative of those that should be part of an intelligent decision system. However, a somewhat different set may be better suited in any given implementation. The leftmost five procedures shown deal with decision-model expansion. In particular, the indirect chance node assessor, the decision alternative suggester, and the preference function elicitor expand the influence diagram model at the level of structure and at the levels of function and number. The probability distribution encoder and the risk attitude encoder expand the model solely at the levels of function and number.

The next two procedures—heuristic model reducer and sensitivity analyzer—help the user reduce the formal decision model. The heuristic model reducer uses domain-specific knowledge to recognize features of the decision model that lend themselves to reduction (e.g., by consolidating a set of similar nodes into a single one). The sensitivity analyzer performs both deterministic and stochastic sensitivity analyses to further help reduce the decision model by identifying low-sensitivity variables. In addition, besides model reduction, the sensitivity analyzer provides an important means of mining the decision model, which is the basis for a recommendation.

The influence diagram checker verifies the syntactic correctness of a decision model. However, given a well-designed set of model expansion procedures (which would not allow illegal additions to the decision model), the primary functions of the checker are to identify incomplete (e.g., unassessed) portions of an influence diagram and to verify that all necessary no-forgetting arrows (discussed in Chapter 4) have been added to the model. If no corrections or additions to the model are needed, then the expected utility maximizer can be used to compute a formal recommendation for action. In addition, as part of the maximization process, several model measurements can be generated and stored for future use.

The value-of-information calculator and the fixed policy evaluator are further examples of model mining procedures. The former evaluates the value of gathering further information on variables explicitly depicted in the model, taking into account the reliability of available information-gathering options. The latter computes the desirability of less-than-optimal decision policies. Both of these procedures can generate many useful model measurements.

The decision model explainer can be used to justify the current decision model. This procedure relies on the rule-based nature of the overall system's operation and produces two types of explanations. First, explanations can describe the rationale for including specific model elements by referring to the facts and rules used in adding those elements to the model. Second, explanation can be more exploratory in nature and respond to user queries about the decision domain. To a large extent, the procedure's ability to justify the current decision model depends on the extent and detail of the trace that has been kept on the interaction between the user and the system (stored in the TRACE knowledge base). Similarly, its ability to respond to exploratory user queries depends on the extent and detail of the domain knowledge base.

The fourth and final part of the proposed architecture for an intelligent decision system is an interface program to interact directly with the user. This program should not only facilitate the use of the procedures and data structures that constitute the intelligent decision system but, ideally, should adapt the system's interaction to the identity and expertise of each individual user.

An important function of the user interface is to keep track of the dynamic nature of a consultation. Thus, the interface program should provide somewhat different functionality when the user is formulating the decision model than when he or she is evaluating it or appraising an evaluated model. This ability to account for the progressive nature of the interaction is particularly useful for providing clear and concise help to the novice user. However, to avoid burdening the user with having to remember the relationship between modes of interaction and system functions, the mode-tracking feature should be implemented automatically and as transparently as possible. In fact, this implementation may benefit from the rule-based structure of the system by exploiting a set of heuristics that make mode transitions more intuitive and explicit.

The architecture described in this section is only an example of how an intelligent decision system might be designed. Many other architectures are possible. For instance, a system based on object-oriented programming would be likely to take quite a different form by, for instance, grouping procedures and data structures into comprehensive objects. However, many of the distinctions made for this example (e.g., distinguishing between various kinds of knowledge) can greatly simplify the design of an intelligent decision system, regardless of its actual implementation.

Part II

Applications

7

Computer-Aided Medical Decision Analysis

The future offers little hope for those who expect that our new mechanical slaves will offer us a world in which we may rest from thinking. Help us they may, but at the cost of supreme demands upon our honesty and our intelligence.
— *God and Golem, Inc.,*
Norbert Wiener

> Intelligent decision systems can make decision analysis available in contexts where it would otherwise be too expensive or too slow to be useful. In particular, the possibility of delivering decision analysis assistance automatically opens the door to a wide range of realistic possibilities for assisting such medical decision-makers as patients, physicians, nurses, and paramedics. This chapter discusses the promise and some of the challenges of using intelligent decision systems in medicine.

We noted in Chapter 1 that the medical field—and, in particular, the area of medical treatment decisions—is a prime candidate for applying intelligent decision systems. This is so because such decisions must typically be made by patients and their physicians at a point where the diagnostic process has produced a relatively stable (albeit incomplete and uncertain) determination of the patient's problem and where specific treatment or more invasive testing options are being considered.

Given the current interest in applying expert-system technology to medical and other diagnostic problems [Shortliffe *et al.*, 1979; Szolovitz, 1982; Clancey and Shortliffe, 1984], it is important to clearly distinguish decision systems from computer-based expert diagnosticians. Whereas a decision system is designed to generate strategies for action, an expert diagnostician concentrates on the inferential task of determining the identity of one or more malfunctions or other forms of disease in the patient's body. Thus, by definition, a decision system performs a prescriptive function, while the task of a diagnostic system is strictly descriptive. Hence, for example, while patient preferences are quite unimportant for diagnosis, they are crucial for decision-making.

SELECTING A MEDICAL DECISION DOMAIN

Selecting a medical domain for an intelligent decision system is a special case of designing a class of decisions. Consequently, in making such a choice, we should take into account the design guidelines proposed in Chapter 5. Here we discuss some of the implications of those guidelines in the context of medical decision-making.

An important criterion for selecting a medical decision domain is the absence of dominating alternatives. For example, given a diagnosis of appendicitis, the best course of action is generally to perform a laparotomy (i.e., surgically opening the abdomen) followed by an appendectomy (i.e., surgically removing the appendix). Although this alternative may not dominate under special circumstances (e.g., when religious beliefs preclude a medical intervention or when there are major medical contraindications), its desirability in most cases is so strong that a decision system for appendicitis decisions would be quite useless. We can compare this situation to that of a patient suffering from end-stage renal disease (ESRD), where both kidneys have ceased to function properly. Currently, an ESRD patient faces a difficult choice between transplantation, dialysis (in its various forms), and a conservative therapy consisting mostly of dietary restrictions. Thus, for ESRD patients, there is rarely a dominating alternative, since no one treatment is better than all others in all respects [Gorry *et al.*, 1973; Holtzman, 1983b].

Another issue that arises in designing a medical intelligent decision system is how much time the patient has to make a decision. Since an intelligent decision system is designed to provide the decision-maker with insight, as opposed to merely giving answers, the design of such a system must assume that there is enough time to make decisions. The environment of an emergency room, for instance, would probably be better suited to a more algorithmic type of decision system that requires less extensive interaction with the patient and physician.[1]

The size of the decision-maker population for which the system is designed is another important factor in the success of an intelligent medical decision system. Consider, for example, the case of heart-lung transplant patients. Although the stakes involved in deciding whether or not to undergo this treatment are very large, the affected patient population is probably too small to make it worthwhile to develop a full-scale intelligent decision system. In these cases, individual decision analyses are likely to be more economical.

A particularly important feature in selecting a medical domain for designing an intelligent decision system is the desire to increase the quality of decision-making on the part of patients, physicians, or both. In the general practice of medicine, the quality of decision-making is diminished by the inability of humans, and physicians in particular, to deal effectively with uncertainty [Pearn, 1973; Black, 1979; Lubs, 1979; Siegelman, 1983; Kong *et al.*, 1986; Kolata, 1986]. Among other consequences, this inability promotes the abuse of diagnostic procedures by encouraging physicians to search for causal relationships without regard for the cost of their search [Bursztajn *et al.*, 1981]. Moreover, poor decision-making also tends to occur in specific medical fields. For example, as we will discuss in more detail in Chapter 8, poor decisions are frequently made in the domain of infertility. In part, we can attribute the prevailing low quality of decision-making in this field to the pervasive nature of sexual taboos in our society [The Boston's Women's Health Book Collective, 1979; Eliasson, 1981]. Our inability to deal openly with sexually related matters often leads to the intentional (i.e., Gordian) ignorance of very basic elements of human reproduction and, therefore, produces very poor decision-making behavior.[2]

The attractiveness of a medical decision domain for intelligent decision systems is also affected by the routine use and overuse of major testing procedures [Hellerstein, 1983]. Examples of such procedures might include biopsies, arteriograms, endoscopies, amniocenteses, exploratory laparotomies, or any other diagnostic task having considerable financial cost, toxicity, invasiveness, and/or threat to life [Pinckney and Pinckney, 1982; Solbel and

---

[1]Given recent technological trends, an interesting possibility would be to develop personal preference and circumstance "dog tags" (e.g., using miniature electromagnetic devices) that could be used as input to emergency-room decision systems. These devices would allow an automatic system to account for the desires and the medical history of the patient. Some of the ethical difficulties that obviously arise in this context are discussed later in this chapter.

[2]For instance, women experiencing difficulties getting pregnant are often subjected to extensive medical workups while their male partners remain untested. Distinguishing the male and female reproductive systems makes anatomic sense, but it severely hinders effective infertility decision-making.

Ferguson, 1985]. These procedures increase the worth of a decision-analytic approach for selecting medical strategies, because value-of-information calculations can be used very effectively to better make the selection.

Beyond decision-analytic considerations, selecting a medical decision domain can also take advantage of the fact that an intelligent decision system is constructed with a rule-based architecture. Consequently, as with traditional expert systems, the intelligent decision system can offer its inferential power to the user as an aid to decision-making. For instance, complex drug interactions can be accounted for in designing a medical strategy. Hence, medical decision domains that require considerable inference for developing treatment strategies are very attractive for developing intelligent decision systems.

As in any other field, a class of medical decisions should be designed from the point of view of the decision-maker, which, in this case, is the patient whose life, pain, and (usually) money are at stake. In general, the patient's interests are largely served by the existing breakdown of specialties within the medical field. However, as discussed in Chapter 5 and as we will see in Chapter 8, an intelligent decision system may have to be designed across medical specialties.

MODELING PATIENT PREFERENCES

Developing a model of patient preferences is a central requirement for designing effective medical intelligent decision systems. As stated in Chapter 6, effective models can consist of a parametric function fitted to each individual decision-maker by assigning parameter values. To be useful, a parametric patient preference function must be both general and simple. Generality is important because the function must represent the wide spectrum of preferences possible within the population of patients for which the decision system is designed. The function must also be simple in the sense that it requires few, well-defined parameter evaluations to be completely specified; if the number of parameters is large, or if the meaning of the parameters is unclear, the assessment process may be infeasible under the time pressures and social constraints of a clinical setting.

We may recall that in the context of decision analysis, a preference (or value) function represents the decision-maker's preferences over the set of possible outcomes that could result given any of the choices being considered and any of the possible ways in which uncertainty could be resolved. Therefore, a value function takes the formal specification of a decision outcome and produces a single number that corresponds to the desirability of that outcome. For intelligent decision systems, it is useful to think of the value function as a computer program, with its input being a description of the outcome scenario to be evaluated and its output being the desired preference measure.

Despite the importance of medical value functions, we currently have only a very limited understanding of how to design them effectively. For instance, to compute its output, the value function must quantify a diverse set of attributes and jointly measure (i.e., commensurate) them according to a single number. Both of these operations, quantification and commensuration, are particularly difficult in a medical decision context [McNeil *et al.*, 1982]. Unlike more traditional application areas for decision analysis—where outcomes are primarily financial—medical decision analysis must account for such attributes as morbidity (i.e., disease and discomfort), life-style, and length of life [Ginsberg and Offensend, 1968; Ginsberg, 1969; Holtzman, 1983b]. In many cases, such medical attributes are simply not well understood by the medical community or the patient. For instance, no one has more than a vague idea of how to describe pain, much less how to measure it. Purely physiological explanations fail to account for the profound effect that semantics has on our perception of even such a basic sensation [Melzack, 1983]. For example, pain feels quite differently when it is inflicted by a dentist than when it is inflicted by a mugger, and different people request vastly different amounts of anesthetic for the same dental procedures. More complex medical outcomes, such as "discomfort," defy all current efforts to define or measure them reliably. Since intelligent decision systems can now make it possible to affordably apply decision analysis to medical treatment decisions, we must deepen our understanding of patient preferences.

Currently, only a very limited number of models have been developed to measure patient preferences. Howard [1979, 1980a, 1984] has designed several models for individuals to make or delegate decisions involving the possibility of death or of a comparable outcome (such as the loss of a limb). Based on these models, a value function has been constructed that commensurates financial cost, morbidity, and lifetime (i.e., remaining length of life) [Holtzman, 1983b]. Other researchers have explored the preferences of patients in a variety of medical situations but have not produced general-purpose preference models based on these studies [McNeil *et al.*,1978; Sackett and Torrance, 1978; McNeil and Pauker, 1979; Pliskin *et al.*, 1980; McNeil *et al.*, 1981; Eraker and Sox, 1981; McNeil *et al.*, 1982; Beck *et al.*, 1982a; Beck *et al.*, 1982b; Ciampi *et al.*, 1982; Harron *et al.*, 1983; Christensen-Szalanski, 1984; Read *et al.*, 1984].

An important prerequisite for designing a patient value function is the ability to clearly and concisely describe complex medical scenarios to patients in meaningful terms, such as their effects on mobility and comfort. Similarly, we must be able to describe the benefits, costs, and risks associated with medical procedures. Recent psychological results indicate that the way we describe possible scenarios and treatments (e.g., in terms of losses and gains) can greatly affect how patients perceive these possibilities [Tversky and Kahneman, 1981; McNeil *et al.*, 1982]. This difficulty primarily occurs because we have to summarize these descriptions to avoid burdening the patient with an unmanageable amount of detail. In addition, contextual semantics play a very important role in the way people visualize hypothetical situations.

As patients become increasingly active participants in the medical decisions that affect them, the need for effective patient value models is likely to become a central issue in decision analysis. Research has been scarce in this area because economic considerations have kept medical decision analysis within the academic realm. As intelligent decision systems are introduced into clinical practice, the cost of analyzing medical decisions should significantly decrease, which is likely to increase the pace of research in the modeling of patient preferences.

ETHICAL CONSIDERATIONS

Using computer-based systems for decision-making raises many important ethical issues, especially when we deal with medical decisions. Even without computerized decision aids, medicine has always produced difficult ethical questions, because physicians often have to decide on their patients' behalfs. That these decisions can directly affect the welfare of patients and even their life only increases the importance of medical ethics. Current technological advances have further complicated the relationship between physicians and patients, forcing medical professionals to review even the most basic concepts on which their discipline is based [Chalk *et al.*, 1980]. For instance, recently acquired abilities to detect living processes and to prolong life artificially have led to an ongoing effort to define death [Veatch, 1978]. Similarly, technological advances in neonatology have challenged our concept of what it means to be a live human being, and new reproductive technology has blurred the meaning of the term *parent* [Austin, 1972; Weaver and Escobar, 1987].

As a result of this adjustment in the philosophical foundations of medical practice, the roles of health-care professionals and of patients are being continuously redefined [Strull *et al.*, 1984]. And, the introduction of a computer-based decision tool into clinical practice is likely to change these roles even further. In particular, using intelligent decision systems implies that decision analysts, knowledge engineers, and domain experts will indirectly participate in the medical decision process. This, in turn, means that we must carefully consider the extent to which such participation is desirable.

The clinical use of intelligent decision systems requires that we be very specific about the identity of the participants in a medical decision. Typically, the patient (who, if not incompetent because of his or her medical condition, should be the ultimate decision-maker) is assisted by an attending physician (or by another health-care professional). Using an intelligent decision system means that several other decision participants will be added. Besides the medical experts whose knowledge has been coded into the system's knowledge base, decision analysts and knowledge engineers who developed the computer-based system can play a significant role in the decision. For example, through the design of the decision system, they can greatly affect what elements of the decision receive attention and, thus, can have a profound effect on the way decision problems are formulated.

Regardless of its apparent expertise, any computer-based decision aid should be viewed strictly as a decision-making tool. Even the most sophisticated tool cannot change the fact that the consequences of a medical decision are borne by the patient and his or her physician. Therefore, these individuals must be held responsible for the quality of decisions. More generally, we must totally avoid assigning the status of a *moral agent* to any computer-based system. To allow the responsibility for poor decisions to be attributed to "computer error" is to pave the way for an Orwellian society [Orwell, 1946, 1949].

The need for individuals to remain responsible for their decisions is particularly severe when a physician must act as a guardian for his or her patient. This situation can arise in a variety of medical contexts, including the treatment of the very young or the very old, the management of comatose patients, and the handling of emergency situations.

The issue of responsibility is closely tied to the assignment of liability when a poor decision is made. It should be apparent that the concept of liability does not apply to amoral agents such as computers. However, liability could definitely be assigned to the designers of a decision tool as well as to its users. This should be an important consideration for potential developers of intelligent decision systems.

As with any new technology, introducing decision systems into the realm of medicine is bound to be met with justifiable skepticism. Technical matters aside, the issue of liability is likely to be central to this skepticism. An interesting question in this regard is whether using a computer-based decision tool could increase the vulnerability of a physician in a medical controversy. However, a possibly more interesting question is whether a physician could be liable for *not* using such a tool when one is available. The latter question reflects the historical reaction of the legal system to the use of technology in medicine much more than the former question.

This brief discussion shows that using intelligent decision systems in medicine requires paying careful attention to ethical matters. Although the potential benefits of these systems can be great, they are also potentially subject to major abuse. Placing these systems in perspective within their human context is an essential factor in our ability to use them wisely.

8

Rachel: An Intelligent Decision System for Infertile Couples

And when Rachel saw that she bore Jacob no children, Rachel envied her sister and she said unto Jacob: "Give me children or else I die."
                                                                    —Bereshit XXX; 1

And God remembered Rachel, and God hearkened to her, and opened her womb. And she conceived, and bore a son, and said: "God hath taken away my reproach." And she called his name Joseph, saying: "The Lord add to me another son."
                                                                    —Bereshit XXX; 22, 23, 24

This chapter describes Rachel, an intelligent decision system for infertile couples seeking medical help. Rachel helps patients and their physician derive a recommended course of action from a model that combines the physician's medical knowledge with the patient's knowledge of his or her preferences and specific circumstances. The Appendix at the end of the book supplements this chapter by presenting a sample session with Rachel.

THE PROBLEM OF INFERTILITY

Although most people take their ability to reproduce for granted, many couples find the joy of bearing children replaced by the anxiety and despair that often follow the realization that they have a fertility problem. In fact, the human reproductive system is so intricate that it should not be surprising to realize that it can sometimes malfunction. What is disturbing, however, is the high prevalence of impaired fertility. For married couples in the United States, estimates of the rate of infertility cluster around 15 percent of the population [Nofziger, 1982; Hatcher *et al.*, 1982]. Thus, about one out of every six married couples in this country is considered infertile.

It is important to distinguish infertility from sterility. As used in this book, **infertility** denotes a condition of *decreased* fertility relative to the over-all population. An infertile couple has the potential to conceive, but only at a rate that is significantly lower than that observed in the general population. **Sterility** refers to the *complete absence* of reproductive faculties, which means that sterile couples cannot conceive at all.

DECISIONS FACED BY INFERTILE COUPLES

There are many medical alternatives available to infertile couples wishing to have children, including surgery, drug therapies, and a variety of other tests and treatments [Lamb, 1972; Silber, 1980; Lamb and Waechter, 1981; Nofziger, 1982; Lamb, 1983–1984; Polansky, 1984; Kessler, 1984–1985]. However, selecting among these alternatives can be quite difficult, primarily because there is often no dominating alternative (i.e., one that is essentially independent of the specific circumstances and preferences of the patient), even when a detailed diagnosis is available. For instance, a tubal blockage[1] can be treated with a laparotomy, with in-vitro fertilization, or sometimes even with a laparoscopy. Furthermore, the option of not treating the blockage can be surprisingly attractive because the risk of an ectopic pregnancy—a highly undesirable situation—is greatly increased after repairing a tubal blockage. Thus, the choice among the available alternatives should account for the patient's specific circumstances and preferences and should not depend solely on medical considerations.

In a clinical context, the need to economically combine medical knowledge with details of the patient's knowledge of his or her situation can place

---

[1] Medical terms used in this chapter are described in the Glossary.

both physician and patient at somewhat of an impasse. Despite everyone's attempts to communicate effectively, the time pressures common in modern medicine make it infeasible for most physicians to get to know their patients well enough to fully understand their detailed circumstances and preferences. Similarly, it is unreasonable to expect most patients to acquire the solid medical background required to make unaided treatment decisions. There is therefore a need to effectively combine the physician's medical knowledge with the patient's personal knowledge to reach a well-informed decision with a reasonable amount of effort.

THE DECISION CONTEXT ADDRESSED BY RACHEL

This chapter describes an intelligent decision system called Rachel, which was designed to aid infertile couples and their physicians at the Stanford University Medical Center infertility clinic in selecting medical treatments given the following setting (a very common occurrence at the clinic) [Holtzman, 1985a, 1985b]. After having been thoroughly examined, an infertile couple undergoes a series of tests—either minor or only slightly invasive—to allow physicians to diagnose the possible sources of their infertility problem. Since the Stanford infertility clinic is typically a tertiary care facility (i.e., patients have often been referred twice—once from a family physician and once from a specialist such as a gynecologist or a urologist—before coming to Stanford), the diagnostic investigation may include the results of any previous relevant tests the couple may bring. At the completion of this diagnosis, physicians and patients meet to discuss diagnostic findings and possible courses of action.

If there is an obvious way to proceed—there is a dominating alternative—then the next action is clear. However, when it is not obvious what course of action is preferable (and this occurs frequently), patients and physicians are faced with a difficult dilemma. The ubiquitous question "Doctor, what would you recommend?" cannot be answered by a responsible physician without a clear understanding of the patient's circumstances and preferences. For instance, occasionally the best treatment from a purely medical standpoint may have serious financial implications for the patient (e.g., in an extreme case, selling the couple's house), since these treatments are often considered elective and, thus, are not covered by insurance (e.g., in-vitro fertilization, vasectomy reversal). Similarly, patients may have difficulty choosing a treatment because they do not really understand the medical and personal implications of their choice.

Rachel was developed to help patients and physicians in this situation. A typical consultation would thus involve one or more physicians and one or both members of the couple sitting at a computer. Each decision participant would contribute his or her knowledge as needed for the decision—medical alternatives and physiological and pathological information would come from the physicians, and personal preferences and details of their individual circumstances would come from the patients. Rachel would then work interactively to analyze the decision and yield a recommendation for action based on all the information gathered during the consultation. The decision participants would then take this recommendation, review it, update the decision basis if necessary to improve the recommendation, and, finally, reach a consensus on how to proceed. It is important to note, however, that Rachel is a laboratory system designed to demonstrate the technology of intelligent decision systems and, as of the writing of this book, is not intended for use in a clinical context.

A PROBABILISTIC VIEW OF INFERTILITY

As discussed in Chapters 5 and 6, an intelligent decision system is a computer implementation of a decision class analysis. For Rachel, this analysis is based on a model of the human reproductive system.

Current medical practice considers a couple to be infertile if the partners have been having regular, unprotected intercourse for at least one year and have not achieved a pregnancy [Silber, 1980]. Although this general view enables us to distinguish highly fertile couples from less fertile ones, it greatly oversimplifies a subtle issue. In particular, this view does not explicitly recognize the probabilistic nature of human reproduction.

To redefine infertility in probabilistic terms, we need to recall that human conception is closely tied to the cyclic physiology of the female reproductive system. Specifically, we should note that ovulation is a periodic process. Since a fresh ovum is required for conception, human reproduction is itself subject to periodicity. In other words, a couple wishing to conceive must ensure that sperm are present for ovum fertilization just after ovulation occurs.

Although it is necessary for successful reproduction, the availability of sperm at ovulation time is insufficient to guarantee that conception will occur or, more importantly, to ensure a successful pregnancy. Many of the processes that occur between intercourse during ovulation and a successful pregnancy are understood to a significant degree. However, many aspects of human reproduction have only been described statistically in an aggregate manner, and others remain essentially unknown [Lamb and Cruz, 1972; Cramer *et al.*, 1979; Lamb, 1983–1984]. Therefore, we must view human conception as an uncertain event and human reproduction as an uncertain process.

A useful way to model human reproduction is as a Bernoulli process [Drake, 1967; Howard, 1971]. A Bernoulli process consists of a series of discrete exchangeable trials, each of which can yield either a success (with probability p) or a failure (with probability $1-p$). A common example of a Bernoulli process is a sequence of tosses of a (possibly biased) coin; success is usually associated with "heads," and failure with "tails." In a model of reproduction, a trial consists of an ovulation cycle at a time when the couple is regularly engaging in intercourse, and a success essentially corresponds to a full-term pregnancy. An important assumption for Bernoulli processes is that the success probability, p, is fixed or, more technically, that the process is stationary. Furthermore, given knowledge of the value of p, the outcome of any trial (success or failure) is probabilistically independent from the outcome of any other trial or from any collection thereof. For human reproduction, the assumption of stationarity is valid as long as the time period being considered falls between puberty and menopause and is not long enough for the effects of aging to come into play.

A significant feature of a Bernoulli process is that consecutive trials need not occur at regular intervals. As is common in most discrete representations, real time has no bearing on the structure of the process. Hence, as long as the stationarity condition holds, trials may occur at any physiologically possible time. Thus, from a mathematical standpoint, we need not be concerned with irregular menstrual cycles or with periods of abstinence, pregnancy, or contraception.

Since much confusion in the field of infertility has resulted from a lack of clear definitions [Cramer *et al.*, 1979], we must be very specific about the meaning of "success" in our previous definition. To more clearly define success, we will introduce the concept of a **take-home baby** (THB). A take-home baby is a newborn child who has passed the neonatal period, that is, a child who is alive 28 days after birth. Of course, most babies go home sooner than their twenty-eighth day of life, but the end of the neonatal period provides a well-defined point where infertility ceases to be a concern. We will thus define the success of a reproductive trial as the creation of a take-home baby. This definition of success is different from that used by others [Guzick and Rock, 1981; Guzick *et al.*, 1982] who consider conception itself as the sought-after event. However, since many disorders can lead to miscarriage after conception, conception (on which the patient has only indirect preferences) is only desirable because it is an important precursor to a take-home baby (on which the patient has direct preferences). Correspondingly, the unfortunate death of an infant after the neonatal period can hardly be labeled an infertility problem. Hence, we will use the concept of a take-home baby as our definition of success for the Bernoulli process representing human reproduction.

The concept of a take-home baby as the meaning of success for infertility treatment was the result of many discussions with physicians at the Stanford infertility clinic over about 3 months. This concept illustrates the need to take culturally accepted distinctions with a healthy degree of skepticism when analyzing a decision and to create new concepts when established ones are unclear or misleading for decision-making. Furthermore, the effort needed to develop a useful new concept should not be underestimated. Representing decision contexts clearly and tersely can be quite challenging.

Figure 8.1 illustrates the Bernoulli representation of the reproductive process as a simple probability tree. Each circular node represents a trial and has two possible outcomes—success (*S*) and failure (*F*)—which are shown as its two emanating branches. Success branches denote events that can occur with probability *p*; failure branches denote events whose probability is 1-*p*. The notation THB$_k$ at the end of the success branches denotes the event of a take-home baby on the kth trial. Although it is certainly possible (even likely) that the process can be restarted sometime after the arrival of the take-home baby, we will assume, for simplicity, that the THB event constitutes an end to the reproductive effort.

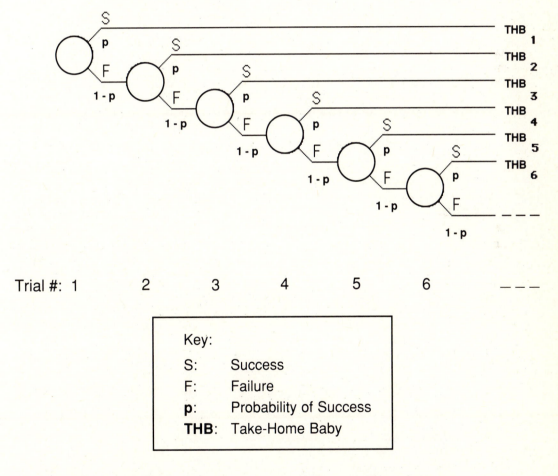

FIGURE 8.1   Human reproduction modeled as a Bernoulli process.

Figure 8.1 depicts what is referred to as the *nonintervention policy*. That is, the figure assumes that nothing is done to change the fertility of the couple (i.e., nothing is done to modify the value of p). Alternatively, if medical intervention takes place, the resulting infertility therapy could be viewed in terms of this figure as a series of medical procedures aimed at determining (tests) and modifying (treatments) the value of the success probability, p. Each of these procedures has an associated cost—financial and otherwise. Therefore, from the standpoint of decision analysis, designing an appropriate therapy for a given couple consists of selecting a set of pertinent procedures that maximize the expected utility of the couple given their desires and abilities, their specific situation, and the limits of the available medical technology.

Some Features of the Bernoulli Model of Human Reproduction[2]

A Bernoulli process has some interesting features that can be exploited to obtain useful information about the human reproductive process. In particular, we are interested in the first-order interarrival time, T_1, that is, the number of trials up to and including the first success. It is simple to show that given p, T_1 is distributed according to a geometric probability mass function. Thus, the distribution of T_1 is

$$\{T_1 | p\} = p (p - 1)^{T_1 - 1}; \quad T_1 = 1, 2, 3, ...; \ 0 \le p \le 1 \tag{8.1}$$

and its expected value and variance are

$$\langle T_1 | p \rangle = \frac{1}{p} \tag{8.2}$$

and

$$^v\langle T_1 | p \rangle = \frac{1 - p}{p^2} \tag{8.3}$$

To ensure clarity, we are using probabilistic inferential notation. Thus, $\{X | Y\}$ denotes the probability distribution of variable X given variable Y, $\langle X | Y \rangle$ denotes the expectation of variable X given variable Y, and $^v\langle X | Y \rangle$ denotes the variance of variable X given variable Y.

---

[2] This section is somewhat more mathematical than the rest of the book and may be skipped without loss of continuity.

Age of Female Partner	Monthly Probability of Success (THB)
Early 20s	0.25
Late 20s	0.20
Early 30s	0.15
Late 30s	0.10
Early 40s	0.08

FIGURE 8.2   Commonly accepted values of the monthly THB probability.

Higher-order interarrival times, that is, the number of trials up to and including the nth success, obey a Pascal probability mass function. The distribution, expected value, and variance of the nth-order interarrival time, T_n, are therefore given by

$$\{T_n \mid p\} = \frac{(T_n - 1)!}{(n - 1)!\,(T_n - n)!}\, p^n\,(1 - p)^{T_n - n}\;;$$

$$T_n = n,\, n + 1,\, n + 2,\, ...;\; n = 1,\, 2,\, 3,\, ...;\; 0 \le p \le 1 \tag{8.4}$$

$$\langle T_n \mid p \rangle = \frac{n}{p} \tag{8.5}$$

and

$$^v\langle T_n \mid p \rangle = \frac{n\,(1 - p)}{p^2} \tag{8.6}$$

Commonly accepted values of the monthly THB probability, p, in the general population are shown in Fig. 8.2, given the age of the female partner [Silber, 1980].[3] Figure 8.3 compares the values of $<T_n \mid p>$ and $^v<T_n \mid p>$ for $n = 1, 2$, and 3 for a wide range of values of p. Figure 8.4 illustrates the shape of $\{T_1 \mid p\}$ for several values of p.

A crucial issue about the Bernoulli model of reproduction is that the parameter p is rarely known with accuracy for a given couple. The next section develops a methodology for assessing p in each individual case.

---

[3]More recent studies of the decline in a couple's fertility as the age of the female partner increases show that the THB probability decreases much less rapidly with age than Figure 8.2 indicates until the few years prior to menopause, when it drops very rapidly.

Monthly THB Probability (p)	$\langle T_1\|p\rangle$	$^V\langle T_1\|p\rangle$	$\langle T_2\|p\rangle$	$^V\langle T_2\|p\rangle$	$\langle T_3\|p\rangle$	$^V\langle T_3\|p\rangle$
0.001	1,000	1,000,000	2,000	2,000,000	3,000	3,000,000
0.002	500	250,000	1,000	500,000	1,500	749,000
0.004	250	62,300	500	125,000	750	187,000
0.006	167	27,600	333	55,200	500	82,800
0.008	125	15,500	250	31,000	375	46,500
0.010	100	9,900	200	20,000	300	29,700
0.020	50	2,450	100	4,900	150	7,350
0.040	25	600	50	1,200	75	1,800
0.060	17	260	33	522	50	783
0.080	13	144	25	287	38	431
0.100	10	90	20	180	30	270
0.150	7	38	13	76	20	113
0.200	5	20	10	40	15	60
0.250	4	12	8	24	12	36
0.300	3	8	7	16	10	23
0.400	3	4	5	8	8	11
0.500	2	2	4	4	6	6
0.600	2	1	3	3	5	3

FIGURE 8.3   The prospects of conception improve as the monthly THB probability increases.

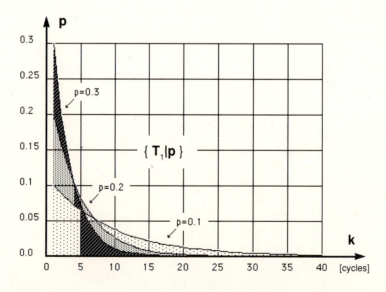

(a)

FIGURE 8.4   First-order interarrival times, $\{T_1\|p\}$, are likely to decrease as the monthly THB probability, p, increases. (a) Probability that the 1st success occurs at the kth cycle. (b) Numerical values of $\{T_1\|p\}$, for $k=1$ to 15 and $p=0.1$ to 0.3.

A MODEL OF THE HUMAN REPRODUCTIVE SYSTEM

In the context of infertility decisions, it is useful to view the human reproductive system as a **transmission network** with uncertain transmission links. Figure 8.5 shows a simple view of this network where the only significant events are ovum production by the female partner (O), sperm production by the male partner (S), fertilization (F), and a take-home baby (THB). In this network, q is the probability the ovum will reach the stage where it can be fertilized, r is the probability the sperm will reach the egg and fertilize it, and s is the probability the fertilized egg will proceed to a take-home baby. Clearly, the overall success probability, p, is equal to the product of q, r, and s.

Although the model shown in Fig. 8.5 might suffice to probabilistically describe the reproductive process for the general population, we need more detail for patients at an infertility clinic. In particular, we need to much more accurately specify the respective paths of sperm, ovum, and embryo from their creation to the arrival of a take-home baby [Behrman and Kistner, 1968; Odell and Moyer, 1971; Edmonds et al., 1982; Overstreet and Blazak, 1983; Collins et al., 1983; Lamb, 1983–1984; Polansky, 1984; Kessler, 1984–1985].

The model shown in Fig. 8.6 describes the human reproductive process in considerably more detail. In this model, transmission must occur from the desire of the female (F) and male (M) partners to conceive through to the completion of the process at THB. Connecting these terminal nodes is a set of milestones (represented by circular nodes), each representing a carefully

k \ P	0.1	0.2	0.3
1	0.1	0.2	0.3
2	0.09	0.16	0.21
3	0.081	0.128	0.147
4	0.073	0.102	0.103
5	0.066	0.082	0.072
6	0.059	0.066	0.05
7	0.053	0.052	0.035
8	0.048	0.042	0.025
9	0.043	0.034	0.017
10	0.039	0.027	0.012
11	0.035	0.021	0.008
12	0.031	0.017	0.006
13	0.028	0.014	0.004
14	0.025	0.011	0.003
15	0.023	0.009	0.002

(b)

FIGURE 8.4 (continued)

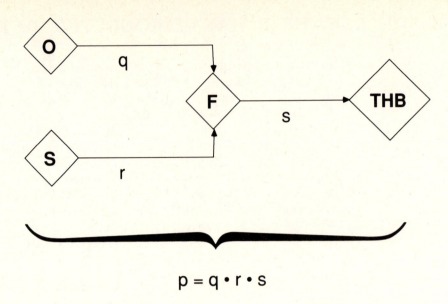

$$p = q \cdot r \cdot s$$

FIGURE 8.5   Human reproductive system as a simple transmission network with uncertain links.

defined event, that must be achieved for overall transmission to succeed in a THB. It is worthwhile to state these definitions in some detail.

At the top of Fig. 8.6 (viewed from the side) are three milestones (ovulation, ovum pickup, and ovum arrival at ampulla) that correspond exclusively to the female partner. **Ovulation** refers to the expulsion of a female germ cell (ovum) from a ruptured Graafian follicle [Hughes, 1972], **ovum pickup** consists of the capture of an ovum by either set of fimbriae, and **ovum arrival at ampulla** denotes the migration of the ovum through either Fallopian tube to its ampulla, where it becomes available for fertilization (although it may not necessarily remain there).

Correspondingly, the middle of Fig. 8.6 depicts three milestones (sperm production, emission, and sperm arrival at cervical mucus—CM) that pertain exclusively to the male partner. **Sperm production** refers to the generation of mature male germ cells (spermatozoa), **emission** is the movement of spermatozoa and associated secretions into the urethra, and **sperm arrival at CM** combines the events of coitus and ejaculation to culminate in the deposit of spermatozoa on the female's cervical mucus [Sadow, 1980]. The last milestone does not include the penetration of sperm into the mucus but refers merely to their arrival there.

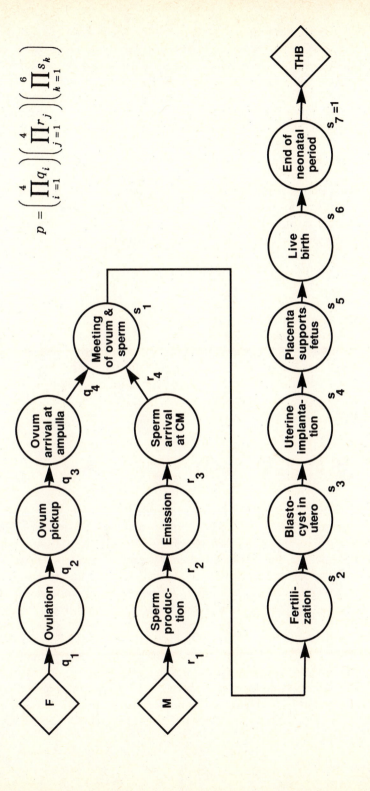

$$p = \left(\prod_{i=1}^{4} q_i \right) \left(\prod_{j=1}^{4} r_j \right) \left(\prod_{k=1}^{6} s_k \right)$$

FIGURE 8.6   More detailed network for a population of infertile couples.

The remaining milestones shown at the bottom of Fig. 8.6 pertain to both partners, because although they take place within the female, both ovum and sperm are necessary for their occurrence. The **meeting of ovum and sperm** refers to the physical encounter of the male and female germ cells prior to any interaction between them. **Fertilization** denotes the termination of the interaction of the ovum and sperm cells and is marked by the initiation of the first cleavage of the resulting zygote [Thomas, 1977; Dorland, 1981]. **Blastocyst in utero** describes the presence of a blastocyst within the uterine cavity prior to implantation. **Uterine implantation** consists of the adherence and penetration of the blastocyst into the endometrium. **Placenta supports fetus** refers to the point in time where the pregnancy becomes independent of ovarian hormonal secretions [Polansky, 1984]. **Live birth** is the expulsion of a live-born infant from the mother. Finally, **end of neonatal period** denotes the beginning of the twenty-eighth day of life of the newly born infant. Since the end of the neonatal period constitutes our definition of success, the probability of THB given this state is unity (i.e., $S_7 = 1$).

Assessing the Bernoulli success probability, $p = \{THB \mid F, M\}$, by assessing the parameters of the model shown in Fig. 8.6 (i.e., q_i, r_j, and s_k) is much easier than assessing p directly—as we would have to do in terms of the more aggregate model shown in Fig. 8.5—because these parameters are both familiar and quantifiable to most medical infertility specialists. The model in Fig. 8.6 assumes that physiological redundancies such as the existence of duplicate ovaries and testicles have been accounted for in assessing probability values. Hence, every milestone is a prerequisite for success. Thus, p is equal to the product of the q_i, r_j, and s_k:

$$p = \left(\prod_{i=1}^{4} q_i \right) \left(\prod_{j=1}^{4} r_j \right) \left(\prod_{k=1}^{6} s_k \right) \tag{8.7}$$

This model of the human reproductive process should be viewed as a starting point for developing individualized models for specific patients. In particular, the model can be modified to reflect the situation of each patient. For instance, Fig. 8.7 shows a sample model for a female patient with ovulatory irregularities. In this case, the male partner has been tested and deemed to have no fertility problems. Consequently, the modified model shows an expanded upper (female) branch and a reduced lower (male) branch. The events represented by the additional milestones are defined as follows. **Endocrine triggers** denotes the availability of follicle-stimulating hormone (FSH) and luteinizing hormone (LH) in the necessary quantities and timing for ovulation to occur. **Graafian stage** refers to the successful development of the follicles from their secondary stage to a vesicular (Graafian) follicle. The **first meiotic division** milestone consists of the completion of the process

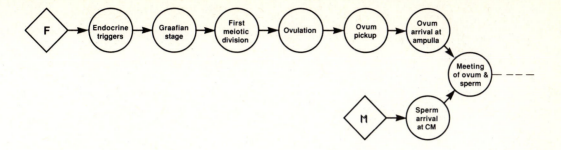

FIGURE 8.7   Modified model for patients with tubal blockage.

leading to the release of the first polar body by a maturing female ovum [Thompson and Thompson, 1980].

Similarly, through a process of expansion and reduction (which was discussed in detail in Chapter 4), the model shown in Fig. 8.6 could be adapted to patients presenting with[4] other infertility problems.

DERIVING AN INFLUENCE DIAGRAM FROM THE MODEL

The transmission network representation used in this discussion can be easily translated into influence diagram notation. Figure 8.8 is a restatement of Fig. 8.6 in terms of an influence diagram. Two points are worth noting. First, while many other equivalent influence diagrams could be developed to represent the network in Fig. 8.6, the diagram shown in Fig. 8.8 is particularly simple to construct from a network because it uses the same probability assessments that exist in the network. Second, the graphic similarity of the two representations is a notational coincidence. The meaning of nodes and arrows in an influence diagram is quite different from that of nodes and links in a transmission network. As discussed in Chapter 4, arrows in an influence diagram without decision nodes, such as the one shown in Fig. 8.8, represent probabilistic dependencies; they do not represent any kind of transition. Probabilistic assessments in an influence diagram are thus associated with nodes and not with arrows, as is the case in a transmission network.

---

[4] In medicine, a patient is said to "present with" a problem—his or her chief complaint—when that problem is the main reason for seeking medical help.

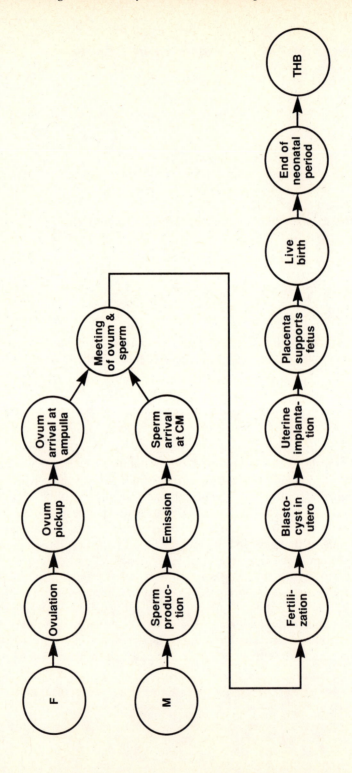

FIGURE 8.8   Influence diagram representation of the human reproduction model.

The model of human reproduction illustrated in Fig. 8.8 can be used directly to assess the Bernoulli probability of success by means of an influence diagram processor in an intelligent decision system.

MODEL CONSTRUCTION FOR INDIVIDUAL PATIENTS

As discussed in Chapters 4 and 5, a decision model for an individual can be constructed interactively. The knowledge necessary for this development falls into three categories: alternative generation, value model formation, and probabilistic assessment.

Alternative generation consists of selecting the set of pertinent alternatives for a specific patient from those that are technologically feasible. In the context of infertility, generating alternatives is usually a simple matching process to produce a list of medical procedures pertinent to an individual's condition. In general, physicians are unlikely to encounter major difficulties in performing this task. Hence, Rachel accepts knowledge about alternatives directly from its physician users and has no explicit alternative generation phase. In other domains, alternative generation could be a much more extensive and creative task.

Value model formation in Rachel is a two-stage process aimed at developing a model of the individual patient's preferences. The first stage is a library search through a set of general-purpose parametric models; the second consists of an assessment protocol for each of the selected model parameters.

Probabilistic assessment addresses the need to obtain distributions for all chance nodes in the decision model. Probabilistic knowledge consists of a collection of rules for directly and indirectly assessing frontier nodes in the model.

Value Model Formation

Rachel has six general-purpose value models, each accounting explicitly for a different set of attributes. According to the general classes of attributes at stake, one of these models is selected for a given consultation. In all cases, we assume that a take-home baby is a valuable attribute. Other general classes of attributes include money, morbidity (i.e., disease and discomfort), and the life of the patient. Each of the six available models is formed by indicating which of these three attribute classes is pertinent to the decision at hand, subject to the restriction that if morbidity is a pertinent attribute, then so is lifetime. The desired parametric value model is constructed by augmenting an initial value function (which accounts exclusively for take-home babies) with modules that can describe preferences in one of the attribute classes.

Although it would be possible to have a single value model for all consultations (i.e., one with all attributes accounted for), such a design would degrade the quality of Rachel's interaction with the user. First (and most importantly), Rachel would need to ask many irrelevant questions; second, because the model would be unnecessarily large, the system would operate at a decreased speed. This delay could be substantial because of the combinatorial size of the decision model. Reducing the size of the value model by explicitly omitting unneeded portions greatly contributes to Rachel's speed and user-friendliness.

This section develops Rachel's value model in significant detail and includes some challenging technical arguments that are important for understanding how the system operates. Readers without the mathematical background necessary to follow these technical arguments would find it useful to skim this section to become acquainted with the reasoning behind Rachel's value model.

The value model in Rachel combines modules accounting for discounted cash flows (labeled "money"), discounted life-quality periods (labeled "morbidity"), and an income-lifetime trade-off function (labeled "life") to yield a single numeraire (i.e., a single aggregate measure for each possible outcome [Howard, 1980a; Holtzman, 1983b]). Specifically, this worth numeraire, w, is obtained by the relation

$$w(c, l) = c\left(\frac{l}{L}\right)^E \tag{8.8}$$

where c is a fixed yearly income equivalent to the individual's current wealth plus his or her future net income stream during his or her actuarial expected lifetime, l is the individual's actual lifetime (appropriately weighed to reflect any treatment-induced morbidity), L is his or her actuarial expected lifetime, and E is the elasticity of w with respect to l [Dorfman, 1972], which needs to be assessed from the individual [Howard, 1980a, 1984].

In general, neither c nor l are directly assessable for a patient and must be calculated from pertinent data. Since the calculation of c is a standard net present value (NPV) conversion of a time-varying cash flow into a fixed annuity, we do not need to discuss it here. This type of calculation is covered in most textbooks on introductory finance [Higgins, 1977; Copeland and Weston, 1979; Van Horne, 1986]. On the other hand, the computation of l requires explanation.

In some cases, where morbidity is not an issue, values for l can be directly assessed probabilistically. However, when the possibility of pain or other forms of discomfort are to be treated explicitly, the value of l can be lowered to reflect the decreased quality of life. For this purpose, we use the concept of a **symptomatic stream**, which is a sequence of **symptomatic periods** where the individual goes through a **symptomatic state** for a certain interval of time. For simplicity, Rachel is designed assuming all symptomatic periods are of the same duration (anywhere from days to months). In general, experience indicates it is useful to deal with only a few (six or so) different symptomatic states for a given case. Commonly used states (and their definitions) include **asymptomatic** (able to conduct business as usual) **hindered** (almost able to conduct business as usual, except for strenuous or otherwise demanding activities), **bed-ridden** (unable to conduct business as usual but capable of essentially unaided survival), **hospitalized** (unable to survive without significant aid from others but not in significant continuous discomfort), **in-pain** (unable to function without significant aid from others and requiring major pain control treatment), and **in-severe-pain** (unable to control pain without rendering unconscious). If we refer to each of these symptomatic states by the symbols AS, HI, BR, HO, PA, and SP, we can illustrate the notion of a symptomatic stream by imagining the outcome of a successful surgery to be represented by the stream

HO, HO, SP, PA, HO, HO, BR, BR, . . ., BR, HI, HI, . . ., HI, AS, . . .

where the operation occurs at the third symptomatic period.

While the set of symptomatic states described here is representative of the kind of situations a patient might face, it is by no means exhaustive. Many other states can be defined, and an appropriate set should be designed to encompass the specific circumstances of the treatments under consideration. In particular, Rachel uses a somewhat different set for the consultation described in the Appendix.

The treatment of symptomatic states in Rachel is based on the idea that if a symptomatic period is of duration d, then there exists a duration d', $0 \leq d' \leq d$, such that the patient is indifferent between living in the given symptomatic state for a time d and living in an asymptomatic state for a time d'. Restricting d' to be positive implies that the patient does not consider any symptomatic state to be worse than death. Under most conditions, and particularly when dealing with infertility, this restriction is very reasonable. However, d' could take negative values if the patient would rather die than be in a given symptomatic state without recourse to suicide or euthanasia. This might be the case, for instance, for victims of massive third-degree burns. Similarly, restricting d' to be less than d implies that the patient does not consider any symptomatic state to be better than being asymptomatic.

Thus, each symptomatic state, s, has an associated quality factor, Q_s, that equals the length of an asymptomatic period the patient deems equivalent to a unit of time spent in state s. Typically, unless the patient prefers the symptoms associated with s to being asymptomatic or considers these symptoms to be worse than death, Q_s will lie in the interval from zero (0) to one (1).

To simplify the assessment of the symptomatic state quality factors, we assume that previous symptomatic periods are a **sunk cost** (i.e., they should have no direct bearing on future actions). More specifically, we assume that if after living in symptomatic state X a person prefers state A to state B, then after living in state Y, $Y \neq X$, the person must still prefer state A to state B for all states A, B, X, and Y. This assumption allows us to state that the quality factor Q_s is unique for state s, regardless of the timing of its occurrence within a symptomatic stream [Holtzman, 1983b].

We can then calculate quality-adjusted lifetime, l, as required by equation 8.8, from a symptomatic stream by the formula

$$l = \sum_{s_i \in S} T_{s_i} Q_{s_i} \tag{8.9}$$

where S is a symptomatic stream composed of periods s_i of duration T_{s_i} and quality factor Q_{s_i}. However, equation 8.9 does not take into account the decision-maker's time preference. Specifically, equation 8.9 is insensitive to the length of time separating the present from the future occurrence of a particular symptomatic state. In general, most people would prefer to be in a given symptomatic state far in the future than in the near term.

Mathematically, this time-preference effect can be represented by adjusting the quality factor coefficient, Q_s, for each symptomatic state, s, with a time-sensitive discount function. This function can be written as $D(Q_s, t)$, where t denotes the time from the present to the occurrence of the symptomatic state, s, in question. A moment of thought should reveal that D must be a continuous, nondecreasing function of t such that $D(Q_s, 0) = Q_s$ and $D(Q_s, \infty) = 1$, for all symptomatic states. The exact nature of the function D is outside the scope of this book; as in the case of the constant yearly income equivalent, c, this type of function is covered in most textbooks on introductory finance and in the professional literature [Higgins, 1977; Copeland and Weston, 1979; Keeler and Cretin, 1983; Van Horne, 1986].

The parameter t can be expressed in terms of the durations, T_{s_i}, of the various symptomatic states, s_i, in a symptomatic stream, S, with k symptomatic periods by

$$t = \sum_{s_i \in S, i \leq k} T_{s_i} \tag{8.10}$$

Thus, by incorporating the patient's time preference, equation 8.9 becomes

$$l = \sum_{s_i \in S} T_{s_i} D\left(Q_{s_i}, \sum_{s_j \in S, j \leq i} T_{s_j}\right) \tag{8.11}$$

Since in Rachel the durations T_{s_i} are assumed to all be equal to a constant duration, T, equation 8.11 can be rewritten as

$$l = T \sum_{s_i \in S} D_T (Q_{s_i}, i), \quad \text{where } D_T (Q_{s_i}, i) = D (Q_{s_i}, iT) \quad (8.12)$$

Thus, equation 8.8 can be rewritten as

$$w (c, S) = c \left(\frac{T \sum_{s_i \in S} D_T (Q_{s_i}, i)}{L} \right)^E \quad (8.13)$$

The last component of the value model is a constant consumption equivalent value, B, to account for the existence of a take-home baby. Using the indicator function[5], I, on the event THB, we can extend equation 8.13 to be

$$w (c, S, \text{THB}) = ([B \cdot I (\text{THB})] + c) \cdot \left(\frac{T \sum_{s_i \in S} D_T (Q_{s_i}, i)}{L} \right)^E \quad (8.14)$$

Finally, using the function $A(W, f)$ to denote a fixed annuity equivalent to the patient's current wealth, W, plus his or her future net income in terms of a cash flow, f, over his or her expected actuarial lifetime, L, we can make explicit the form of the fixed wealth and income equivalent, c, to yield

$$w (f, S, \text{THB}) = ([B \cdot I (\text{THB})] + A (W, f)) \cdot \left(\frac{T \sum_{s_i \in S} D_T (Q_{s_i}, i)}{L} \right)^E \quad (8.15)$$

which is a value model that accounts for all desired attributes: money, morbidity, lifetime, and the existence of a take-home baby.

As stated previously, it is not necessary to use all the aspects of the model described in equation 8.15 for all cases. For instance, a situation where

---

[5]An indicator function, I, of an event, A, is equal to 1 when A occurs and is equal to 0 when A does not occur.

financial issues are not sufficiently important to warrant explicit consideration could use the following value function:

$$w\,(S\,,\,\text{THB}) = ([B\,\bullet I\,(\text{THB})] + A\,(W\,)) \bullet \left(\frac{T\,\displaystyle\sum_{s_i \in S} D_T\,(Q_{s_i},\,i\,)}{L} \right)^{E}$$

(8.16)

This might be the case of someone cared for at a health-maintenance organization (HMO). Alternatively, if neither lifetime nor morbidity are important
problem dimensions (as in the case of a mild drug therapy), the value function could be stated simply as

$$w\,(\text{THB}) = [B\,\bullet I\,(\text{THB})]$$

(8.17)

Thus, the choice of an appropriate form for the value function should be
determined by the nature of the specific case at hand.

Once a functional form has been developed, Rachel proceeds to assess
values for the parameters of the value function. (See the Appendix.) These
parameters can include L, W, f, B, T, E, a financial discount rate, i, and as
many quality factors, Q_{s_i}, as there are symptomatic states being considered.
In addition, Rachel assumes an exponential utility function so that a risk-
tolerance coefficient, R, is also assessed.

Probabilistic Assessment

When the value function has been fully specified, the interactive process of
building a decision model begins in earnest. For simplicity, Rachel assumes a
single decision node, which represents the alternative courses of action available to the patient. This decision node is initially connected by Rachel to the
value node, thus forming a minimal influence diagram for the decision
problem. As discussed in Chapter 4, the probabilistic assessment process
determines a probability distribution for the value node given each possible
decision alternative. In general, these distributions will need to be assessed
indirectly, so Rachel introduces the immediate predecessors i.e., the arguments of the value node (producing an incipient influence diagram) and
places the decision node as the sole predecessor of these new nodes. From
that point on, the assessment process attempts to obtain a distribution for
every frontier node in the model (either directly or indirectly) until no frontier border nodes exist and the model is completed.

An Example Case

To illustrate the probabilistic assessment process Rachel performs, we will consider, as an example, the case of a male patient presenting with a left scrotal varicocele and low motile sperm count (total sperm count times the fraction of motile sperm). In other words, the patient in question has some varicose veins near his left testicle and has very few moving sperm in his semen as detected by inspection with a microscope. We will discuss this case at a level that suffices for our example; more detailed discussions can be found in the literature [Bain, 1981; Bustos-Obregón *et al.*, 1981; Vermeulen, 1981a, 1981b; Swerdloff and Boyers, 1982; Meistrich and Brown, 1983].

Current medical knowledge indicates the surgical suppression of blood flow into the varicocele is somewhat correlated with an increase in the percent of normal motile sperm and, to a lesser extent, with an increase in the concentration of sperm in the semen. The surgical procedure involved is known as an internal spermatic vein ligation (or, less accurately, a varicocelectomy), and its effects commonly improve the patient's fertility.

A theory underlying this procedure is based on the observation that healthy sperm production in humans normally occurs at a slightly lower temperature than that of the rest of the body, which is strongly confirmed by the fact that male genitalia reside within the scrotum. The scrotal sac not only is directly exposed to the environment (which acts as a cooling agent) but typically contracts and expands in response to variations in environmental temperature and heat conductivity. The presence of a scrotal varicocele appears to disrupt this physiological mechanism by supplying a significant source of heat. Thus, suppressing the flow of blood into the scrotal varicocele should improve scrotal temperature control and, in principle, should improve the quality and number of sperm in the semen.

Although this theory is quite plausible, it is still quite controversial. Strictly speaking, the etiology of scrotal varicoceles as a cause of male infertility has not been fully elucidated. Statistically, however, the results of internal spermatic vein ligation (ISVL) upon infertility seem encouraging [Kessler, 1984–1985].

The incidence of varicoceles in the general population is approximately 10 percent. In many cases, however, the varicocele does not seem to affect the patient's fertility. By contrast, 25 to 40 percent of the infertile male population presents with a varicocele. Roughly 60 percent of all ligated patients experience a return of spermatogenesis at a level considered fertile. Of these, about 75 percent eventually produce a pregnancy. Surprisingly, about 13 percent of those patients whose spermatogenesis does not improve also succeed in producing a pregnancy. Thus, an infertile patient presenting with a left scrotal varicocele faces roughly a 50 percent overall chance of producing a pregnancy following an ISVL [Amelar and Dubin, 1975; Abdelmassih *et al.*, 1982; Kessler, 1984–1985].

To begin our example of Rachel's probabilistic assessment process, we need to specify a value node (with its associated value function) and a decision node describing the available alternatives. Since ISVL involves major surgery, we will consider a value function accounting for all four classes of attributes: money, morbidity, lifetime, and THB. Hence, we will use the value function, $w(c, S, THB)$, described by equation 8.14. (Recall that the symptomatic stream argument, S, accounts for both morbidity and lifetime. Also, we are abbreviating the assessment of c and thus not using equation 8.15.) The decision node, D_v, consists of the choice between undergoing an ISVL and not doing anything. This decision clearly influences all four classes of attributes. The starting-point incipient influence diagram for this problem is shown in Fig. 8.9.

This starting-point model has three frontier nodes—c, THB, and S—which correspond to each of the arguments of the value function, w, and which must be fully assessed to complete the decision model. Note that frontier nodes are shaded for easy recognition.

For this example, we will assume the patient has average medical insurance coverage. Specifically, if he opts for surgery and if the operation proceeds without complications, he would have to pay the equivalent of an incremental out-of-pocket $100 annuity for the duration of his expected lifetime. If he opts for surgery and the operation has complications requiring prolonged hospitalization, his yearly equivalent payment would be $250 in incremental out-of-pocket expenses after all insurance payments have been received. If the patient does not undergo surgery, he would incur no incremental surgical costs. Thus, node c is deterministically dependent on the patient's decision to have surgery and on the occurrence of postsurgical complications given that surgery is chosen. Figure 8.10 shows a plausible deterministic expansion rule that embodies this decision knowledge.

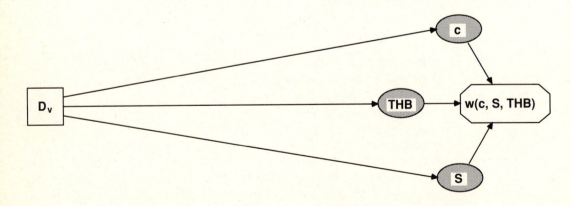

FIGURE 8.9   Beginning of a decision model for an internal spermatic vein ligation candidate.

IF   the patient has insurance coverage with company XYZ under plan ABC,

THEN   his incremental medical costs, Δc, (in annuity form) can be indirectly assessed by means of the following relation:

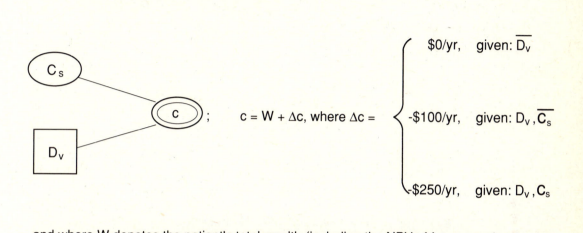

and where W denotes the patient's total wealth (including the NPV of future earnings) as an equivalent fixed yearly income, C_s denotes the advent of postsurgical complications requiring hospitalization (a binary chance variable), and D_v denotes the internal spermatic vein ligation (varicocelectomy) decision (a binary decision variable).

FIGURE 8.10   Deterministic expansion rule for medical costs.

Similarly, we will assume the patient and his physician are willing to describe the space of symptomatic streams, S, in terms of three possible scenarios (labeled, respectively, surgery without complications, surgery with complications, and no surgery). As in the case of variable c, the occurrence of these symptomatic states also depends deterministically on the advent of surgical complications, C_s, and on the surgical decision, D_v. Figure 8.11 shows the influence diagram after applying deterministic expansion rules to nodes c and S.

The assessment of node *THB* is somewhat more complex than that of the other two immediate predecessors of the value node. It is based on the model of human reproduction shown in Figs. 8.6 and 8.8, which can be considerably simplified because the pathological effects of a scrotal varicocele pertain exclusively to the male partner. Rules such as the one shown in Fig. 8.12 embody this kind of context-dependent decision knowledge in Rachel. The influence diagram that results from applying this stochastic indirect assessment rule is illustrated in Fig. 8.13.

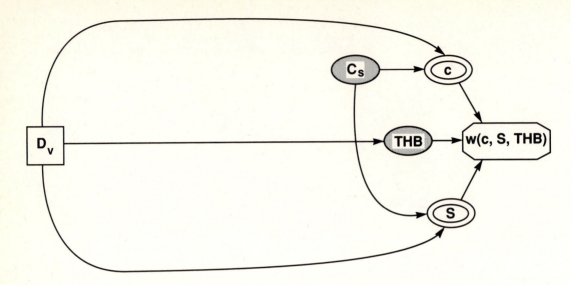

FIGURE 8.11   Decision model after two deterministic expansions.

Similar rules can be triggered to expand the diagram with nodes labeled FERT (for "fertilization"), SCM (for "sperm in the cervical mucus"), and HSP (for "healthy sperm production," i.e., number of motile sperm), as shown in Fig. 8.14. At this point, there are two remaining frontier nodes: C_s and HSP. The rule described in Fig. 8.15 can be used to assess node C_s through a simple stochastic indicated assessment that relates possible postsurgical complications to the track record of the surgical team.

IF   the diagnosed pathology believed to be leading to the couple's infertility pertains exclusively to the male partner,

THEN   the event THB can be indirectly assessed by means of the following relation:

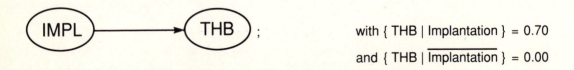

with { THB | Implantation } = 0.70

and { THB | $\overline{\text{Implantation}}$ } = 0.00

FIGURE 8.12   Stochastic indirect assessment rule for node THB.

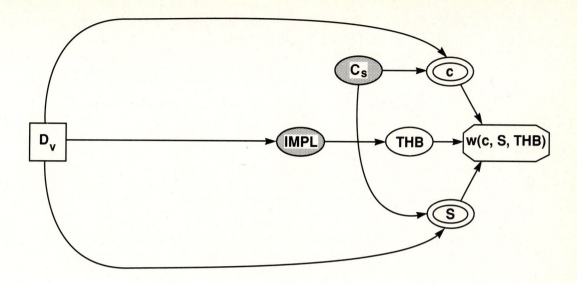

FIGURE 8.13   Evolving decision model after a stochastic expansion.

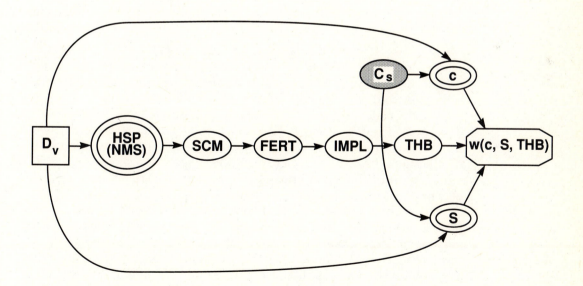

FIGURE 8.14   Influence diagram model after three more stochastic expansions.

IF   the patient is in good health, the internal spermatic vein ligation is performed by Dr. PQR, and the attending anesthesiologist is Dr. STW,

THEN   the event C_s can be indirectly assessed by means of the following relation:

$$\text{with } \{\, C_s \mid D_v \,\} = 0.002$$
$$\text{and } \{\, C_s \mid \overline{D_v} \,\} = 0.0$$

FIGURE 8.15   Rule relating the probability of postsurgical complications to the track record of the surgical team.

Node HSP represents the production of sperm of sufficient quality to produce a pregnancy. A natural way to assess this node is by realizing that a close surrogate for the existence of healthy sperm is the availability of a sufficiently large number of motile sperm. Thus, node HSP can be indirectly assessed through the deterministic relation

$$NMS = NS \times PM/100 \tag{8.18}$$

where NMS is the total number of motile sperm, NS is the total number of sperm regardless of motility, and PM is the percentage of motile sperm in the patient's semen. Figure 8.16 shows the nearly complete decision model after having assessed nodes C_s and HSP.

Finally, nodes NS and PM can be directly assessed given values for the decision D_v. Figure 8.17 shows plausible distributions for NS and PM given D_v. The data in this figure would be displayed for approval, with possible modifications, by the physician using Rachel. Figure 8.18 shows a complete influence diagram decision model for the internal spermatic vein ligation patient.

It is important to note that at every point in the probabilistic assessment process, many more than a single indirect assessment rule may be available to guide the expansion process. For conciseness, we only showed one such rule for each frontier node. In general, it will be necessary to select one among a (possibly large) set of applicable expansion rules, according to the features of the specific case and to the preferences and knowledge of both physician and patient.

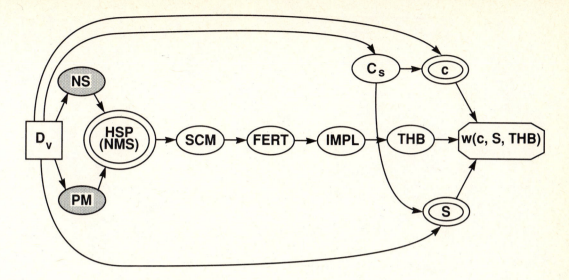

FIGURE 8.16   Decision model after indirectly assessing nodes C_s and HSP.

Possible Cases	Sperm Concentration		Percent Motile	
	Million Sperm per Cubic Centimeter	Probability	Percent	Probability
$\overline{D_v}$	7	0.25	3	0.25
	10	0.50	5	0.50
	13	0.25	10	0.25
D_v	10	0.40	5	0.15
	20	0.05	10	0.20
	30	0.20	25	0.30
	50	0.35	35	0.25
			45	0.10

NOTE: These values are specific to the hypothetical patient under consideration.

FIGURE 8.17   Plausible distributions for the total number of sperm and for the percentage of motile sperm in the internal vein ligation patient.

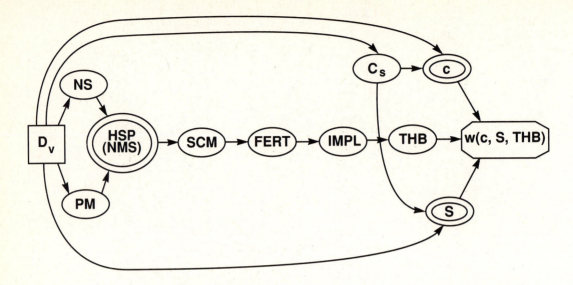

FIGURE 8.18 Complete influence diagram model for an internal spermatic vein ligation decision.

THE STYLE OF RACHEL

Within the overall framework for intelligent decision systems presented in this book, Rachel concentrates almost exclusively on the knowledge-based process of formulating infertility decision problems. Thus, Rachel has been developed to select a preference function, determine the values of the function's parameters, and indirectly assess its distribution using a knowledge base of expansion objects. By directly evaluating the resulting influence diagram, Rachel then produces an optimal decision strategy [Breese and Holtzman, 1984]. The task of clarifying the modeling process in Rachel is addressed by providing a simple on-line explanation facility throughout the consultation. Although rudimentary, this facility demonstrates the ease with which a declarative representation of decision knowledge can be used as the basis for clarifying the model design process.

As mentioned earlier in this chapter, Rachel's design takes advantage of several simplifying assumptions. These assumptions make the task of programming the system feasible within the constraints imposed by the severely limited resources available for its development while retaining sufficient generality to demonstrate the attractiveness of intelligent decision systems technology. One such simplification is the existence of a single decision node with no predecessors. Furthermore, the alternative choices associated with this node are assumed to be known prior to using Rachel. The restriction of a single, fully assessed decision node for each model greatly reduces the complexity of the computer-based system without significantly reducing its experimental value. In addition, this restriction has little effect on Rachel's usefulness in the context for which it is designed: that of a physician and patient at the point of selecting among available therapies given a diagnosis.

Another important assumption made in designing Rachel is that the user has at least a working familiarity with first-order prefix predicate calculus (FOPPC) and with the concepts and process of decision analysis. Readers unfamiliar with FOPPC notation should refer to the Glossary for some examples. Thus, Rachel has only a primitive front end and does little to aid the user in assessing model parameters such as probabilities. These parameters are simply entered in response to direct queries. Furthermore, the form of most of Rachel's queries is very close to that of existential queries in FOPPC. For other parameters, such as risk-tolerance and value-model coefficients, which are somewhat more difficult to assess, Rachel has simple interview protocols that replace corresponding FOPPC queries.

Figure 8.19 illustrates three typical instances of Rachel's query mechanism when there are, respectively, no unknown variables, an unknown variable that needs to be bound to a single value, and an unknown variable that needs to be bound to a collection of values.[6] In the latter two cases, the acronym WFF stands for a "well-formed formula" in FOPPC. Moreover, following a common FOPPC convention, variable names are noted by appending an initial $ sign. Although not shown in the figure, Rachel can also handle single and multiple bindings to several variables in the same WFF. Also, Rachel can bind a variable to a single value that is a list (vector) of distinct symbols. For notational clarity, Fig. 8.19 and all subsequent figures follow the convention that all user inputs are indicated by underlined italics; all other text is displayed by the program. In addition, the computer-generated text can be separated into two classes. Capitalized text between double quotes is derived from the system's knowledge base; otherwise, text is displayed verbatim (i.e., canned) as it appears in the query programs.

User-typed text in FOPPC-like queries falls into two categories: truth value and bindings. The truth value of a query is entered in response to a question such as the one shown on the second line in Fig. 8.19 (indicated by the symbol [Y/N]). At this point, Rachel is trying to ascertain whether it is at all possible (given appropriate bindings) for the WFF in question to be true. The user can respond with an "n" for "no" or a "y" for "yes." In addition, other possible answers are valid at this point and are discussed below. If the WFF contains unknown variables that need to be bound, either singly or multiply, and if the answer to the truth-value question is *y*, then the user must type one or more symbols (i.e., strings of characters) as needed to bind

---

[6] In general, Rachel's queries are of the form shown in Fig. 8.19. However, for clarity, all queries shown in the Appendix were automatically processed with very simple, special-purpose procedures to make them appear more English-like.

```
    a)  Without  Unknown  Variables

Is  it  true  that  "(IS-OVER-60-YEARS-OF-AGE  MR-SMITH)"?  [Y/N]>    n


    b)  With  One  Unknown  Variable  Requiring  a  Single  Value

Could  WFF  "(PATIENT-NAME  $X)"  be  satisfied?  [Y/N]>               y
$X:  MR-SMITH


    c)  With  One  Unknown  Variable  Requiring  Multiple  Values

Could  WFF  "(MODEL-ATTRIBUTE  MR-SMITH  $X)"  be  satisfied?  [Y/N]> y
1>  $X:  MONEY
2>  $X:  LIFE
3>  $X:  quit
```

Note: The word **quit** is restricted to the termination of input.

FIGURE 8.19   Form of Rachel's queries.

the WFF variables in a manner that satisfies the WFF truthfully. The semantics of the symbols used in this open-ended binding process are left entirely to the user.

Besides responding with a "yes" or a "no" to the truth-value query, the user can respond in various other useful ways. Closely associated with these two common responses are "m" for "maybe" or "O.K. for now" and "u" for "unprovable at this point." The latter two responses correspond almost exactly to *y* and *n*, respectively, except that *m* and *u* do not make the system store the newly proven WFF in its knowledge base, whereas *y* and *n* do trigger this storage process. Strictly speaking, the responses *m* and *u* can lead to logical inconsistencies and are used primarily for debugging purposes.

Other useful responses to the truth-value query have the effect of placing Rachel in its on-line explanation mode. Ultimately, a positive or negative response must be given to terminate the query process, but explanatory requests can be issued to aid in assigning the requested truth value. One of these requests is "f" for "facts," which prompts Rachel to display part or all of its factual knowledge base. A similar request is "r" for "rules," which helps the user determine the contents of Rachel's collection of rules. Since both f and r requests can potentially lead to the display of substantial quantities of text and since Rachel is implemented in a single-screen, text-only environment, it is entirely possible that the currently active query may be scrolled out of the screen. To help the user remember the question being asked, the response "q" for "query" constitutes a request to Rachel to redisplay the currently active truth-value query. Another helpful aid to the user is the response "?," which at any point displays a listing of the currently valid responses (e.g., y, n, m, u, q, f, r, w, $?$).

The most important explanatory response that can be given to a truth-value query is "w" for "why." Specifically, this response represents a request for Rachel to answer the question "Why are you asking me this?" or, more accurately, "Why are you trying to prove this WFF?" Algorithmically, a w response uncovers the stack of subgoals whose satisfaction depends on the truth value and bindings (if necessary) of the WFF in question. The existence of this stack is a consequence of the depth-first, backward-reasoning design underlying Rachel's inference engine.[7]

Therefore, responding to a truth-value query with a w displays the subgoal that immediately precedes the current query in Rachel's dynamic goal stack. After displaying the preceding subgoal, Rachel repeats the truth-value query. (The original WFF is not redisplayed.) The user once again has access to the full set of responses available after the original query. Any assertive response would pertain to the truth value of the WFF in this original query. Alternatively, the user could respond with another w. In this case, the response would pertain not to the original query but rather to the previously displayed subgoal. If the user were to issue a sequence of w responses, the goal stack would be recursively unfolded until its end. In most instances, such unfolding can yield considerable insight about the context in which the current query is being issued and, consequently, can serve as an explanation for why the original question is being asked. Of course, as in the rest of Rachel, the display of subgoals occurs in FOPPC-like notation and is not intended for the untrained user. A friendlier (e.g., pseudo-natural language) front end to aid this process might allow a wider class of users to take advantage of Rachel's explanation facility.

Figure 8.20 illustrates the process of unfolding Rachel's subgoal stack at a point in the consultation where an appropriate value function is being selected, that is, where the relevant value attributes (e.g., morbidity) are being determined. The first subgoal display tells the user that Rachel needs to find the pertinent attributes for Mr. Smith's decision model because it is trying to determine whether the function template labeled MON-LIF, which accounts

---

[7] A "how" explanation facility that responds to the question "How are you going about proving the current goal" and that usually accompanies a "why" explanation facility in standard inference engine implementations would be a straightforward addition to Rachel, but because of tight computer memory constraints, it was not implemented.

for money and lifetime (i.e., a form that disregards morbidity), is an appropriate value function template for Mr. Smith's case. Pursuing his or her curiosity, the user asks for the next higher subgoal. Rachel then responds that it needs to satisfy the previous subgoal to establish whether there is an exact match between the attributes pertinent to Mr. Smith and those represented by the MON-LIF function template. Subsequent subgoals reveal Rachel's need to find an appropriate value function (i.e., to bind variable $X4$), to fully specify the value node for Mr. Smith's model and, ultimately, to complete a decision model for him. Finally, the highest goal is to satisfy the user's desire for a decision model. (See the epigraph at the beginning of Chapter 6 for a comment on this last goal.)

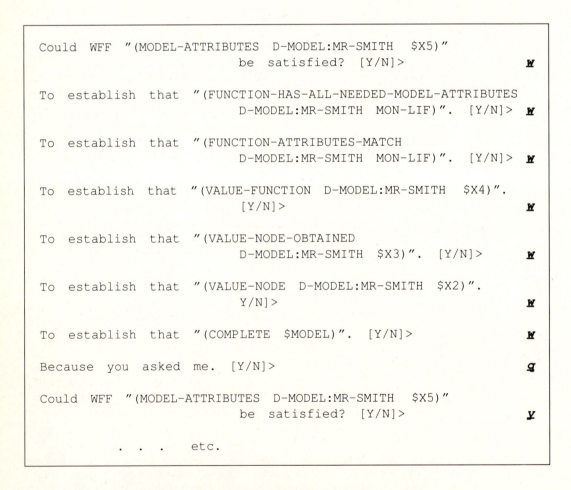

```
Could WFF "(MODEL-ATTRIBUTES D-MODEL:MR-SMITH $X5)"
                    be satisfied? [Y/N]>                    N

To establish that "(FUNCTION-HAS-ALL-NEEDED-MODEL-ATTRIBUTES
              D-MODEL:MR-SMITH MON-LIF)". [Y/N>  N

To establish that "(FUNCTION-ATTRIBUTES-MATCH
              D-MODEL:MR-SMITH MON-LIF)". [Y/N>  N

To establish that "(VALUE-FUNCTION D-MODEL:MR-SMITH $X4)".
              [Y/N]>                                       N

To establish that "(VALUE-NODE-OBTAINED
              D-MODEL:MR-SMITH $X3)". [Y/N]>               N

To establish that "(VALUE-NODE D-MODEL:MR-SMITH $X2)".
              Y/N]>                                        N

To establish that "(COMPLETE $MODEL)". [Y/N]>             N

Because you asked me. [Y/N]>                              g

Could WFF "(MODEL-ATTRIBUTES D-MODEL:MR-SMITH $X5)"
                    be satisfied? [Y/N]>                    y

     . . .   etc.
```

FIGURE 8.20 Rachel's subgoal-based explanation facility.

Once the goal stack is exhausted, the user may want to have the original query redisplayed. This can be done by responding with a *q* to the truth-value prompt. However, it is not necessary to redisplay the original query to be able to respond to it. In fact, at any point in the explanation process, the user can assert, either positively or negatively, the query's truth value.

Other examples of Rachel's subgoal-based explanation facility are shown in Figs. 8.21 and 8.22. Figure 8.21 shows the unfolding of a stack that might occur in the context of determining whether a given frontier node is suitable for direct assessment. In this case, the subgoals represent Rachel's attempt to fully assess Mr. Smith's model by, among other things, assessing the node labeled LIFE (i.e., Mr. Smith's remaining lifetime in years) and, in particular, by assessing that node directly. Figure 8.22 illustrates Rachel's explanation of the reasoning behind its question about the necessity of surgery for the patient. As shown in the figure, Rachel issues this query in an attempt to find an indicated distribution to assess node LIFE (i.e., to find a rule in its knowledge base whose consequent constitutes a direct assessment for the node).

In addition to the standard FOPPC-style queries, Rachel has special-purpose procedures for inputting specific data structures such as the range of possible outcomes and probability distributions for variables that are directly assessed. These procedures do not require special mention, since they follow a straightforward sequential input protocol and since they are displayed in the Appendix.

To further describe the nature of Rachel's operation, it is useful to discuss some aspects of the system's architecture. In particular, it is important to outline the structure of Rachel's knowledge base (KB).

```
Is it true that "(OK-FOR DIRECT-ASSESSMENT LIFE)"? [Y/N]>          w

To establish that "(DIRECTLY-ASSESSED LIFE)". [Y/N]>               w

To establish that "(ASSESSED  LIFE)". [Y/N]>                      w

To establish that "(FULLY-ASSESSED D-MODEL:MR-SMITH)". Y/N]>       w

To establish that "(COMPLETE  $MODEL)". [Y/N]>                    w

Because you asked me. [Y/N]>                                      n

          . . .   etc.
```

FIGURE 8.21   Rachel's explanation of why it is trying to directly assess the node labeled LIFE.

```
Is it true that "(COULD-REQUIRE-SURGERY MR-SMITH)"? [Y/N]>        N

To establish that "(INDICATED-ASSESSMENT LIFE $X27 $X28
                            $X29)". [Y/N]>                        N

To establish that "(ASSESSED-BY-INDICATION LIFE)". [Y/N]>        N

To establish that "(ASSESSED LIFE)". [Y/N]>                      N

To establish that "(FULLY-ASSESSED D-MODEL:MR-SMITH)". [Y/N]>   N

To establish that "(COMPLETE $MODEL)". [Y/N]>                    N

Because you asked me. [Y/N]>                                     Y


        . . .    etc.
```

FIGURE 8.22   Rachel's explanation of why it is trying to determine whether the patient needs surgery.

The knowledge used by Rachel can be divided into two distinct categories. Of immediate concern to the user is a set of rules and facts that embody Rachel's decision knowledge about infertility treatment choices. These rules and facts are placed in two separate KBs. The first of these KBs concerns developing a value model and is referred to as VALKB; the other pertains to indirectly assessing the value node by using medical knowledge and is referred to as MEDKB. The second category of knowledge in Rachel is only indirectly apparent to the user (since it does not generate queries), but it is centrally important to the system's design. The latter category embodies Rachel's knowledge about the decision-analytic process. The corresponding set of rules and facts resides in a knowledge base labeled DAKB.

It has been useful to distinguish the highly domain-dependent knowledge in the first category from the much more general and highly portable knowledge in the second category. To emphasize this distinction, the former category is commonly referred to as Rachel's knowledge base, whereas the latter can be referred to as its **wisdom base**. It would be hard to justify as strong a term as *wisdom* in reference to a knowledge area without having carefully understood the implications of this knowledge and without evidence that these implications embody substantial normative power. In the case of knowledge about decision analysis, this evidence has been presented in Chapters 2 and 3. It is rare to find as thorough an analysis of the underlying methodology outside the decision-analytic realm. It is worth noting that most current knowledge-based decision systems reside outside this realm.

To complete our description of Rachel's features and limitations, we should comment on a few other characteristics of the system's operation. Rachel was implemented directly on MACLISP (a dialect of the LISP computer language) [Winston and Horn, 1980; Charniak *et al.*, 1980]. To simplify the design of Rachel's inference engine (and keeping in mind that the system in its current implementation is experimental), little, if any, backtracking is allowed during a consultation. Hence, the only way to correct an erroneous entry of data is to rerun a substantial portion of the consultation.

Another feature of Rachel's operation is that it can continually report the status of its reasoning. Thus, at all times, the user can be made aware of how any given inference was made, including unsuccessful proof attempts. This feature is particularly convenient during lengthy, time-consuming inferences that would otherwise give the user the impression that Rachel is idle or no longer functioning. Moreover, these reports of Rachel's lines of reasoning can greatly enhance the clarity of the resulting decision model.

The verbosity of Rachel's reports about its reasoning, as well as that of its query and subgoal-based explanation facilities, can be very accurately controlled. This control is available directly from the system's knowledge bases and is implemented through simple syntactic pattern matching applied to the WFFs to be displayed. Thus, Rachel provides a declarative language to control the "askability" and the "tellability" of specific WFF patterns.

Finally, the influence diagram decision models that result from Rachel's formulation process can be subjected to full formal analysis by using decision-theoretic techniques. In addition to evaluating the model's optimal policy (i.e., the policy that maximizes expected utility), Rachel can make value-of-information and other sensitivity calculations that mine the model. These calculations are carried out by a closely associated influence diagram processing system, called SUPERID, whose description is outside the scope of this book [Breese and Holtzman, 1984].

The Appendix at the end of the book contains an annotated version of a typical Rachel consultation. To exhibit as many features of the system as possible, the consultation was conducted with a high level of reporting and explanation verbosity. Focusing on a specific case of tubal blockage, this consultation gives an indication of the capabilities of Rachel as an aid for infertility decision-making. In turn, despite the limitations of its implementation, Rachel provides a glimpse at the potential of intelligent decision systems for helping decision-makers in difficult decision situations.

9

The Promise of Intelligent Decision Systems

The creation of a new device . . . can have far-reaching significance—it can create new ways of being that previously did not exist and a framework for actions that would not have previously made sense.
—Understanding Computers and Cognition,
Terry Winograd and Fernando Flores

This chapter concludes our discussion of intelligent decision systems by indicating important design criteria, by contrasting their potential benefits to those of expert systems, and by suggesting a taxonomy for future application areas. We finish by reflecting on the promise of intelligent decision systems.

WHERE DO WE GO FROM HERE?

Rachel in Perspective

Built and developed primarily as an initial demonstration of intelligent decision system (IDS) technology, Rachel served its purpose well. Despite its limitations, Rachel demonstrates that intelligent decision systems can deliver decision analysis assistance through a computer. Moreover, it shows that this assistance can be provided for significant decisions—such as selecting a medical treatment for infertility.

However, while exhibiting many key features of IDS technology, Rachel greatly lacks the flexibility and robustness that make computer systems truly useful. Furthermore, Rachel focuses primarily on formulating and evaluating the user's decision problem, providing only minimal support for appraising the resulting decision models and recommendations.

Thus, Rachel should be viewed not as a comprehensive IDS example but rather as a window into a realm of new possibilities. Based on the ideas developed in this book, we could conceive of systems that would go far beyond Rachel to assist decision-makers in many important arenas. In that sense, Rachel represents the tip of an iceberg whose full impact remains to be discovered through future IDS applications. Intelligent decision systems could be built to assist decision-making in such arenas as finance, capital investments, contract bidding, product marketing, real estate, medicine, litigation, emergency management, space exploration, and personal investments. From the business person trying to determine whether to build a new factory to the individual who has been sued and needs to decide whether to go to trial or settle out of court, from the patient for whom undergoing exploratory surgery does not seem like an obvious choice to the prospective house buyer contending with an overwhelming selection of mortgage possibilities, IDS applications can help clarify and simplify the decisions at hand.

Realizing this vision will, of course, require significant effort and resources. Yet the benefits of intelligent decision systems seem so clearly to outweigh their cost that commercial IDS development appears imminent.

Design Criteria for Intelligent Decision Systems

Just how effective future IDS applications will be depends on the characteristics of their target class of decisions and on how well the application addresses the needs of individuals facing those decisions. As a guide for future IDS efforts, we now outline some key design criteria that follow from our discussion in this book. To a large extent, these criteria help map the philosophical underpinnings of decision analysis onto the realm of practical system design.

An IDS should not simply select among known choices or assume (except in very simple cases) that the decision-maker can clearly state his or her preferences. Professional decision analysts spend a great deal of their time helping clients generate a rich set of distinct alternatives (mere perturbations on a fixed theme will not suffice), clarifying the possible outcomes of these alternatives, and explicitly describing the decision-maker's preferences over these outcomes. Intelligent decision systems should be designed to support this highly creative task, and the ideas developed in Chapters 2, 3, and 5 provide a solid foundation for addressing this issue. In addition, the decision analysis literature [Howard and Matheson, 1983–1984] describes specific techniques for generating alternatives and eliciting preferences.

With few exceptions, we must confront uncertainty when we make important decisions. Intelligent decision systems provide an exceptional platform for capturing and reasoning with uncertain decision elements. Their ability to reliably capture uncertainty follows from the recognition in decision analysis that uncertain decision elements must be determined for the specific problem at hand rather than from a previous analysis of generic decision situations. In addition, intelligent decision systems should accurately reflect the structure of uncertain decision elements by explicitly incorporating specific information unique to the decision-maker.

Recognizing the unique aspects of each decision implies that a well-designed intelligent decision system must develop every decision model from the unique perspective of each specific decision-maker. Such a system should be flexible enough to allow the user to easily incorporate new elements into the decision model to account for aspects of the decision that were either totally or partially unanticipated in the system's knowledge bases. Furthermore, if the system contains previously defined model elements (e.g., "canned" distributions or decision variables), its designers should provide a means for ensuring the validity of these model elements every time they are used in the context of a specific decision problem.

Effective intelligent decision systems should also assist the user in assessing key decision model elements. For instance, these systems should provide a framework for assessing probability distributions that avoids introducing biases, explores possible dependencies, and encourages consistency. Similarly, the systems should help elicit the decision-maker's risk attitude. Time-preference (discount rate) parameters, outcome attribute trade-off parameters, and critical deterministic model parameters also warrant special attention. Identifying the decision model elements that merit special attention in the specific context of an IDS application should be a major design task.

To a large extent, intelligent decision systems derive their normative power by using the MEU action axiom to produce recommendations for action. Thus, designers of IDS applications should not be tempted to include non-MEU condition-recommendation rules in the system, because such rules would greatly reduce the reliability of the system's recommendations for action.[1] Since most expert systems contain a large body of heuristic (hence non-MEU) condition-recommendation rules, keeping this IDS design criterion in mind is particularly important.

---

[1] Admissible condition-recommendation rules that are simpler than MEU may be developed for the rare cases where deterministic and/or stochastic dominance can be established. These rules would implement an abbreviated version of MEU, and their recommendations would be consistent with those obtained using the full MEU action axiom.

Because intelligent decision systems are ultimately intended to clarify otherwise confusing decision situations and yield the insight necessary for action, they focus attention on important decision elements and away from unimportant ones. This attention-focusing process produces a series of increasingly refined models of the decision and a corresponding series of recommendations for action. Achieving the desired insight requires the decision-maker to play an active role in the analysis by continually appraising the proposed recommendations and the model on which they are based. Thus, effective IDSs should assist the user in this task by providing a means for mining and justifying the decision basis at every stage of the analysis process.

Another key design criterion is that intelligent decision systems should be built for specific domains and not as general-purpose tools (except, possibly, for designs aimed at assisting trained decision analysts). Focusing on a well-defined domain is essential for developing meaningful knowledge bases. Furthermore, having an explicit domain focus allows IDS designers to identify and incorporate into the system particular IDS features that address key aspects of decisions in the given domain.

Decision situations never arise in a vacuum, which means that besides being intuitive to the decision-maker, decisions must often be defensible to others (e.g., superiors or family members) and be consistent with related decisions (e.g., within an organization or with respect to a higher-level objective). Thus, decision analysts are usually careful to document the analysis process and its conclusions, something that IDS designers must recognize and for which they should provide appropriate system features.

We have addressed several key IDS design criteria. Other issues, such as the security of knowledge bases and real-time response, are common considerations for designing computer-based systems that may be important for some IDS applications and not for others. In general, however, intelligent decision systems imply a new way of thinking about decisions; as such, successful IDS designs (independent of their implementation details) should reflect this way of thinking in terms that are meaningful and useful within their specific application domain.

USING INTELLIGENT DECISION SYSTEMS AND EXPERT SYSTEMS

Although both intelligent decision systems and expert systems can provide knowledge-based assistance to decision-makers, there are major differences in the type of help these two technologies can offer, and it is worth clarifying this distinction. In doing so, we must recall that when decision-makers face a difficult decision, they need a means to develop the *insight* necessary for action. A system that merely *answers* their possibly misformulated decision problems would be of limited value and could do more harm than good.

Different Types of Help for Decision-Making

Recalling Fig. 2.1, we can distinguish the domain of a decision from its situation (i.e., the decision-maker's circumstances and preferences). Expert systems can offer decision-makers valuable assistance for dealing with the *domain* of their decision, because the skills and factual knowledge of experienced domain experts can be represented in extensive knowledge bases. These knowledge bases enable the system to assist its users by simplifying and clarifying the effects of relations and constraints inherent to its domain and by suggesting plausible courses of action. However, as discussed in Chapter 6, these suggestions for action cannot reflect the unique issues that are often central in decision-making. Clearly, this type of help is *generic*, since it applies to the whole domain addressed by the expert system.

In contrast, decision analysts are most valuable in helping decision-makers understand their specific *circumstances* and *preferences* and the effect these have on the availability and desirability of various possible actions. Because decision analysis directly addresses the decision-maker's alternatives, information, and preferences, it ensures that key decision elements (many of which are usually unanticipated and even surprising to the decision participants) are quickly identified and incorporated in the decision model and reflected in any corresponding recommendations for action. Hence, decision analysis offers help that is *unique* to the decision situation at hand.

As illustrated in Fig. 9.1, intelligent decision systems provide the benefits of both decision analysis and expert systems. Therefore, IDS applications can address both the generic and unique aspects of a class of decisions. Furthermore, by providing extensive domain knowledge to assist the decision-analytic process, intelligent decision systems can go significantly beyond simply automating decision analysis.

A Sample Decision Situation

A simplified, yet realistic, example helps illustrate the different types of decision-making help that expert systems and intelligent decision systems provide. Consider the predicament of the chief operating engineer (or, possibly, the plant manager) at a large power-generating plant who, during a hot summer night, is informed by an operator that the internal temperature of the largest of three generators has risen somewhat above normal values. By asking only a few key questions, a generator diagnosis expert system helps the chief operating engineer quickly identify a low-grade electrical leakage between adjacent generator windings as the most likely source of the problem. The diagnosis is greatly speeded because, through a multitude of automatic sensors, the expert system has an accurate description of the current

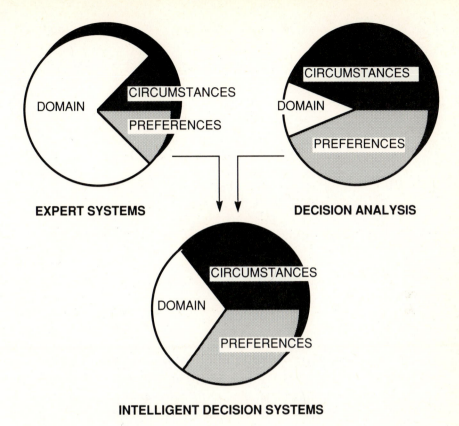

FIGURE 9.1   Intelligent decision systems can assist decision-makers with both the generic and the unique aspects of their decisions.

state of the generator. In this case, unusual gas impurities inside the generator casing (possibly from insulation breakdown), together with a faint, yet clearly recognizable electrical disturbance pattern, led directly to identifying the general nature of the malfunction.

Moreover, while a minor short seems by far the most likely source of the problem, it is also possible for the damage to be much more widespread. The latter is less likely but could potentially have catastrophic consequences should the generator burn and could easily lead to a lengthy—and extremely costly—forced outage. However, as long as the situation does not get worse, the temperature rise is still low enough that the generator could continue to operate without intervention.

The chief operating engineer (quite likely in consultation with the system dispatcher) faces a tough decision. He could stop the offending generator as soon as possible to carry out the necessary unscheduled maintenance.

Choosing this option would allow him to inspect and repair the generator before any further damage has a chance to occur; however, this action would also involve his having to purchase expensive replacement power from other generating facilities on the network. Alternatively, he could keep the overheated generator in operation and risk a forced outage. If all goes well, any needed maintenance could be performed during next month's scheduled shutdown, for which replacement power has already been purchased at competitive rates.

While the expert system greatly helped in identifying the nature—and maybe even the likelihood—of possible problems affecting the generator and could suggest relevant repair actions, it can do little to help the chief engineer decide what to do. In particular, this system cannot take into account such factors as the unanticipated availability of inexpensive spot-market power, or the effect that the company's traditional focus on safety and reliability (a fact that has been recently emphasized by top management) should have on his attitude toward taking risks.

The chief operating engineer therefore turns to the plant management intelligent decision system he has at his facility. Since the intelligent decision system communicates with the diagnosis expert system, it already has a description of the possible generator problems and has outlined a set of alternative courses of action. Furthermore, it has been kept up to date on such matters as the company's cost of capital and top management's risk tolerance. In addition, it contains information about the current usage costs and availability of other generating units and sources of replacement power—information that, without the benefit of an intelligent decision system, would not be normally accessible to plant operating engineers. Thus, the chief operating engineer can focus quickly and effectively on the decision at hand.

As is often the case, this decision has some important complications. First, the West Coast (where the plant is located) is going through a major heat wave—implying heavy use of air-conditioners, which greatly increases demand for electrical power—and it is uncertain how long this weather will last. Second, the company has recently signed a major new contract with nearby cogenerators (companies that generate electricity as a by-product of some other production process), and government regulations require that the company purchase this power even if it costs more than network power. Depending on where and how this cogenerated power is produced, it may or may not meet the company's reliability standards. The company can also purchase replacement power from neighboring utilities. Cogeneration and power from nearby utilities are particularly important for our discussion, since they introduce decision elements that could not have been anticipated a couple of years ago, when both the expert system and the intelligent decision system were developed.

True to its decision-analytic underpinnings, the intelligent decision system helps the chief operating engineer capture the unique power-generation and weather-related circumstances that affect his decision. And it readily handles the new possibilities introduced by cogeneration as a potential source of power by developing new decision and chance variables in the overall decision model.[2]

Based on the analysis, the chief operating engineer determines that before deciding whether to perform unscheduled maintenance on the overheated generator, he should accurately assess the actual reliability of currently available cogenerator power. A few telephone calls and a review of the present load and expected power needs for the next few days provide the desired information, making it obvious that in this particular case the best course of action is to perform unscheduled maintenance on the malfunctioning generator and to purchase replacement power from a nearby utility and specific cogenerators.

Selecting the Appropriate Decision-Making Technology

Figure 9.2 shows that intelligent decision systems fill an important gap in decision-making technology. *Standard decision methods* (shown in the lower left-hand corner of the figure), whether heuristic or formal, are all that are needed in many decision situations. However, there are times when the effectiveness of standard decision methods relies on the expertise of a few key individuals. When this occurs, overall decision effectiveness can be improved by automating the skills and factual knowledge of these key individuals with *expert systems* (shown in the upper left-hand corner of the figure) and by then making the resulting systems available in quantity to less-skilled decision-makers. When decisions are difficult because they require an extraordinary understanding of the complexities of a particular domain, expert systems perform particularly well.

In contrast, expert systems do not perform well when difficult decisions must be made in the face of significant uncertainty, unclear alternatives, or complex preferences. To improve their quality, such decisions call for the normative power of *decision analysis* (shown in the lower right-hand corner of the figure). Typically, however, undertaking a professional decision analysis is a relatively lengthy and expensive process and is reserved for major, one-of-a-kind decisions.

---

[2]An expert system could not handle a similar situation, because it would require new condition-recommendation rules to cover the new possibilities—rules that would take considerable time and effort to produce. Furthermore, even if the necessary rules were added for the system to handle this specific case, other cases would introduce additonal unanticipated complications that could not all be incorporated into the expert system's knowledge bases. Since intelligent decision systems base all their recommendations on the MEU action axiom, no additional condition-recommendation rules are necessary to deal with unanticipated circumstances.

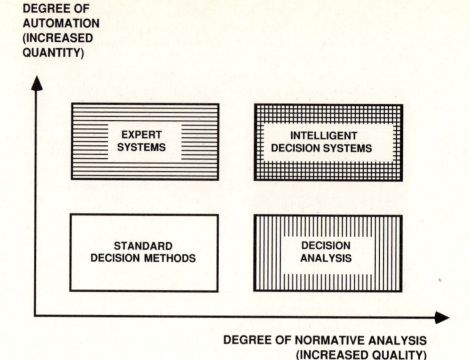

DEGREE OF AUTOMATION (INCREASED QUANTITY)

EXPERT SYSTEMS

INTELLIGENT DECISION SYSTEMS

STANDARD DECISION METHODS

DECISION ANALYSIS

DEGREE OF NORMATIVE ANALYSIS (INCREASED QUALITY)

FIGURE 9.2 Decision-makers have a choice of four kinds of decision-making technology.

Thus, a different approach is needed when decisions requiring the normative power of decision analysis are frequent or require a faster response than is possible through traditional analysis. These situations call for *intelligent decision systems* (shown in the upper right-hand corner of the figure). Intelligent decision systems make high-quality decision-making available in greater quantity. They are particularly effective for addressing decisions that, although recurrent, involve uncertainty and depend strongly on the specific decision situation at hand. Furthermore, since they contain much of the functionality of expert systems, they can also be used to distribute the expertise of domain experts.

Given the characteristics of the decision situation, the flowchart in Fig. 9.3 provides an easy guide for selecting an appropriate decision technology when the decision is important enough to warrant careful thought. Central to this selection process is determining whether similar decisions are made frequently enough to benefit from automation. If this is the case, then the resulting economies of scale would make either expert systems or intelligent

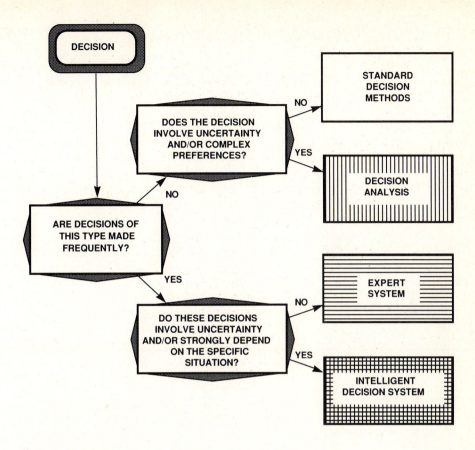

FIGURE 9.3   The nature of a decision allows a decision-maker to select an appropriate decision technology.

decision systems the preferred choice. An expert system would be appropriate when the decisions in question do not involve uncertainty and do not depend strongly on the specific situation at hand. However, an intelligent decision system would be appropriate when, besides being frequent, the decisions involve uncertainty or are sensitive to preferences and circumstances unique to each situation.

If the decision is infrequent or one-of-a-kind, then standard decision methods or decision analysis would be appropriate. Decision analysis should be chosen when the decision involves a high degree of uncertainty or complexity of preferences and when the magnitude of the resources at stake justify the associated expense. If this is not the case, standard decision methods should be used.

THE BIRTH OF A NEW INDUSTRY

Delivering on the Rhetoric of Fifth-Generation Computing

Much is said these days about the promise of fifth-generation computing—an attempt to revolutionize the use of computers by exploiting the latest advances in artificial intelligence [Moto-oka, 1981a; Feigenbaum and McCorduck, 1983]. Issued jointly by the Japanese government and Japanese industry, the fifth-generation challenge has been met in the United States and in Europe with national and even multinational efforts. A central focus of the rhetoric that surrounds this worldwide initiative is a desire to assist decision-makers. For example, in his keynote speech at the International Conference on Fifth-Generation Computer Systems, Tohru Moto-oka, leader of Japan's fifth-generation project and the conference's program committee chairman, indicated that "one of the most important tasks facing mankind in this century is the effective use of finite resources" [Moto-oka, 1981b, p. 15]. He goes on to state the following [Moto-oka, 1981b, p. 25]:

> The following are some effects that fifth-generation computers can be expected to have on main fields which will be rapidly systematized up to the 1990's and in which computer systems will produce great advantages. . . . [Decision Support Systems (DSS) provide] high-level information and support thinking processes to decision-making individuals and groups for increasing the validity and reducing the time required for making decisions, as well as reducing the costs involved in decision-making. With DSS, due to the fact that consistency in decision-making is improved, and group decision-making is rendered more efficient and adaptable, more sophisticated decision-making becomes possible, thus enabling industries to increase productivity rationally and smoothly.

Yet despite the promise, the rhetoric, and the gargantuan size of these efforts, there is little evidence that genuine decision-making help will be provided.

At the heart of this skepticism lies the almost exclusive reliance on expert systems technology for developing advanced fifth-generation software. As we have discussed, expert systems can only assist decision-makers in the simplest of decision situations—hardly the ones that such an initiative aims to address. Other technologies that have been suggested to supplement expert systems for decision assistance, such as those collectively referred to as "decision support systems" [Keen and Scott Morton, 1978; McCosh and Scott Morton, 1978; Bonczek et al., 1981], also fail to address the real needs of decision-makers, because they focus on providing information and do little to help define and incorporate alternatives and preferences.

This book supports the belief that intelligent decision systems can deliver the decision-making assistance promised by the proponents of fifth-generation computing. Free from many of the constraints inherent in expert system technology, intelligent decision systems are fully capable of handling the uncertainty, complexity, and dynamics often at the source of decision difficulty. Furthermore, an IDS can account for the unique preferences and circumstances that shape the decision situation to yield sound, consistent, and defensible decisions.

From a broader perspective, the technology of intelligent decision systems is sufficiently general and flexible to potentially change the way many of us make decisions. While its initial progress may be in the form of special-purpose decision tools, IDS technology could go far beyond isolated applications to become the basis of a new industry.

Different Types of Intelligent Decision Systems

So far, we have discussed intelligent decision systems without saying much about the particular purpose of specific applications. However, while all IDS applications would be expected to share a common philosophy and its associated technological implications, individual intelligent decision systems could serve very different purposes, and their implementations could take strikingly different forms.

Like Rachel, an IDS application can be designed to deliver substantial decision-modeling knowledge within a particular domain. Much of the value of knowledge-delivery IDS applications would reside in how trustworthy their associated knowledge bases are, rather than in any raw analytical assistance they might provide. In most of these applications, information about user preferences and circumstances would primarily guide the use of previously defined model elements. Only under exceptional circumstances should the user need to incorporate totally unanticipated decision elements.

Other IDS applications could help in delegating decision authority. Typically, such intelligent decision systems would have two groups of users: those delegating authority and those to whom the authority is being delegated. In most organizations, the delegation of authority often takes the form of a policy. These policies, while usually effective, tend to err on the side of bureaucratic rigidity. Intelligent decision systems that delegate decision authority, however, could implement policies that, although strict regarding critical parameters, remain sensitive to the unique circumstances that arise in specific decision situations. An attractive feature of these IDS applications may be the possibility of designing an appropriate set of "control knobs," allowing key individuals throughout the organization to guide the behavior of others without imposing overly rigid rules. These knobs could reflect organization-wide decision parameters, such as risk tolerance and cost of capital.

A very different type of IDS application could address decisions that, although recurrent, hinge strongly on the unique aspects of each specific situation. For example, such decisions could arise within large capital investment activities, competitive strategy generation and evaluation efforts, plaintiff and defendant decisions in tort cases, company mergers and acquisitions, and experimental medical procedures. An intelligent decision system designed to assist with this type of decisions would be generally referred to as a *decision analysis workbench*. Unlike the more operational IDS applications discussed above, where a streamlined interaction may be more desirable, a decision analysis workbench would typically offer its users considerable assistance for capturing and quantifying unique decision elements. For this purpose, it should provide users with a wide range of pertinent decision-analytic methods and tools, each supported by an appropriate level of expert decision analysis guidance.

Autonomous decision systems constitute yet another type of IDS application. These systems would be designed to operate with little or no direct human intervention. Obvious application areas for this kind of intelligent decision system include unattended manufacturing and the exploration and use of deep space and ocean environments. Since it would be difficult or impossible for a human to participate in the decision process in such situations, unanticipated circumstances could impair the operation of an autonomous decision system. This places an exceptionally heavy burden on the extent and reliability of the knowledge contained in the system. However, should an unanticipated circumstance arise, IDS technology would ease the corresponding task of updating the system, because only domain knowledge (rather than new condition-recommendation rules) would need to be added.

CONCLUSION

Intelligent decision systems can greatly simplify and improve the way people make difficult choices by providing expert-level automated decision analysis assistance rapidly and inexpensively. Yet as with any technology that embodies a new way of thinking, intelligent decision systems will need to contend with the same cultural limitations they were conceived to improve upon. In the near term, their success will hinge on how well they can meet the current needs of decision-makers without compromising fundamental principles. Their long-term success will depend on how much these fundamental principles become part of our culture.

The decision to spend the time and effort to develop intelligent decision systems was very good when I made it. Participating in the outcome of this decision has been, and promises to be, very exciting.

Appendix

A Sample Session with Rachel

This appendix presents an example of Rachel's operation. The example begins with a case description that is sufficiently detailed to allow specific medical alternatives to be determined; however, it is much less rigorous than what should normally appear in the patient's records. This description is then followed by an annotated version of a verbatim consultation report (which can be requested of Rachel). The report illustrates the construction and evaluation of a decision model for the patient.

The reader should be warned of two important issues about the contents of this Appendix. First, the case under consideration is totally fictitious, although an attempt has been made to make it realistic. Furthermore, the various parametric assessments associated with the case were obtained with only a minimal attempt to correct for psychological biases[1] and, hence, should be considered merely as reasonable guesses for a patient in the situation being considered. The second warning concerns the current implementation of Rachel. The system was developed with very limited computational and human resources. In a more extensive development environment, it would have been possible to display many more features of the methodology of intelligent decision systems (e.g., the "palette" approach to decision model design illustrated in Fig. 4.9).

---

[1]Psychologists have identified many important sources of assessment biases that must be accounted for in reliable assessment interviews. Some important biases are cognitive and motivational in nature and are discussed in Chapters 3, 5, and 7 and in the literature [Kahneman *et al.*, 1982].

As an aside, it is interesting to note that the consultation shown below constitutes a constructive proof of the theorem stating that a complete influence diagram can be built for the hypothetical patient. That this proof was generated by a computer is irrelevant in this regard; even if the consultation report were typed by hand, it would still prove the theorem.

CASE DESCRIPTION: TUBAL BLOCKAGE

A 28-year-old female patient has come to the infertility clinic complaining of an inability to conceive despite having had regular intercourse with her husband for the past two years. Her husband has had a normal semen analysis (i.e., normal seminal volume, sperm concentration, sperm motility, and sperm morphology), and the couple has had a positive postcoital test (i.e., presence of motile sperm in the cervical mucus following intercourse). Moreover, the patient experiences regular menstrual periods, which indicates a healthy endocrine (i.e., hormonal) system. The results of an endometrial biopsy showing a secretory, in-phase endometrium provide further evidence of her normal ovulatory function.

A pertinent element of the patient's medical history is that ten years before coming to the clinic she suffered from pelvic inflammatory disease. A common consequence of this disease in females is the partial or total obstruction of the individual's Fallopian tubes.

The results of a recent hysterosalpingogram (i.e., an X-ray of the Fallopian tubes and of the uterus) are available, and they show bilateral hydrosalpinges (i.e., both tubes are blocked at their ovarian—fimbrial—end and are distended with fluid inside). A subsequent laparoscopic observation (i.e., a view of the pelvic organs through a fiber-optic instrument introduced through a small abdominal incision) reveals that, in fact, both tubes are totally blocked and that their outer diameter is approximately two centimeters (which is considerably larger than normal). Otherwise, the uterus and ovaries appear healthy, except for a few filmy adhesions between the tubes and their corresponding ovaries.

Finally, for general background, the patient is in good health, smokes, drinks alcohol moderately, and has no known allergies. In conclusion, the couple's infertility can be safely attributed to a tubal blockage in the female partner.

This patient has essentially three possible medical courses of action. An important surgical option is to undergo a laparotomy (i.e., abdominal surgery) during which the blockages could be corrected and the adhesions removed. An alternative strategy would be for the patient to undergo a series of in-vitro fertilization attempts, thus mechanically bypassing the blockage. Each fertilization attempt would involve a laparoscopy to harvest developed eggs, an actual in-vitro fertilization procedure, and a reintroduction of fertilized eggs (if any become available) through the cervical opening and into the uterine cavity. A final alternative is to forgo medical intervention. This strategy can be quite attractive, because tubal repair requires major surgery (which involves significant risks). Furthermore, both surgery and in-vitro fertilization imply considerable discomfort and financial cost. Moreover, the probability of the patient having an ectopic pregnancy (i.e., a pregnancy outside the uterus—typically in a Fallopian tube) is significantly increased following corrective tubal surgery. For simplicity, less common medical alternatives, such as laparoscopic repair of the hydrosalpinges or donor embryo transfer techniques (as well as nonmedical alternatives such as adoption), will not be considered here.

CONSULTATION REPORT

The report illustrates Rachel's analysis of the case discussed above. This decision example was chosen over a smaller, less representative problem to show the power of the methodology of intelligent decision systems in a realistic clinical situation. In addition, the report shows Rachel's explanation and tracing facilities in detail. Thus, the report is relatively lengthy.

To facilitate the task of reading the report, Fig. A.1 at the end of the Appendix shows the influence diagram built by Rachel during the consultation. For further clarity, explanatory notes have been added throughout the consultation report, canned text output has been edited, various computer messages of no consequence have been deleted, and blank space has been added where necessary to improve readability. Otherwise, the report is a facsimile of Rachel's operation as seen on a computer terminal. As discussed previously, the consultation begins with the construction of a value model and proceeds to assess the corresponding value node by indirect means. The report concludes with an evaluation of the optimal strategy for the patient (i.e., the decision that maximizes her expected utility) given the model constructed. However, this consultation only takes the patient and physician through a first pass at formulating, evaluating, and appraising the decision problem. Further passes would probably be necessary to develop the desired insight.

RACHEL

> ```
> Welcome to Rachel, an experimental intelligent decision system
> for infertile couples seeking medical help.
> ```

> ```
> Please be aware that because it is an experimental system,
> Rachel is quite limited in scope and is unsuitable for clinical
> use.
> ```

|| NOTE: Explanatory notes (such as this one) appear at appropriate places throughout the consultation report. For clarity, they are always marked by a double line on the left margin.

|| NOTE: User input is highlighted in *underscore italic* characters.

```
Before proceeding, would you like some introductory information?
[Y/N]> y

Rachel is designed to aid infertile couples and their physician in
selecting a medical treatment.  Specifically, it addresses the
situation commonly faced by infertile couples who have been diagnosed
and who are presented with a set of alternative treatments, none of
which is an obvious best choice (i.e., a dominating alternative).

Reflecting the characteristics of this situation, Rachel's
interactive style assumes that all decision participants — one or
both partners and their physician — are present throughout the
consultation.  However, it also assumes that it is interacting
directly with the physician.

Rachel determines a recommended course of action by combining the
physician's pertinent medical knowledge with relevant aspects of the
patient's preferences and personal circumstances.

More? [Y/N]> y

Rachel's recommendation relies on its ability to represent a couple's
decision problem in an intuitively simple form.  This representation
— known as an influence diagram — is built in accordance with the
principles of decision analysis and, hence, constitutes a well-
```

defined model of the decision.   From this decision model, a recommended course of action is mathematically deduced.

It is worth noting that although obtaining a recommendation for action is an important result of the analysis, the main purpose of constructing and evaluating a decision model and of deducing a corresponding recommendation is to help both the couple and their physician gain a clear understanding of the decision at hand. Because it focuses on developing this understanding and not merely on producing a recommendation, Rachel can be an effective aid for arriving at a well-thought-out course of action.

More? [Y/N]> y

Rachel was motivated by the fact that because professional decision analysis is prohibitively expensive and slow, it is not useful for most individuals in many important decision situations.   However, despite its cost and time requirements, decision analysis is highly desirable for dealing with difficult decisions, such as selecting a medical course of action in the absence of a dominating alternative.

In an attempt to overcome this economic and speed barrier, intelligent decision systems — of which Rachel is the first example — deliver decision analysis assistance through a knowledge-based system.   In the specific context of infertility treatments, Rachel provides a fast and inexpensive way for infertile couples to analyze their medical decisions.

Would you like instructions for using RACHEL? [Y/N]> y

Every time a decision problem is presented to Rachel, the system sets out to satisfy the top-level goal of completing a corresponding well-formed influence diagram.   As part of this model formulation task, Rachel needs to ask a variety of questions about the particular case being analyzed.   In general, these questions should be clear and self-explanatory.   However, if there is a need for further clarification, Rachel can provide a simple explanation of why it needs to ask any given question by displaying the current state of its dynamic subgoal stack.

To activate Rachel's explanation facility, the user can simply type "W" or "WHY" to any query. Rachel will then exhibit the subgoal it is trying to satisfy at the time it asked the last question. Responding "W" or "WHY" once again will uncover the next higher subgoal.   This process can be repeated until the topmost goal is displayed. Once the topmost goal is displayed, further "W" or "WHY" responses will continue to redisplay it.   At any time throughout this explanation process, the user can return to the original query by typing "Q" or "Question".

Rachel is currently implemented at an experimental level. Thus, it runs slowly and its interaction style requires that the user be familiar with rule-based technology, particularly in the second half of the consultation. Specifically, Rachel assumes the user can understand simple, first-order prefix predicate calculus well-formed formulas (FOPPC WFFs) and has at least a rough idea of the operation of a backward-chaining, depth-first automatic inference system.

More? [Y/N]>y

Other useful responses are:

```
Y, Yes       : YES, and STORE the corresponding assertion;
N, No        : NO, and STORE the corresponding (negated) assertion;
M, Maybe     : YES, but DO NOT STORE the corresponding assertion;
U, Unprovable: NO, but DO NOT STORE the corresponding assertion;
Q, Question  : Repeat the question;
F, Facts     : Display the currently known FACTS;
R, Rules     : Display the currently known RULES;
?            : Display all currently valid responses.
```

The first four responses — Y, N, M, U — can be used to answer any YES/NO question throughout the consultation. The last four responses — Q, F, R, ? — (as well as "W") can be used prior to answering any question.

NOTE: Responses "M" and "U" are available for debugging purposes only and can be made unavailable to the user.

More? [Y/N]>y

Rachel's influence diagram processing facility is called SUPERID. Rachel uses SUPERID to construct, evaluate, and analyze decision models. In addition to its function within Rachel, SUPERID can be used as a stand-alone influence diagram workbench. (In fact, SUPERID is the first program ever built that evaluates influence diagrams directly, without first converting them into equivalent decision trees.)

If you would like information on SUPERID, please consult the following reference:

Breese, J.S. and Holtzman, S. 1984. <u>SUPERID: Influence Diagram Processing Environment—User's Guide</u>. Stanford, California: Department of Engineering-Economic Systems, Stanford University.

```
RACHEL is now about to load its knowledge bases.  This process may
take anywhere from a few seconds to several minutes, depending on the
status of the (time-shared) computer system on which it is imple-
mented.  Thank you for your patience.
```

```
Loading DAKB  [Decision Analysis Knowledge Base] ...  ... Done.
Loading VALKB [Value Model Knowledge Base] ...        ... Done.
Loading MEDKB [Medical Knowledge Base] ...            ... Done.
```

```
RACHEL is now ready to begin the consultation.
```

```
To begin the consultation, we need to get some basic patient informa-
tion.
```

```
What is the patient's name? [single string, e.g., Sally_Jones]> Marsha
What is the patient's age?  [years]> 28
What is the patient's sex?  [M/F]> f
```

```
Proved: "(DECISION-MODEL-INITIALIZED D-MODEL:MARSHA)".
Proved: "(DECISION-NODE-NAME D-MODEL:MARSHA D-NODE:MARSHA)".
```

NOTE: Statements beginning with the term "Proved:" are issued by Rachel's inference engine primarily to allow the user to monitor the inference process.
Although the user can request that all or some of these statements not be displayed, they have been included in this consultation report to exhibit the
reasoning underlying Rachel's operation.

The term "proved" is being used because Rachel's inference engine is, in fact,
a formal theorem prover. In a system intended for a less technical audience,
most of these statements would be suppressed. However, in cases where it is
useful to issue messages of this nature to the user, terms like "established" or
"completed" may be easier to understand and, hence, preferable to the term
"proved."

```
What alternative courses of action does MARSHA have?
Please type "quit" to finish the list.
```

```
Alternative   #1:    [single_string]> laparotomy
Alternative   #2:    [single_string]> ivf-4
Alternative   #3:    [single_string]> do-nothing
Alternative   #4:    [single_string]> quit
```

NOTE: The term "IVF-4" stands for a commonly prescribed regimen of up to four in-vitro fertilization (IVF) attempts. Typically, this regimen is administered in accordance with relatively well-defined guidelines to determine whether it makes sense for a patient to continue undergoing in-vitro fertilization attempts if implantation has not been achieved. These guidelines take into account the large amount of physiological and pathological information obtained as a side effect of each in-vitro fertilization attempt (particularly the first one).

```
Proved: "(DECISION-ALTERNATIVES D-MODEL:MARSHA
                                D-NODE:MARSHA
                                (LAPAROTOMY IVF-4 DO-NOTHING))".
Proved: "(DECISION-NODE D-MODEL:MARSHA D-NODE:MARSHA)".
Proved: "(VALUE-NODE-NAME D-MODEL:MARSHA V-NODE:MARSHA)".
```

We now need to determine the general classes of attributes that must be accounted for by the value function.

More information? [Y/N]> y

At present, Rachel can only account for four (4) classes of attributes:

```
    - MONEY        (i.e., financial costs);
    - MORBIDITY    (i.e., disease and discomfort);
    - LIFE         (i.e., duration of life);
    - THB          (i.e., a take-home baby).
```

The term "THB" refers to a newborn infant ready to go home following birth. The concept of a THB is explained in more detail later in the consultation.

Given the alternatives under consideration and given the patient's specific situation (e.g., in terms of insurance coverage and tolerance for pain), you will be asked to select pertinent attributes for the decision at hand. Note that a THB is assumed to be of concern in every infertility case.

More? [Y/N]> y

For instance, if surgery is being contemplated, then morbidity and life are probably pertinent. In contrast, if only a mild drug therapy is under consideration, then money might be the only attribute, other than THB, that should be explicitly considered. If the patient's insurance policy covers all medical costs, then money is likely not to be an issue (except perhaps for lost wages, if any) regardless of the treatment under consideration.

```
Should "MONEY" be considered?     [Y/N]> y
Should "LIFE" be considered?      [Y/N]> y
Should "MORBIDITY" be considered? [Y/N]> y


Proved: "(MODEL-ATTRIBUTES D-MODEL:MARSHA (LIFE MONEY MORBIDITY THB))".
Proved: "(VALUE-FUNCTION-NAME MON-MOR-LIF)".
Proved: "(VALUE-FUNCTION-NAME MON-LIF)".
Proved: "(VALUE-FUNCTION-NAME MON)".
```

> NOTE:
>
> For the case in question, all three optional classes of attributes were deemed pertinent. To find a corresponding value function, Rachel has just searched its knowledge base for all available value function forms—MON (exclusively for monetary outcomes), MON-LIF (for monetary and life outcomes), and MON-MOR-LIF (for monetary, morbidity, and life outcomes). Because of memory constraints in Rachel's implementation, its knowledge base does not contain all six value function forms discussed in Chapter 8; in particular, it only contains forms that account for money, THB, and (possibly) morbidity, and/or life.
>
> These are function forms and not actual functions because they are not completely specified to allow them to be parametrically adjusted to better fit the patient's preferences. As the consultation proceeds, values for all necessary parameters will be obtained and the forms will become fully specified functions.
>
> Having found these function forms, Rachel is about to check their suitability for dealing with all attribute classes pertinent to the decision at hand. In this case, the testing process is quite short because the very first function form tested (MON-MOR-LIF) succeeds.
>
> Once Rachel identifies MON-MOR-LIF as the function form to be used, it proceeds to add the corresponding direct predecessors of the value node (with appropriate outcome restrictions). In doing so, it converts what started as a minimal influence diagram into an incipient influence diagram. (See Chapter 4 for a definition of minimal and incipient influence diagrams.)

```
Proved: "(FUNCTION-ATTRIBUTES MON-MOR-LIF (THB MONEY MORBIDITY LIFE))".
Proved: "(FUNCTION-HAS-ALL-NEEDED-MODEL-ATTRIBUTES D-MODEL:MARSHA
                                                  MON-MOR-LIF))".
Proved: "(FUNCTION-ATTRIBUTES-MATCH D-MODEL:MARSHA MON-MOR-LIF)".
Proved: "(FUNCTION-PRED-OUT-TYPES MON-MOR-LIF
                    ((THB (EXACTLY THB NO-THB))
                     (MONEY (INTEGER))
                     (MORBIDITY (LIST-OF N I B H U))
                     (LIFE (NUMBER))))".
```

NOTE: The list "N I B H U" refers to five symptomatic state quality factors: NOR-
MAL (N), IMPAIRED (I), BED-RIDDEN (B), HOSPITALIZED (H), UNCON-
SCIOUS (U).

Proved: "(VALUE-FUNCTION D-MODEL:MARSHA
                (LIFE MONEY MORBIDITY THB)
                MON-MOR-LIF)".

NOTE: The function form MON-MOR-LIF now needs to be parametrically fitted to
the patient's specific preferences. For each functional parameter in the function form, Rachel activates a corresponding assessment module. The nature
of each of the six functional parameters (ACTUARIAL-LIFETIME,
WEALTH-EQUIVALENT, THB-VALUE-EQUIVALENT, ELASTICITY-
COEFF, S-PERIOD-DURATION, and S-PERIOD-Q-FACTORS) of MON-
MOR-LIF will be explained as we proceed with the consultation report.

Proved: "(FUNCTION-ASSESSMENT-NEEDS MON-MOR-LIF
                    (ACTUARIAL-LIFETIME
                    WEALTH-EQUIVALENT
                    THB-VALUE-EQUIVALENT
                    ELASTICITY-COEFF
                    S-PERIOD-DURATION
                    S-PERIOD-Q-FACTORS))".

```
We now need to assess MARSHA's preferences as they affect her selec-
tion of an infertility therapy.  However, as a preliminary step, we
need to estimate her expected remaining lifetime and her current net
worth.

Would you like some introductory information on how Rachel assesses
MARSHA's expected remaining lifetime? [Y/N]> y

The patient's expected lifetime can depend on a variety of factors,
the most important of which are age and sex (which Rachel has already
asked about).  In addition, we are concerned with the patient's smok-
ing and drinking habits.  For simplicity, Rachel does not consider
such other relevant factors as weight and occupation.

More? [Y/N]> y

Given the patient's age, sex, and various habits, Rachel calculates
an expected remaining lifetime from the appropriate actuarial table
compiled (as of 1977) by the United States National Center for Health
Statistics.
```

Reference: [U.S. Bureau of the Census, Department of Commerce, 1977]

We will now proceed with the assessment of MARSHA's expected life-time.

To account for MARSHA's smoking habits, we need to be specific about what we mean by being a heavy smoker. Let us say, somewhat arbitrarily, that MARSHA is a heavy smoker if she smokes over half a pack (i.e., more than ten (10) cigarettes) a day, on average. We are not concerned with the size of the cigarettes (most of the harm is done when the cigarette is nearly finished) nor with smoking pipes or cigars (unless their smoke is inhaled).

Does MARSHA smoke ten or more cigarettes per day? [Y/N]> y

By the way, MARSHA may want to know that smoking heavily during pregnancy can impair her baby's health.

To evaluate MARSHA's drinking habits, we want to know if she consumes over two (2) drinks (any type) a day, on average. Note that a beer or two with dinner every day and a few extra drinks on the weekend can easily add up to more than two drinks a day on average.

Does MARSHA drink two or more drinks per day? [Y/N]> n

We will now compute MARSHA's remaining expected lifetime from the actuarial tables.

Please, wait a few seconds ...   ... Done.

MARSHA's remaining actuarial expected lifetime is 48.4 years.
Thank you for your help in assessing this number.

Proved: "(PARAMETER-VALUE ACTUARIAL-LIFETIME 48.4)".

We now need to assess MARSHA's net worth. Would you like some introductory information? [Y/N]> y

An individual's net worth has two primary components: current wealth and future income. Current wealth is measured as the difference between the patient's current assets and liabilities. Future income is measured as the net present value of future cash flows.

More? [Y/N]> _y_

Rachel estimates the patient's net worth simply as the sum of two parameters: current net wealth and the present value of typical yearly income for the patient's actuarial lifetime. Furthermore, it assumes a 3%/year real time-preference (discount) rate. While a considerably fancier assessment could be used for this purpose, Rachel's simple model suffices for selecting infertility treatments.

We now proceed to assess MARSHA's wealth.

What is MARSHA's current wealth? Be sure to account for all large assets (e.g., house, car, jewelry, securities, bank accounts, etc.) and liabilities (e.g., mortgage, school loans, consumer loans, court-directed payments, etc.). [number_of_dollars—no commas or periods]> _117000_

The assessed CURRENT-WEALTH value is $117,000.00 . Thank you for your help.

Proved: "(PARAMETER-VALUE CURRENT-WEALTH 117,000)".

| NOTE: Rachel uses standard annuity calculations to compute a fixed yearly consumption equivalent to the patient's current wealth (assuming she lives exactly her actuarial expected lifetime).

Proved: "(PARAMETER-VALUE YEARLY-WEALTH-EQUIVALENT 4600)".

We will now assess MARSHA's typical yearly income.

What figure (in today's dollars) would be typical of the amount MARSHA expects to earn on a yearly basis for the rest of her life? Be sure to account for all sources of income (e.g., wages, interest, dividends, inheritances, gifts, etc.) but, for simplicity, ignore tax effects. [number_of_dollars—no commas or periods]> _45000_

The assessed TYPICAL-INCOME value is $45,000.00 . Thank you for your help.

Proved: "(PARAMETER-VALUE TYPICAL-INCOME 45,000)".
Proved: "(PARAMETER-VALUE WEALTH-EQUIVALENT 49600)".

We can now proceed to assess MARSHA's preferences, and we begin by evaluating how much MARSHA desires to become pregnant and deliver a

live baby. For clarity, as mentioned earlier in the consultation, we
will refer to this event as the arrival of a take-home baby (THB).
The notion of a THB is useful to remind us that while becoming pregnant is an important milestone in treating infertility, it is not
MARSHA's final objective.

Before we proceed with the assessment of MARSHA's preferences toward
a THB, would you like some introductory information? [Y/N]> y

A THB is defined as a newborn child that has survived the neonatal
period of twenty-eight (28) days — about one menstrual cycle. It is
important to note that the arrival of a THB includes the usual "costs"
of pregnancy, including money, labor pains, postpartum blues, and all
the risks of delivery. Given the patient's specific circumstances,
these costs should be taken into account when assessing the desirability of a THB.

More? [Y/N]> y

To assess a value for the event THB, we will introduce a mythical
character referred to as the Wizard. By definition, the wizard can
make any clearly defined situation become reality — usually for a
fee. In particular, he can guarantee the patient a THB. This character allows us to ask the question: "How much is the most that the
patient would be willing to pay the wizard for this feat?" We will
assume the amount stated is the value to the patient of having a THB.

NOTE: It is important to realize that given no better alternative, the patient *could*
and *would* pay this amount to the mythical wizard. To be realistic, the THB-
VALUE should reflect her desire to have a child in the context of her wealth.
However, the possibility of invoking a wizard is clearly hypothetical and the
THB-VALUE should *not* be interpreted as anything other than a reference
point in the patient's preferences obtained by eliminating the effect of uncertainty.

We now proceed to assess MARSHA's THB value.

In the absence of other alternatives, how much would MARSHA be willing to pay an
omnipotent wizard to guarantee a THB (with all the associated pregnancy and delivery
costs)? [number of dollars—no commas or periods]> *25000*

The assessed THB value is $25,000.00 . Thank you for your help.

Proved: "(PARAMETER-VALUE THB-VALUE 25000)".

NOTE: Rachel uses standard annuity calculations to obtain a fixed yearly consump-
             tion equivalent to the lump-sum THB value assessed from the patient.

Proved: "(PARAMETER-VALUE THB-VALUE-EQUIVALENT 989).

         We now need to assess MARSHA's desired trade-off between consumption
         and lifetime. Would you like some introductory information? [Y/N]> N

NOTE: At this point, the user chooses to reveal Rachel's current goal stack before
             answering the question. In this explanation, it is interesting to note the pre-
             cise way in which assessing the consumption/lifetime elasticity coefficient is
             part of assessing the overall decision model. It is also worth noting that the
             topmost goal is "Because you asked me.". The reader may want to refer to the
             epigraph at the beginning of Chapter 6 for a philosophical perspective on this
             feature.

NOTE: Predicates preceded by a caret (^) are proved by procedural attachment (i.e.,
             by using a special-purpose procedure rather than by using Rachel's general-
             purpose inference engine). Attached procedures are used to implement text-
             oriented queries and to provide Rachel's inference engine with an iteration
             mechanism.

```
To establish that "(^ELASTICITY-COEFF $%%%VALUE-TO-BE-GOTTEN)".
  Consumption/lifetime trade-off information? [Y/N]> N
To establish that "(^PARAMETER-VALUE ELASTICITY-COEFF $PVAL)".
  Consumption/lifetime trade-off information? [Y/N]> N
To establish that "(PARAMETER-VALUE ELASTICITY-COEFF $PVAL)".
  Consumption/lifetime trade-off information? [Y/N]> N
To establish that "(^PARAMETER-VALUES-ASSESSED MON-MOR-LIF
                                        (ACTUARIAL-LIFETIME
                                        WEALTH-EQUIVALENT
                                        THB-VALUE-EQUIVALENT
                                        ELASTICITY-COEFF
                                        S-PERIOD-DURATION
                                        S-PERIOD-Q-FACTORS))".
       Consumption/lifetime trade-off information? [Y/N]> N
To establish that "(PARAMETER-VALUES-ASSESSED MON-MOR-LIF
                                        (ACTUARIAL-LIFETIME
                                        WEALTH-EQUIVALENT
                                        THB-VALUE-EQUIVALENT
                                        ELASTICITY-COEFF
                                        S-PERIOD-DURATION
                                        S-PERIOD-Q-FACTORS))".
       Consumption/lifetime trade-off information? [Y/N]> N
```

```
To establish that "(PARAMETRICALLY-ASSESSED MON-MOR-LIF)".
   Consumption/lifetime trade-off information? [Y/N]> w
To establish that "(VALUE-NODE-OBTAINED D-MODEL:MARSHA $V14)".
   Consumption/lifetime trade-off information? [Y/N]> w
To establish that "(VALUE-NODE D-MODEL:MARSHA $V3)".
   Consumption/lifetime trade-off information? [Y/N]> w
To establish that "(COMPLETE $MODEL)".
   Consumption/lifetime trade-off information? [Y/N]> w
Because you asked me.
   Consumption/lifetime trade-off information? [Y/N]> q
```

We now need to assess MARSHA's desired trade-off between consumption and lifetime. Would you like some introductory information? [Y/N]> y

Just about everyone would prefer to live longer and make more money. However, we must frequently make choices likely to increase either lifetime or money while reducing the other attribute. For instance, working overtime can increase one's income, but it can also decrease one's lifetime by, for example, adding to the risk of suffering a heart attack. In contrast, moving to a better neighborhood (with better air quality and lower crime rates) is likely to lead to a longer lifetime, but it usually implies a considerable monetary cost.

Infertility and other medical treatments have an unpleasant double effect on monetary costs and lifetime. Their financial cost can be both directly related to the medical treatment (e.g., surgical and hospital expenses) and indirectly related to it (e.g., lost wages and travel expenses). In terms of lifetime, any treatment involving anesthesia and surgery (or, to a lesser extent, drugs) poses a risk to life.

We now want to assess the patient's preferences over possible outcomes involving various amounts of cost and risk to life.

More information? [Y/N]> y

The specific model we are using to measure the desirability of a given income/lifetime pair is given by the formula:

$$W(C, L) = C \times \left(\frac{L}{AL}\right)^{E}, \text{ where}$$

- W is a joint income/lifetime worth function — a numeraire — measured in uninflated (i.e., real) dollars;
- C represents a constant yearly consumption equivalent for the patient's current wealth plus lifetime income — beyond bare survival income — measured in real dollars;

- L represents the patient's remaining lifetime — measured in years;
- AL represents the patient's actuarial expected remaining lifetime — measured in years;
- E (> 0) is an elasticity coefficient and represents the patient's desired trade-off rate between income and lifetime. E is dimensionless — typical values for E tend to lie between two (2) and ten (10).

Rachel derives values for C, L, and AL from pertinent data elicited elsewhere throughout the consultation. However, a value for E needs to be obtained at this point.

More? [Y/N]> _y_

To obtain a value for the trade-off parameter, E, it is sufficient for Rachel to obtain an answer to a question like the following.

Suppose we could increase the patient's lifetime by x percent. What percentage decrease, y, in annual consumption would compensate for this increase so that the new situation is neither preferred nor disliked over the original one?

We now proceed with the assessment of the consumption/lifetime trade-off parameter.

Would you prefer a direct assessment (i.e., by typing the appropriate number) or an indirect assessment (i.e., guided through pertinent questions) of the consumption/lifetime trade-off parameter, E? [D/I]> _i_

Suppose we could offer the patient a 10 percent increase in lifetime. What percentage reduction in annual consumption would just about compensate for this increase in lifetime?

That is:

What percentage decrease in annual consumption would make MARSHA indifferent between getting a 10 percent increase in lifetime at the reduced consumption level and leaving things as they are now? [percent]> _eighty_

Your answer must be a number.
Please try again: [percentage]> _n_

Your answer must be a number.
Please try again: [percentage]> _80_

Please wait a few seconds ... ... Done.

> NOTE: The physician in charge of the consultation—who is assumed to have the necessary training—should ascertain whether the indifference value just assessed is a valid representation of the patient's preferences by explicitly showing her key implications of her assessment. A more fully developed version of Rachel would perform this validation automatically.

```
              The corresponding consumption/lifetime trade-off parameter is: 16.89

Is that value acceptable to MARSHA? [Y/N]> n

Let's try again ...

What percentage decrease in annual consumption would make MARSHA indifferent be-
tween getting a 10 percent increase in lifetime at the reduced consumption level and
leaving things as they are now? [percent]> 20

              Please wait a few seconds ... ... Done.

              The corresponding consumption/lifetime trade-off parameter is:  2.34

Is that value acceptable to MARSHA? [Y/N]> n

Let's try again ...

What percentage decrease in annual consumption would make MARSHA indifferent be-
tween getting a 10 percent increase in lifetime at the reduced consumption level and
leaving things as they are now? [percent]> 25

              Please wait a few seconds ... ... Done.

              The corresponding consumption/lifetime trade-off parameter is:  3.02

Is that value acceptable to MARSHA? [Y/N]> y

              MARSHA's consumption/lifetime trade-off parameter is 3.02
              Thank you for your help assessing it.


Proved: "(PARAMETER-VALUE ELASTICITY-COEFF 3.0183775)".




              We now need to determine a unit of time to use in describing the
              possible outcomes associated with MARSHA's alternative therapies.

              Would you like some introductory information? [Y/N]> y
```

The time unit chosen must be small enough to allow sufficient detail for describing the treatments under consideration. It should also be large enough to lead to simple outcome descriptions. For infertility treatments involving invasive procedures, the most commonly selected time unit is one day. For strictly drug-based treatments, the time unit chosen is often a week or a month.

More? [Y/N]> y

In other areas of medicine where treatments can be lengthy and debilitating (as might be the case with physical therapy after an accident, dialysis therapy for kidney failure patients, or cancer radiotherapy and chemotherapy), a better choice of time unit might be a month or even a year. For infertility, where most treatments occur in a much shorter period of time, a smaller time unit is usually more appropriate.

We will now determine a unit of time for describing infertility treatments.

Please choose a descriptive time unit for MARSHA's case.
Valid choices are: (DAY D WEEK WK MONTH M YEAR Y)> d

The descriptive time unit is 1 day.

Proved: "(PARAMETER-VALUE S-PERIOD-DURATION 1)".

To complete the value function, we need to measure how much MARSHA dislikes various amounts of discomfort. For simplicity, we will restrict our assessment to a few specific situations, which we will refer to as symptomatic states. Each symptomatic state has an associated quality factor that can range from zero (0) — worst case — to one hundred (100) — best case. This factor represents the percentage of MARSHA's remaining lifetime without discomfort that she would consider equivalent to living the remainder of her life in the given symptomatic state.

Do you want more information on quality factors? [Y/N]> y

Rachel can account for five (5) distinct symptomatic states. These states are characterized by their effect on the patient's lifestyle rather than by their specific symptoms. They are: NORMAL (N), IMPAIRED (I), BED-RIDDEN (B), HOSPITALIZED (H), and UNCONSCIOUS (U).

More? [Y/N]> y

More specifically, these five states are defined as follows.

1.- NORMAL	Business as usual.
2.- IMPAIRED	Activity level somewhat below business-as-usual, but with no major geographical confinement and little or no discomfort.
3.- BED-RIDDEN	Activity level significantly below business-as-usual and limited to specific locations (e.g., home). Also, the patient experiences moderate discomfort. However, the patient can survive without constant direct intervention by others.
4.- HOSPITALIZED	Severely restricted activities limited to a very specific location (e.g., hospital). The patient may experience some pain. Constant direct intervention by others (e.g., nurse) is needed for comfort and survival.
5.- UNCONSCIOUS	Little or no activity; the patient is unaware of surroundings and requires extensive care by others to survive. The patient could be in severe pain if not sedated.

To assess a quality factor for each symptomatic state, Rachel will ask for a comparison between two hypothetical situations: living the remainder of the patient's lifetime in that particular symptomatic state or living it for some percentage of that remaining lifetime in the NORMAL state. Rachel's model is based on the assumption that most people would prefer to give up some lifetime in exchange for not suffering discomfort.

More? [Y/N]> y

By definition, state NORMAL corresponds to a quality factor of 100 percent. The other four symptomatic states need to be assessed individually. For most people, a state such as HOSPITALIZED would be considered to be worse than, say, IMPAIRED. Rachel therefore expects the user to enter a lower quality factor for the former than for the latter. This is just a convention and Rachel will not enforce it. However, it will give a warning if this decreasing order is not followed, just in case there was a mistake in input.

We will now ask for the quality factors that correspond to each symptomatic state.

Quality factor for state NORMAL: [percentage]> 100
Quality factor for state IMPAIRED: [percentage]> 89
Quality factor for state BED-RIDDEN: [percentage]> 92
Quality factor for state HOSPITALIZED: [percentage]> 80
Quality factor for state UNCONSCIOUS: [percentage]> 20

The symptomatic state quality factors are:

```
(State: NORMAL        Quality factor:  100%)
(State: IMPAIRED      Quality factor:   89%)
(State: BED-RIDDEN    Quality factor:   92%)
(State: HOSPITALIZED  Quality factor:   80%)
(State: UNCONSCIOUS   Quality factor:   20%)
```

Your quality factor assignments are not in the usual decreasing order. Do you wish to keep them as they are? [Y/N]> n

```
Quality factor for state NORMAL:        [percentage]> 100
Quality factor for state IMPAIRED:      [percentage]> 98
Quality factor for state BED-RIDDEN:    [percentage]> 92
Quality factor for state HOSPITALIZED:  [percentage]> 80
Quality factor for state UNCONSCIOUS:   [percentage]> 20
```

The symptomatic state quality factors are:

```
(State: NORMAL        Quality factor:  100%)
(State: IMPAIRED      Quality factor:   98%)
(State: BED-RIDDEN    Quality factor:   92%)
(State: HOSPITALIZED  Quality factor:   80%)
(State: UNCONSCIOUS   Quality factor:   20%)
```

```
Proved: "(PARAMETER-VALUE S-PERIOD-Q-FACTORS ((N . 1.0)
                                             (I . 0.98)
                                             (B . 0.92)
                                             (H . 0.8)
                                             (U . 0.2)))".
```

NOTE: A more fully developed system would interact with the user at this point to verify the validity of the quality-factor assessments.

```
Proved: "(PARAMETER-VALUES-ASSESSED MON-MOR-LIF
                               (ACTUARIAL-LIFETIME
                                WEALTH-EQUIVALENT
                                THB-VALUE-EQUIVALENT
                                ELASTICITY-COEFF
                                S-PERIOD-DURATION
                                S-PERIOD-Q-FACTORS))".
Proved: "(PARAMETRICALLY-ASSESSED MON-MOR-LIF)".
Proved: "(VALUE-NODE-OBTAINED D-MODEL:MARSHA V-NODE:MARSHA)".
Proved: "(VALUE-NODE D-MODEL:MARSHA V-NODE:MARSHA)".
```

NOTE: Having finished the value-model assessment process, Rachel deactivates its corresponding knowledge-base context to make space for the influence diagram decision model.

```
RACHEL-KB: Deactivating context: "VALUE".
```

```
We now need to assess the patient's (i.e., MARSHA's) attitude toward
taking risks.
```

```
Would you like some introductory information? [Y/N]> w
```
```
To establish that "(^RISK-TOLERANCE D-MODEL:MARSHA $V41)".
  Introductory information? [Y/N]> w
To establish that "(ASSESSED-RISK D-MODEL:MARSHA)".
  Introductory information? [Y/N]> w
To establish that "(COMPLETE $MODEL)".
  Introductory information? [Y/N]> w
Because you asked me.
  Introductory information? [Y/N]> q
```

```
We now need to assess the patient's (i.e., MARSHA's) attitude toward
taking risks.
```

```
Would you like some introductory information? [Y/N]> y
```

```
Most people are averse to taking risks.  This is evidenced by the fact
that many of us buy insurance of various types.  Hence, to make an
appropriate recommendation for the patient, Rachel needs to measure
her risk attitude.
```

```
More? [Y/N]> y
```

```
Rachel assumes an exponential utility function of the form:
```

$$U(x) = 1 - e^{-(x/R)}$$
```
, where R is referred to as the (constant)
                              risk-tolerance coefficient.
```

```
Note that using an exponential utility function implies that the
patient's risk attitude satisfies the "delta" property (i.e., that
risk tolerance is invariant to changes in wealth).
```

```
More? [Y/N]> y
```

To assess a value for R, it is sufficient to obtain an answer to a question of the form:

What is the highest amount, X, for which the patient would be willing to accept a gamble giving 7 out of 10 chances of winning the amount X against 3 out of 10 chances of losing a third of that amount?

Graphically, the gamble looks like this:

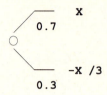

The value of R can then be mathematically derived from the highest acceptable value for X.

| NOTE: | The decision analysis literature often uses 50-50 lotteries with corresponding prizes of **X** and -**X**/2 to assess risk tolerance. This form of lottery is useful because it eliminates the need for computing the desired risk-tolerance coefficient, **R**, since it is nearly equal to the value of **X** (**R** = 1.04 **X**, approximately). Rachel uses a different assessment lottery because we want to present the patient with a gamble that more closely resembles her real decision situation. Mathematically, both forms of the assessment question are equivalent. The only burden added by using the 30-70 form is computational, and within an intelligent decision system, such a burden is negligible. |

More? [Y/N]> *y*

The formula to obtain R from X in the above hypothetical gamble is:

$0.7 \, U(X^*) = -0.3 \, U(-X^* / 3)$,   where U(x) is the utility funtion described above (which has R as a parameter), and X^* is the maximum amount for which the gamble would be acceptable.

We now proceed with the risk-tolerance assessment.

We can assess MARSHA's risk tolerance by either
  a. Direct assessment (i.e., by simply typing a number), or
  b. Indirect assessment (i.e., through a graphical indifference question).

Which would you prefer, DIRECT or INDIRECT assessment? [D/I]> _i_

Consider the following lottery:

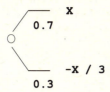

What is the highest amount, X, for which the patient would be willing to accept this gamble (giving 7 out of 10 chances of winning the amount X, against 3 out of 10 chances of losing a third of that amount)?

That is:

What is the MAXIMUM amount of money, X, for which MARSHA would willingly accept a 7/10 chance of winning X versus a 3/10 chance of losing X/3?
[number_of_dollars]> _15000_

       Please wait a few seconds ... ... Done.

       The corresponding risk-tolerance value is: $4224.10
Is that value acceptable to MARSHA? [Y/N]> _n_

> NOTE: To determine whether the risk tolerance value just assessed is truly acceptable to the patient, the physician in charge of the consultation—who is assumed to have the appropriate training in using Rachel—would discuss its implications with the patient in terms of simple hypothetical gambles. A more developed version of Rachel would be able to do this validation automatically.

       Let's try again.

What is the MAXIMUM amount of money, X, for which MARSHA would willingly accept a 7/10 chance of winning X versus a 3/10 chance of losing X/3?
[number_of_dollars]> _20000_

       Please wait a few seconds ... ... Done.

       The corresponding risk-tolerance value is: $5632.14
Is that value acceptable to MARSHA? [Y/N]> _y_

       Thank you. We have finished assessing MARSHA's risk tolerance and found it to be: $5632.14 .

Proved: "(ASSESSED-RISK D-MODEL:MARSHA)".

NOTE: Rachel assesses the patient's risk tolerance with respect to gambles involving lump sums and then converts this quantity into an equivalent risk tolerance with respect to gambles involving fixed yearly consumption equivalents. Alternatively, it could assess the latter form of risk tolerance directly [Howard, 1980a].

Having assessed the value function and risk attitude for the patient, RACHEL will now construct a full decision model. This assessment process is based on knowledge about infertility obtained from experts in the field.

More information? [Y/N]> y

The model will be implemented as an influence diagram and will be built through direct and indirect assessment of frontier nodes.

NOTE: During the following assessment process, Rachel will refer to the following influence diagram nodes (in assessment order). The complete influence diagram is illustrated in Fig. A.1 at the end of the Appendix.

Node Name	Brief Description of Node [Units]
LIFE	Length of the patient's remaining life [years]
MONEY	Lifetime annuity equivalent to medical treatment costs [dollars]
MORBIDITY	Treatment discomfort [symptomatic stream]
THB	Take-home baby [indicator]
IVF-MON (*)	Total cost of an in-vitro fertilization (IVF) procedure [dollars]
IVF-MOR (*)	Discomfort from the full IVF procedure [symptomatic stream]
IVF-THB (*)	Take-home baby obtained through IVF [indicator]
LAP-MON (*)	Total cost of a laparotomy procedure [dollars]
LAP-MOR (*)	Discomfort from the laparotomy [symptomatic stream]
LAP-THB (*)	Take-home baby obtained through laparotomy [indicator]
SURG-COMP	Surgical complications [indicator]
TREATMENT	Actual treatment undergone by the patient [indicator]
ANES-DEATH	Death from anesthesia [indicator]
IVF-ACCEPT	Acceptance in an IVF program [indicator]
IVF-IMPLANT	Blastocyst implantation through IVF [indicator]
NUM-HOSP-DAYS	Number of days spent as an inpatient [days]
NUM-IVF-CYCLES	Number of IVF cycles administered [cycles]
T-MUCOSA	State of the patient's tubal mucosa [indicator]
T-WTHICK	Thickness of the patient's Fallopian tube wall [indicator]

(*)   These nodes are introduced solely to reduce the combinatorial size of the model. They could be removed in a straightforward manner by simply passing their predecessors onto their successors and updating the distributions of the latter nodes accordingly. An alternate implementation of Rachel might not even show these nodes to the user.

NOTE: The goal-oriented influence diagram assessment process begins in earnest at this point. Rachel starts the process by generating an agenda with the names of the current frontier nodes (which were created when the value node was assessed). It then assesses each of these nodes and creates a new agenda with all newly added frontier nodes.

In this respect, Rachel's frontier node generation and assessment process is much more rigid than it could be in a more fully developed system. Chapters 4 and 6 discuss a much more interactive palette-like IDS facility.

```
Proved: "(FRONTIER D-MODEL:MARSHA LIFE)".
Proved: "(FRONTIER D-MODEL:MARSHA MONEY)".
Proved: "(FRONTIER D-MODEL:MARSHA MORBIDITY)".
Proved: "(FRONTIER D-MODEL:MARSHA THB)".
```

NOTE: Every time Rachel attempts to indirectly assess a frontier node using expansion objects (either indicated, deterministic, or stochastic) from its knowledge base, it does so in three steps. First, it verifies that, in fact, expansion objects (i.e., potential assessments) that match the frontier node in question exist in the knowledge base. A successful match requires, among other things, that the outcomes of the expansion object that is a potential assessment satisfy any outcome restrictions imposed by the successors of the frontier node being assessed.

Second, Rachel exhibits its set of potential assessments to the user, who must endorse any assessment actually used in the decision model. In general, these potential assessments could include several indicated, deterministic, and/or stochastic expansion objects applicable to the frontier node in question (e.g., LIFE). However, for brevity and because of severe memory constraints in its current implementation, Rachel's knowledge base has been constructed with a single applicable expansion object for each frontier node being assessed.

Assuming at least one potential assessment is accepted (perhaps with some modifications), Rachel proceeds to the third and last step of the indirect assessment. In this final step, Rachel incorporates the accepted indirect assessment—including all needed predecessors of the node being assessed—into the decision model.

```
Would you like to assess node "LIFE" by DIRECT-ASSESSMENT? [Y/N]> w
To establish that "(^OK-FOR DIRECT-ASSESSMENT LIFE)".
  DIRECT-ASSESSMENT? [Y/N]> w
To establish that "(OK-FOR DIRECT-ASSESSMENT LIFE)".
  DIRECT-ASSESSMENT? [Y/N]> w
To establish that "(DIRECTLY-ASSESSED LIFE)".
  DIRECT-ASSESSMENT? [Y/N]> w
To establish that "(ASSESSED LIFE)".
  DIRECT-ASSESSMENT? [Y/N]> w
To establish that "(^ASSESSED-ALL-FRONTIER-NODES D-MODEL:MARSHA)".
  DIRECT-ASSESSMENT? [Y/N]> w
To establish that "(FULLY-ASSESSED D-MODEL:MARSHA)".
  DIRECT-ASSESSMENT? [Y/N]> w
To establish that "(COMPLETE $MODEL)".
  DIRECT-ASSESSMENT? [Y/N]> w
Because you asked me.
  DIRECT-ASSESSMENT? [Y/N]> q

Would you like to assess node "LIFE" by DIRECT-ASSESSMENT? [Y/N]> n
```

NOTE: Realizing that the user does not wish to assess node "LIFE" directly, Rachel proceeds to look for potential assessments—indicated, deterministic, and stochastic—in its knowledge base.

```
Proved: "(STOCHASTIC-ASSESSMENT LIFE
                    (0.0   0.8   1.05)
                    (SURG-COMP TREATMENT)
                    ((ONE-OF DEATH PERF-BOWEL NO-COMP)
                     (ONE-OF LAPAROTOMY IVF-4 DO-NOTHING))
                    NIL
                    ((1       0     0)
                     (1       0     0)
                     (0       0.1   0.9)
                     (0.005   0.3   0.695)
                     (0.001   0.1   0.899)
                     (0       0.1   0.9)
                     (0.001   0.1   0.899)
                     (0.001   0.1   0.899)
                     (0       0.1   0.9)))".
```

NOTE: Rachel has not found any indicated or deterministic expansion objects for node "LIFE", but it did find a stochastic expansion object for it. This expansion object is constructed as a frame with 7 slots: assessment type, name of the node being assessed, outcome list, predecessor list, predecessor outcome restrictions, relation to the decision node, and probability distribution.

Specifically, this expansion consists of a stochastic assessment for node "LIFE" with outcome list "(0.0 0.8 1.05)"—expressed as fractions of the patient's expected remaining actuarial lifetime—and predecessors "SURG-COMP" and "TREATMENT". For this assessment to be valid, the outcomes of the node "SURG-COMP" must be members of the list "(DEATH PERF-BOWEL NO-COMP) "—meaning, respectively, death during or shortly after surgery, perforated bowel, and no major complications. Similarly, the outcomes of node "TREATMENT" must belong to the list "(LAPAROTOMY IVF-4 DO-NOTHING)".

The term "NIL" following the list of predecessor outcome restrictions denotes the fact that according to this assessment, the treatment selection decision is not a predecessor of node "LIFE". (Note that the node "TREAT-MENT" is a chance node representing the treatment received, which may differ from the one chosen. See Figure A.1.)

Finally, the distribution assigned to the node "LIFE" by this assessment consists of nine triplets, each corresponding to a conditional probabilistic assignment to the three possible outcomes of the node. Each of these triplets corresponds to one of the nine possible combinations of predecessor outcomes, with the outcomes of node "TREATMENT" varying first and those of node "SURG-COMP" varying second. For example, the first triplet corresponds to the conditioning path: "DEATH" and "LAPAROTOMY", whereas the fourth triplet corresponds to the path: "PERF-BOWEL" and "LAPAROTOMY".

Rachel now asks the user whether this type of assessment would be satisfactory.

```
Would you like to assess node "LIFE" by STOCHASTIC-ASSESSMENT? [Y/N]> w
To establish that "(^OK-FOR STOCHASTIC-ASSESSMENT LIFE)".
   STOCHASTIC-ASSESSMENT? [Y/N]> w
To establish that "(OK-FOR STOCHASTIC-ASSESSMENT LIFE)".
   STOCHASTIC-ASSESSMENT? [Y/N]> w
To establish that "(STOCHASTICALLY-ASSESSED LIFE)".
   STOCHASTIC-ASSESSMENT? [Y/N]> w
To establish that "(ASSESSED LIFE)".
   STOCHASTIC-ASSESSMENT? [Y/N]> w
To establish that "(^ASSESSED-ALL-FRONTIER-NODES D-MODEL:MARSHA)".
   STOCHASTIC-ASSESSMENT? [Y/N]> w
To establish that "(FULLY-ASSESSED D-MODEL:MARSHA)".
   STOCHASTIC-ASSESSMENT? [Y/N]> w
To establish that "(COMPLETE $MODEL)".
   STOCHASTIC-ASSESSMENT? [Y/N]> w
Because you asked me.
   STOCHASTIC-ASSESSMENT? [Y/N]> g
```

```
Would you like to assess node "LIFE" by STOCHASTIC-ASSESSMENT? [Y/N]> y
```

NOTE: After reviewing Rachel's current goal stack, the user agrees to explore the possibility of assessing node "LIFE" with a stochastic indirect assessment.

> **Note that although RACHEL has already found at least one possible STOCHASTIC-ASSESSMENT for node "LIFE", it still needs to check its suitability given previous assessments. Thus, it is possible that no actual STOCHASTIC-ASSESSMENTs will be attempted.**

NOTE: As indicated in the preceding statement, it is entirely possible for Rachel to reject any and all potential indirect assessments it identifies. However, in addition to having a single applicable expansion object for each frontier node being assessed, for brevity and because of memory constraints, each expansion object has been designed to successfully match its corresponding frontier node in every case.

These limitations apply only to Rachel's current knowledge base and not to the overall system, which is designed to handle much richer knowledge bases. Hence, although we know the test will succeed, Rachel will now check whether the expansion object previously identified matches the node being assessed.

This match must account for any and all restrictions imposed by the successors of the node being assessed on its outcomes. It must also account for the feasibility of adding any required new predecessors without creating cycles in the influence diagram. Finally, it must account for any and all restrictions imposed by the expansion object being tested on the outcomes of the already existing nodes that are to become immediate predecessors of the node being assessed.

```
Proved: "(OK-FOR STOCHASTIC-ASSESSMENT LIFE)".
Proved: "(STOCHASTIC-ASSESSMENT LIFE
                        (0.0   0.8   1.05)
                        (SURG-COMP  TREATMENT)
                        ((ONE-OF DEATH PERF-BOWEL NO-COMP)
                         (ONE-OF LAPAROTOMY IVF-4 DO-NOTHING))
                        NIL
                        ((1       0     0)
                         (1       0     0)
                         (0       0.1   0.9)
                         (0.005   0.3   0.695)
```

```
              (0.001  0.1  0.899)
              (0      0.1  0.9)
              (0.001  0.1  0.899)
              (0.001  0.1  0.899)
              (0      0.1  0.9)))".
```
Proved: "(CHECK-OUTCOMES LIFE (0.0 0.8 1.05))".
Proved: "(CHECK-PRED-OUT-TYPES (SURG-COMP TREATMENT)
                        ((ONE-OF DEATH PERF-BOWEL NO-COMP)
                        (ONE-OF LAPAROTOMY IVF-4 DO-NOTHING)))".

NOTE: Rachel has found a matching expansion object for the node "LIFE" and now reveals it to the user for acceptance.

NOTE: The outcomes of node "LIFE" represent possible lengths of the patient's lifetime expressed as fractions of her remaining actuarial expected lifetime. The outcome "0.0" stands for the possibility of death during or shortly after surgery.

The following stochastic assessment has been found for node "LIFE". Please review it and determine whether it is acceptable.

```
Outcomes:      (0.0  0.8  1.05)

Predecessors:  (SURG-COMP TREATMENT)

Distribution:  ((1      0    0)
               (1      0    0)
               (0      0.1  0.9)
               (0.005  0.3  0.695)
               (0.001  0.1  0.899)
               (0      0.1  0.9)
               (0.001  0.1  0.899)
               (0.001  0.1  0.899)
               (0      0.1  0.9))
```

Is it acceptable? [Y/N]> *y*

NOTE: The user is assumed to have a list with descriptions of all anticipated node names and their outcomes. Clearly, a more fully developed system would have an automated version of this set of descriptions.

NOTE: Having found the proposed stochastic expansion object acceptable for indirect assessment by the user, Rachel proceeds to incorporate it into the decision model.

```
Proved: "(CHECK-FULL-STOCH-ASSESSMENT LIFE
                                 (0.0  0.8  1.05)
                                 (SURG-COMP TREATMENT)
                                 NIL
                                 ((1          0    0)
                                  (1          0    0)
                                  (0        0.1  0.9)
                                  (0.005   0.3  0.695)
                                  (0.001   0.1  0.899)
                                  (0        0.1  0.9)
                                  (0.001   0.1  0.899)
                                  (0.001   0.1  0.899)
                                  (0        0.1  0.9)))".
Proved: "(ENTER-D-PRED LIFE NIL)".
Proved: "(ENTER-NEW-C-PREDS LIFE
                       (SURG-COMP TREATMENT)
                       ((ONE-OF DEATH PERF-BOWEL NO-COMP)
                       (ONE-OF LAPAROTOMY IVF-4 DO-NOTHING)))".
Proved: "(ENTER-OUTCOMES LIFE (0.0 0.8 1.05))".
Proved: "(ENTER-DISTRIBUTION LIFE
                          ((1          0    0)
                           (1          0    0)
                           (0        0.1  0.9)
                           (0.005   0.3  0.695)
                           (0.001   0.1  0.899)
                           (0        0.1  0.9)
                           (0.001   0.1  0.899)
                           (0.001   0.1  0.899)
                           (0        0.1  0.9)))".
Proved: "(STOCHASTICALLY-ASSESSED LIFE)".
Proved: "(ASSESSED LIFE)".
```

|| NOTE: The stochastic indirect assessment of node "LIFE" is now complete. Rachel
|| will now proceed to assess the next frontier node in its agenda.

```
Would you like to assess node "MONEY" by DIRECT-ASSESSMENT? [Y/N]> n
```

```
Proved: "(DETERMINISTIC-ASSESSMENT MONEY
                           (INTEGER)
                           (LAP-MON IVF-MON TREATMENT)
                           ((INTEGER)
                           (INTEGER)
                           (ONE-OF LAPAROTOMY IVF-4 DO-NOTHING))
                           NIL
                           (%%MEDKB-MONEY IVF-MON LAP-MON TREATMENT))".
```

NOTE: In this case, Rachel has found a deterministic expansion object for node "MONEY". The assessment process follows the same three steps used for the case of a stochastic assessment, except that instead of a distribution, a deterministic indirect assessment attaches a deterministic function (%%MEDKB-MONEY) to the node being assessed.

```
Would you like to assess node "MONEY" by DETERMINISTIC-ASSESSMENT? [Y/N]> y
```

> Note that although RACHEL has already found at least one possible DETERMINISTIC-ASSESSMENT for node "MONEY", it still needs to check its suitability given previous assessments. Thus, it is possible that no actual DETERMINISTIC-ASSESSMENTs will be attempted.

```
Proved: "(OK-FOR DETERMINISTIC-ASSESSMENT MONEY)".
Proved: "(DETERMINISTIC-ASSESSMENT MONEY
                        (INTEGER)
                        (LAP-MON IVF-MON TREATMENT)
                        ((INTEGER)
                         (INTEGER)
                         (ONE-OF LAPAROTOMY IVF-4 DO-NOTHING))
                        NIL
                        (%%MEDKB-MONEY IVF-MON LAP-MON TREATMENT))".
Proved: "(CHECK-OUT-TYPE MONEY (INTEGER))".
Proved: "(CHECK-PRED-OUT-TYPES (LAP-MON IVF-MON TREATMENT)
                        ((INTEGER)
                         (INTEGER)
                         (ONE-OF LAPAROTOMY IVF-4 DO-NOTHING)))".
```

> The following deterministic assessment has been found for node "MONEY". Please review it and indicate whether it is acceptable.
>
> Predecessors: (LAP-MON IVF-MON TREATMENT)
>
> Deterministic Function: (%%MEDKB-MONEY IVF-MON LAP-MON TREATMENT)
>
> Is it acceptable? [Y/N]> y

NOTE: For brevity, the user is assumed to have access to a listing of Rachel's library of deterministic assessment functions. Hence, the statement "(%%MEDKB-MONEY IVF-MON LAP-MON TREATMENT)", which refers to the function "%%MEDKB-MONEY" with arguments "IVF-MON", "LAP-MON", and "TREATMENT", can be used within the query without explanation. Here, and throughout Rachel, function arguments have the same name as the node whose outcome they represent. If the user were not to have access to a deterministic assessment function listing, it would be simple, albeit lengthy at times, to include the full function definition in the query.

```
Proved: "(CHECK-FULL-DET-ASSESSMENT MONEY
                           (LAP-MON IVF-MON TREATMENT)
                           NIL
                           (%%MEDKB-MONEY IVF-MON LAP-MON TREATMENT)))".
Proved: "(ENTER-D-PRED MONEY NIL)".
Proved: "(ENTER-NEW-C-PREDS MONEY
                       (LAP-MON IVF-MON TREATMENT)
                        ((INTEGER)
                         (INTEGER)
                         (ONE-OF LAPAROTOMY IVF-4 DO-NOTHING)))".
Proved: "(MAKE-DET-NODE MONEY)".
```

> NOTE: Node MONEY was originally created as a stochastic chance node. Rachel has now converted it into a deterministic chance node.

```
Proved: "(ENTER-D-FUNCTION MONEY (%%MEDKB-MONEY IVF-MON LAP-MON TREATMENT))".
Proved: "(DETERMINISTICALLY-ASSESSED MONEY)".
Proved: "(ASSESSED MONEY)".

Would you like to assess node "MORBIDITY" by DIRECT-ASSESSMENT? [Y/N]> n

Proved: "(DETERMINISTIC-ASSESSMENT MORBIDITY
                           (LIST-OF N I B H U)
                           (LAP-MOR IVF-MOR TREATMENT)
                           ((LIST-OF N I B H U)
                            (LIST-OF N I B H U)
                            (ONE-OF LAPAROTOMY IVF-4 DO-NOTHING))
                            NIL
                            (%%MEDKB-MORBIDITY IVF-MOR
                                               LAP-MOR
                                               TREATMENT)))".
```

> NOTE: The list "N I B H U" refers to the five previously elicited symptomatic state quality factors: NORMAL (N = 1.0), IMPAIRED (I = 0.98), BED-RIDDEN (B = 0.92), HOSPITALIZED (H = 0.8), and UNCONSCIOUS (U = 0.2).

```
Would you like to assess node "MORBIDITY" by DETERMINISTIC-ASSESSMENT? [Y/N]> y
```

```
              Note that although RACHEL has already found at least one possible
              DETERMINISTIC-ASSESSMENT for node "MORBIDITY", it still needs to
              check its suitability given previous assessments. Thus, it is pos-
              sible that no actual DETERMINISTIC-ASSESSMENTs will be attempted.
```

Proved: "(OK-FOR DETERMINISTIC-ASSESSMENT MORBIDITY)".
Proved: "(DETERMINISTIC-ASSESSMENT MORBIDITY

                                  (LIST-OF N I B H U)
                                  (LAP-MOR IVF-MOR TREATMENT)
                                  ((LIST-OF N I B H U)
                                    (LIST-OF N I B H U)
                                    (ONE-OF LAPAROTOMY IVF-4 DO-NOTHING))
                              NIL
                              (%%MEDKB-MORBIDITY IVF-MOR
                                                  LAP-MOR
                                                  TREATMENT))".
Proved: "(CHECK-OUT-TYPE MORBIDITY (LIST-OF N I B H U))".
Proved: "(CHECK-PRED-OUT-TYPES (LAP-MOR IVF-MOR TREATMENT)
                        ((LIST-OF N I B H U)
                        (LIST-OF N I B H U)
                        (ONE-OF LAPAROTOMY IVF-4 DO-NOTHING)))".

        The following deterministic assessment has been found for node "MOR-
        BIDITY". Please review it and indicate whether it is acceptable.

        Predecessors: (LAP-MOR IVF-MOR TREATMENT)

        Deterministic Function: (%%MEDKB-MORBIDITY IVF-MOR LAP-MOR
        TREATMENT)

        Is it acceptable? [Y/N]> _y_

Proved: "(CHECK-FULL-DET-ASSESSMENT MORBIDITY

                                  (LAP-MOR IVF-MOR TREATMENT)
                              NIL
                              (%%MEDKB-MORBIDITY IVF-MOR
                                                  LAP-MOR
                                                  TREATMENT))".
Proved: "(ENTER-D-PRED MORBIDITY NIL)".
Proved: "(ENTER-NEW-C-PREDS MORBIDITY
                        (LAP-MOR IVF-MOR TREATMENT)
                        ((LIST-OF N I B H U)
                        (LIST-OF N I B H U)
                        (ONE-OF LAPAROTOMY IVF-4 DO-NOTHING)))".
Proved: "(MAKE-DET-NODE MORBIDITY)".
Proved: "(ENTER-D-FUNCTION MORBIDITY
                        (%%MEDKB-MORBIDITY IVF-MOR
                                            LAP-MOR
                                            TREATMENT))".
Proved: "(DETERMINISTICALLY-ASSESSED MORBIDITY)".
Proved: "(ASSESSED MORBIDITY)".

```
Would you like to assess node "THB" by DIRECT-ASSESSMENT? [Y/N]> n


Proved: "(STOCHASTIC-ASSESSMENT THB
                        (THB NO-THB)
                        (IVF-THB LAP-THB SURG-COMP TREATMENT)
                        ((ONE-OF  THB NO-THB)
                         (ONE-OF  THB NO-THB)
                         (ONE-OF  DEATH PERF-BOWEL NO-COMP)
                         (ONE-OF  LAPAROTOMY IVF-4 DO-NOTHING))
                        NIL
                        ((0   1)  (0   1)  (0   1)
                         (0   1)  (0   1)  (0   1)
                         (1   0)  (1   0)  (0   1)
                         (0   1)  (0   1)  (0   1)
                         (0   1)  (0   1)  (0   1)
                         (0   1)  (1   0)  (0   1)
                         (0   1)  (0   1)  (0   1)
                         (0   1)  (0   1)  (0   1)
                         (1   0)  (0   1)  (0   1)
                         (0   1)  (0   1)  (0   1)
                         (0   1)  (0   1)  (0   1)
                         (0   1)  (0   1)  (0   1)))".
```

NOTE: The above stochastic expansion object could have been encoded as a deterministic expansion object, since all its conditional distributions place all probability mass on a single outcome. This expansion object is encoded stochastically to show that deterministic nodes are just a special case of stochastic nodes. Deterministic nodes are used primarily because they enhance the model's clarity and greatly increase the efficiency of the influence diagram evaluation algorithm.

```
Would you like to assess node "THB" by STOCHASTIC-ASSESSMENT? [Y/N]> y


          Note that although RACHEL has already found at least one possible
          STOCHASTIC-ASSESSMENT for node "THB", it still needs to check its
          suitability given previous assessments.  Thus, it is possible that no
          actual STOCHASTIC-ASSESSMENTs will be attempted.

Proved: "(OK-FOR STOCHASTIC-ASSESSMENT THB)".
Proved: "(STOCHASTIC-ASSESSMENT THB
                        (THB NO-THB)
                        (IVF-THB LAP-THB SURG-COMP TREATMENT)
```

```
                            ((ONE-OF THB NO-THB)
                             (ONE-OF THB NO-THB)
                             (ONE-OF DEATH PERF-BOWEL NO-COMP)
                             (ONE-OF LAPAROTOMY IVF-4 DO-NOTHING))
                            NIL
                            ((0  1)  (0  1)  (0  1)
                             (0  1)  (0  1)  (0  1)
                             (1  0)  (1  0)  (0  1)
                             (0  1)  (0  1)  (0  1)
                             (0  1)  (0  1)  (0  1)
                             (0  1)  (1  0)  (0  1)
                             (0  1)  (0  1)  (0  1)
                             (0  1)  (0  1)  (0  1)
                             (1  0)  (0  1)  (0  1)
                             (0  1)  (0  1)  (0  1)
                             (0  1)  (0  1)  (0  1)
                             (0  1)  (0  1)  (0  1)))".
Proved: "(CHECK-OUTCOMES THB (THB NO-THB))".
Proved: "(CHECK-PRED-OUT-TYPES (IVF-THB LAP-THB SURG-COMP TREATMENT)
                            ((ONE-OF THB NO-THB)
                             (ONE-OF THB NO-THB)
                             (ONE-OF DEATH PERF-BOWEL NO-COMP)
                             (ONE-OF LAPAROTOMY IVF-4 DO-NOTHING)))".
```

The following stochastic assessment has been found for node "THB".
Please review it and determine whether it is acceptable.

```
    Outcomes:      (THB NO-THB)

    Predecessors:  (IVF-THB LAP-THB SURG-COMP TREATMENT)

    Distribution: ((0  1)  (0  1)  (0  1)
                   (0  1)  (0  1)  (0  1)
                   (1  0)  (1  0)  (0  1)
                   (0  1)  (0  1)  (0  1)
                   (0  1)  (0  1)  (0  1)
                   (0  1)  (1  0)  (0  1)
                   (0  1)  (0  1)  (0  1)
                   (0  1)  (0  1)  (0  1)
                   (1  0)  (0  1)  (0  1)
                   (0  1)  (0  1)  (0  1)
                   (0  1)  (0  1)  (0  1)
                   (0  1)  (0  1)  (0  1))
```

Is it acceptable? [Y/N]> _y_

```
Proved: "(CHECK-FULL-STOCH-ASSESSMENT THB
                                      (THB NO-THB)
                                      (IVF-THB LAP-THB SURG-COMP TREATMENT)
                                      NIL
                                      ((0  1)   (0  1)   (0  1)
                                       (0  1)   (0  1)   (0  1)
                                       (1  0)   (1  0)   (0  1)
                                       (0  1)   (0  1)   (0  1)
                                       (0  1)   (0  1)   (0  1)
                                       (0  1)   (1  0)   (0  1)
                                       (0  1)   (0  1)   (0  1)
                                       (0  1)   (0  1)   (0  1)
                                       (1  0)   (0  1)   (0  1)
                                       (0  1)   (0  1)   (0  1)
                                       (0  1)   (0  1)   (0  1)
                                       (0  1)   (0  1)   (0  1)))".
Proved: "(ENTER-D-PRED THB NIL)".
Proved: "(ENTER-NEW-C-PREDS THB
                            (IVF-THB LAP-THB SURG-COMP TREATMENT)
                            ((ONE-OF THB NO-THB)
                             (ONE-OF THB NO-THB)
                             (ONE-OF DEATH PERF-BOWEL NO-COMP)
                             (ONE-OF LAPAROTOMY IVF-4 DO-NOTHING)))".
Proved: "(ENTER-OUTCOMES THB (THB NO-THB))".
Proved: "(ENTER-DISTRIBUTION THB ((0  1)   (0  1)   (0  1)
                                  (0  1)   (0  1)   (0  1)
                                  (1  0)   (1  0)   (0  1)
                                  (0  1)   (0  1)   (0  1)
                                  (0  1)   (0  1)   (0  1)
                                  (0  1)   (1  0)   (0  1)
                                  (0  1)   (0  1)   (0  1)
                                  (0  1)   (0  1)   (0  1)
                                  (1  0)   (0  1)   (0  1)
                                  (0  1)   (0  1)   (0  1)
                                  (0  1)   (0  1)   (0  1)
                                  (0  1)   (0  1)   (0  1)))".
Proved: "(STOCHASTICALLY-ASSESSED THB)".
Proved: "(ASSESSED THB)".
```

NOTE: At this point, Rachel has successfully assessed all the frontier nodes in its
         initial agenda. In the process, by attaching direct predecessors to the indi-
         rectly assessed nodes, it has added new frontier nodes to the diagram. Rachel
         now needs to update its agenda and to assess all new frontier nodes.

```
Proved: "(FRONTIER D-MODEL:MARSHA IVF-MON)".
Proved: "(FRONTIER D-MODEL:MARSHA IVF-MOR)".
Proved: "(FRONTIER D-MODEL:MARSHA IVF-THB)".
Proved: "(FRONTIER D-MODEL:MARSHA LAP-MON)".
Proved: "(FRONTIER D-MODEL:MARSHA LAP-MOR)".
Proved: "(FRONTIER D-MODEL:MARSHA LAP-THB)".
Proved: "(FRONTIER D-MODEL:MARSHA SURG-COMP)".
Proved: "(FRONTIER D-MODEL:MARSHA TREATMENT)".
```

NOTE: The next eight node assessments follow a pattern that closely resembles the assessment of the previous four nodes. Most readers will want to either skip or skim this material, which is included for completeness. New features of Rachel are once again exhibited starting with the assessment of node ANES-DEATH, following Rachel's next agenda update (p. 212).

```
Would you like to assess node "IVF-MON" by DIRECT-ASSESSMENT? [Y/N]> n
```

```
Proved: "(STOCHASTIC-ASSESSMENT IVF-MON
                    (0 750 2500)
                    (NUM-IVF-CYCLES)
                    ((ONE-OF 0 1 2 3 4))
                    NIL
                    ((1.0   0.0    0.0)
                     (0.0   0.75   0.25)
                     (0.0   0.5    0.5)
                     (0.0   0.25   0.75)
                     (0.0   0.0    1.0)))".
```

```
Would you like to assess node "IVF-MON" by STOCHASTIC-ASSESSMENT? [Y/N]> y
```

> Note that although RACHEL has already found at least one possible STOCHASTIC-ASSESSMENT for node "IVF-MON", it still needs to check its suitability given previous assessments. Thus, it is possible that no actual STOCHASTIC-ASSESSMENTs will be attempted.

```
Proved: "(OK-FOR STOCHASTIC-ASSESSMENT IVF-MON)".
Proved: "(STOCHASTIC-ASSESSMENT IVF-MON
                    (0 750 2500)
                    (NUM-IVF-CYCLES)
                    ((ONE-OF 0 1 2 3 4))
                    NIL
                    ((1.0   0.0    0.0)
                     (0.0   0.75   0.25)
                     (0.0   0.5    0.5)
                     (0.0   0.25   0.75)
                     (0.0   0.0    1.0)))".
Proved: "(CHECK-OUTCOMES IVF-MON (0 750 2500))".
Proved: "(CHECK-PRED-OUT-TYPES (NUM-IVF-CYCLES) ((ONE-OF 0 1 2 3 4)))".
```

The following stochastic assessment has been found for node "IVF-MON". Please review it and determine whether it is acceptable.

Outcomes: (0 750 2500)

Predecessors: (NUM-IVF-CYCLES)

Distribution: ((1.0 0.0   0.0)
                (0.0 0.75 0.25)
                (0.0 0.5   0.5)
                (0.0 0.25 0.75)
                (0.0 0.0   1.0))

Is it acceptable? [Y/N]> y

Proved: "(CHECK-FULL-STOCH-ASSESSMENT IVF-MON
                        (0 750 2500)
                        (NUM-IVF-CYCLES)
                        NIL
                        ((1.0 0.0   0.0)
                         (0.0 0.75 0.25)
                         (0.0 0.5   0.5)
                         (0.0 0.25 0.75)
                         (0.0 0.0   1.0)))".
Proved: "(ENTER-D-PRED IVF-MON NIL)".
Proved: "(ENTER-NEW-C-PREDS IVF-MON (NUM-IVF-CYCLES) ((ONE-OF 0 1 2 3 4)))".
Proved: "(ENTER-OUTCOMES IVF-MON (0 750 2500))".
Proved: "(ENTER-DISTRIBUTION IVF-MON
                        ((1.0 0.0   0.0)
                         (0.0 0.75 0.25)
                         (0.0 0.5   0.5)
                         (0.0 0.25 0.75)
                         (0.0 0.0   1.0)))".
Proved: "(STOCHASTICALLY-ASSESSED IVF-MON)".
Proved: "(ASSESSED IVF-MON)".

Would you like to assess node "IVF-MOR" by DIRECT-ASSESSMENT? [Y/N]> n

Proved: "(DETERMINISTIC-ASSESSMENT IVF-MOR
                        (LIST-OF N I B H U)
                        (NUM-IVF-CYCLES)
                        ((ONE-OF 0 1 2 3 4))
                        NIL
                        (%%MEDKB-IVF-MOR NUM-IVF-CYCLES))".

Would you like to assess node "IVF-MOR" by DETERMINISTIC-ASSESSMENT? [Y/N]> y

Note that although RACHEL has already found at least one possible DETERMINISTIC-ASSESSMENT for node "IVF-MOR", it still needs to check its suitability given previous assessments. Thus, it is possible that no actual DETERMINISTIC-ASSESSMENTs will be attempted.

Proved: "(OK-FOR DETERMINISTIC-ASSESSMENT IVF-MOR)".
Proved: "(DETERMINISTIC-ASSESSMENT IVF-MOR
                        (LIST-OF N I B H U)
                        (NUM-IVF-CYCLES)
                        ((ONE-OF 0 1 2 3 4))
                        NIL
                        (%%MEDKB-IVF-MOR NUM-IVF-CYCLES))".
Proved: "(CHECK-OUT-TYPE IVF-MOR (LIST-OF N I B H U))".
Proved: "(CHECK-PRED-OUT-TYPES (NUM-IVF-CYCLES) ((ONE-OF 0 1 2 3 4)))".

The following deterministic assessment has been found for node "IVF-MOR". Please review it and indicate whether it is acceptable.

Predecessors: (NUM-IVF-CYCLES)

Deterministic Function: (%%MEDKB-IVF-MOR NUM-IVF-CYCLES)

Is it acceptable? [Y/N]> y

Proved: "(CHECK-FULL-DET-ASSESSMENT IVF-MOR
                        (NUM-IVF-CYCLES)
                        NIL
                        (%%MEDKB-IVF-MOR NUM-IVF-CYCLES))".
Proved: "(ENTER-D-PRED IVF-MOR NIL)".
Proved: "(ENTER-NEW-C-PREDS IVF-MOR (NUM-IVF-CYCLES) ((ONE-OF 0 1 2 3 4)))".
Proved: "(MAKE-DET-NODE IVF-MOR)".
Proved: "(ENTER-D-FUNCTION IVF-MOR (%%MEDKB-IVF-MOR NUM-IVF-CYCLES))".
Proved: "(DETERMINISTICALLY-ASSESSED IVF-MOR)".
Proved: "(ASSESSED IVF-MOR)".

Would you like to assess node "IVF-THB" by DIRECT-ASSESSMENT? [Y/N]> n

```
Proved: "(STOCHASTIC-ASSESSMENT IVF-THB
                          (THB NO-THB)
                          (IVF-IMPLANT)
                          ((ONE-OF IMPLANT NO-IMPLANT))
                          NIL
                          ((0.7  0.3) (0  1)))".
```

Would you like to assess node "IVF-THB" by STOCHASTIC-ASSESSMENT? [Y/N]> y

> Note that although RACHEL has already found at least one possible
> STOCHASTIC-ASSESSMENT for node "IVF-THB", it still needs to check its
> suitability given previous assessments. Thus, it is possible that no
> actual STOCHASTIC-ASSESSMENTs will be attempted.

```
Proved: "(OK-FOR STOCHASTIC-ASSESSMENT IVF-THB)".
Proved: "(STOCHASTIC-ASSESSMENT IVF-THB
                          (THB NO-THB)
                          (IVF-IMPLANT)
                          ((ONE-OF IMPLANT NO-IMPLANT))
                          NIL
                          ((0.7  0.3) (0  1)))".
Proved: "(CHECK-OUTCOMES IVF-THB (THB NO-THB))".
Proved: "(CHECK-PRED-OUT-TYPES (IVF-IMPLANT) ((ONE-OF IMPLANT NO-IMPLANT)))".
```

> The following stochastic assessment has been found for node
> "IVF-THB". Please review it and determine whether it is acceptable.

> Outcomes: (THB NO-THB)

> Predecessors: (IVF-IMPLANT)

> Distribution: ((0.7 0.3) (0 1))

> Is it acceptable? [Y/N]> y

```
Proved: "(CHECK-FULL-STOCH-ASSESSMENT IVF-THB
                               (THB NO-THB)
                               (IVF-IMPLANT)
                               NIL
                               ((0.7  0.3) (0  1)))".
Proved: "(ENTER-D-PRED IVF-THB NIL)".
Proved: "(ENTER-NEW-C-PREDS IVF-THB (IVF-IMPLANT)
                               ((ONE-OF IMPLANT NO-IMPLANT)))".
Proved: "(ENTER-OUTCOMES IVF-THB (THB NO-THB))".
Proved: "(ENTER-DISTRIBUTION IVF-THB ((0.7  0.3) (0  1)))".
Proved: "(STOCHASTICALLY-ASSESSED IVF-THB)".
```

Proved: "(ASSESSED IVF-THB)".

Would you like to assess node "LAP-MON" by DIRECT-ASSESSMENT? [Y/N]> n

Proved: "(STOCHASTIC-ASSESSMENT LAP-MON
                     (0 300 450)
                     (NUM-HOSP-DAYS)
                     ((ONE-OF 0 4 6 8))
                     NIL
                     ((1   0   0)
                      (0 0.75 0.25)
                      (0 0.75 0.25)
                      (0 0.25 0.75)))".

Would you like to assess node "LAP-MON" by STOCHASTIC-ASSESSMENT? [Y/N]> y

       Note that although RACHEL has already found at least one possible STOCHASTIC-ASSESSMENT for node "LAP-MON", it still needs to check its suitability given previous assessments. Thus, it is possible that no actual STOCHASTIC-ASSESSMENTs will be attempted.

Proved: "(OK-FOR STOCHASTIC-ASSESSMENT LAP-MON)".
Proved: "(STOCHASTIC-ASSESSMENT LAP-MON
                     (0 300 450)
                     (NUM-HOSP-DAYS)
                     ((ONE-OF 0 4 6 8))
                     NIL
                     ((1   0   0)
                      (0 0.75 0.25)
                      (0 0.75 0.25)
                      (0 0.25 0.75)))".
Proved: "(CHECK-OUTCOMES LAP-MON (0 300 450))".
Proved: "(CHECK-PRED-OUT-TYPES (NUM-HOSP-DAYS) ((ONE-OF 0 4 6 8)))".

       The following stochastic assessment has been found for node "LAP-MON". Please review it and determine whether it is acceptable.

   Outcomes: (0 300 450)

   Predecessors: (NUM-HOSP-DAYS)

   Distribution: ((1   0   0)
                      (0 0.75 0.25)
                      (0 0.75 0.25)
                      (0 0.25 0.75))

       Is it acceptable? [Y/N]> y

Proved: "(CHECK-FULL-STOCH-ASSESSMENT LAP-MON
                                    (0 300 450)
                                    (NUM-HOSP-DAYS)
                                    NIL
                                    ((1   0   0)
                                     (0   0.75 0.25)
                                     (0   0.75 0.25)
                                     (0   0.25 0.75)))".
Proved: "(ENTER-D-PRED LAP-MON NIL)".
Proved: "(ENTER-NEW-C-PREDS LAP-MON (NUM-HOSP-DAYS) ((ONE-OF 0 4 6 8)))".
Proved: "(ENTER-OUTCOMES LAP-MON (0 300 450))".
Proved: "(ENTER-DISTRIBUTION LAP-MON ((1   0   0)
                                       (0   0.75 0.25)
                                       (0   0.75 0.25)
                                       (0   0.25 0.75)))".
Proved: "(STOCHASTICALLY-ASSESSED LAP-MON)".
Proved: "(ASSESSED LAP-MON)".

Would you like to assess node "LAP-MOR" by DIRECT-ASSESSMENT? [Y/N]> n

Proved: "(DETERMINISTIC-ASSESSMENT LAP-MOR
                                    (LIST-OF N I B H U)
                                    (NUM-HOSP-DAYS)
                                    ((ONE-OF 0 4 6 8))
                                    NIL
                                    (%%MEDKB-LAP-MOR NUM-HOSP-DAYS))".

Would you like to assess node "LAP-MOR" by DETERMINISTIC-ASSESSMENT? [Y/N]> y

> Note that although RACHEL has already found at least one possible
> DETERMINISTIC-ASSESSMENT for node "LAP-MOR", it still needs to check
> its suitability given previous assessments. Thus, it is possible
> that no actual DETERMINISTIC-ASSESSMENTs will be attempted.

Proved: "(OK-FOR DETERMINISTIC-ASSESSMENT LAP-MOR)".
Proved: "(DETERMINISTIC-ASSESSMENT LAP-MOR
                                    (LIST-OF N I B H U)
                                    (NUM-HOSP-DAYS)
                                    ((ONE-OF 0 4 6 8))
                                    NIL
                                    (%%MEDKB-LAP-MOR NUM-HOSP-DAYS))".
Proved: "(CHECK-OUT-TYPE LAP-MOR (LIST-OF N I B H U))".
Proved: "(CHECK-PRED-OUT-TYPES (NUM-HOSP-DAYS) ((ONE-OF 0 4 6 8)))".

The following deterministic assessment has been found for node "LAP-MOR". Please review it and indicate whether it is acceptable.

    Predecessors: (NUM-HOSP-DAYS)

    Deterministic Function: (%%MEDKB-LAP-MOR NUM-HOSP-DAYS)

    Is it acceptable? [Y/N]> *y*

Proved: "(CHECK-FULL-DET-ASSESSMENT LAP-MOR
                              (NUM-HOSP-DAYS)
                              NIL
                              (%%MEDKB-LAP-MOR NUM-HOSP-DAYS))".
Proved: "(ENTER-D-PRED LAP-MOR NIL)".
Proved: "(ENTER-NEW-C-PREDS LAP-MOR (NUM-HOSP-DAYS) ((ONE-OF 0 4 6 8)))".
Proved: "(MAKE-DET-NODE LAP-MOR)".
Proved: "(ENTER-D-FUNCTION LAP-MOR (%%MEDKB-LAP-MOR NUM-HOSP-DAYS))".
Proved: "(DETERMINISTICALLY-ASSESSED LAP-MOR)".
Proved: "(ASSESSED LAP-MOR)".

Would you like to assess node "LAP-THB" by DIRECT-ASSESSMENT? [Y/N]> *n*

Proved: "(STOCHASTIC-ASSESSMENT LAP-THB
                         (THB NO-THB)
                         (T-MUCOSA T-WTHICK)
                         ((ONE-OF BAD GOOD)
                          (ONE-OF THIN NORMAL THICK))
                         NIL
                         ((0.21 0.79)
                          (0.3   0.7)
                          (0.21 0.79)
                          (0.42 0.58)
                          (0.51 0.49)
                          (0.42 0.58)))".

Would you like to assess node "LAP-THB" by STOCHASTIC-ASSESSMENT? [Y/N]> *y*

The following note that although RACHEL has already found at least one possible STOCHASTIC-ASSESSMENT for node "LAP-THB", it still needs to check its suitability given previous assessments. Thus, it is possible that no actual STOCHASTIC-ASSESSMENTs will be attempted.

Proved: "(OK-FOR STOCHASTIC-ASSESSMENT LAP-THB)".

```
Proved: "(STOCHASTIC-ASSESSMENT LAP-THB
                         (THB NO-THB)
                         (T-MUCOSA T-WTHICK)
                       ((ONE-OF BAD GOOD) (ONE-OF THIN NORMAL THICK))
                         NIL
                         ((0.21 0.79)
                          (0.3  0.7)
                          (0.21 0.79)
                          (0.42 0.58)
                          (0.51 0.49)
                          (0.42 0.58)))".
Proved: "(CHECK-OUTCOMES LAP-THB (THB NO-THB))".
Proved: "(CHECK-PRED-OUT-TYPES (T-MUCOSA T-WTHICK)
                        ((ONE-OF BAD GOOD)
                         (ONE-OF THIN NORMAL THICK)))".
```

The following stochastic assessment has been found for node
"LAP-THB". Please review it and determine whether it is acceptable.

```
    Outcomes:      (THB NO-THB)

    Predecessors:  (T-MUCOSA T-WTHICK)

    Distribution:  ((0.21  0.79)
                    (0.3   0.7)
                    (0.21  0.79)
                    (0.42  0.58)
                    (0.51  0.49)
                    (0.42  0.58))
```

    Is it acceptable? [Y/N]> y

```
Proved: "(CHECK-FULL-STOCH-ASSESSMENT LAP-THB
                              (THB NO-THB)
                              (T-MUCOSA T-WTHICK)
                              NIL
                              ((0.21  0.79)
                               (0.3   0.7)
                               (0.21  0.79)
                               (0.42  0.58)
                               (0.51  0.49)
                               (0.42  0.58)))".
Proved: "(ENTER-D-PRED LAP-THB NIL)".
Proved: "(ENTER-NEW-C-PREDS LAP-THB
                         (T-MUCOSA T-WTHICK)
                        ((ONE-OF BAD GOOD)
                         (ONE-OF THIN NORMAL THICK)))".
Proved: "(ENTER-OUTCOMES LAP-THB (THB NO-THB))".
```

```
Proved: "(ENTER-DISTRIBUTION LAP-THB
                              ((0.21   0.79)
                               (0.3    0.7)
                               (0.21   0.79)
                               (0.42   0.58)
                               (0.51   0.49)
                               (0.42   0.58)))".
Proved: "(STOCHASTICALLY-ASSESSED LAP-THB)".
Proved: "(ASSESSED LAP-THB)".
```

Would you like to assess node "SURG-COMP" by DIRECT-ASSESSMENT? [Y/N]> n

```
Proved: "(STOCHASTIC-ASSESSMENT SURG-COMP
                              (DEATH PERF-BOWEL NO-COMP)
                              (ANES-DEATH TREATMENT)
                              ((ONE-OF DIE LIVE)
                               (ONE-OF LAPAROTOMY IVF-4 DO-NOTHING))
                              NIL
                              ((1       0      0)
                               (1       0      0)
                               (0       0      1)
                               (0.001  0.002  0.997)
                               (0.001  0      0.999)
                               (0       0      1)))".
```

Would you like to assess node "SURG-COMP" by STOCHASTIC-ASSESSMENT? [Y/N]> y

> Note that although RACHEL has already found at least one possible
> STOCHASTIC-ASSESSMENT for node "SURG-COMP", it still needs to check
> its suitability given previous assessments. Thus, it is possible
> that no actual STOCHASTIC-ASSESSMENTs will be attempted.

```
Proved: "(OK-FOR STOCHASTIC-ASSESSMENT SURG-COMP)".
Proved: "(STOCHASTIC-ASSESSMENT SURG-COMP
                              (DEATH PERF-BOWEL NO-COMP)
                              (ANES-DEATH TREATMENT)
                              ((ONE-OF DIE LIVE)
                               (ONE-OF LAPAROTOMY IVF-4 DO-NOTHING))
                              NIL
                              ((1       0      0)
                               (1       0      0)
                               (0       0      1)
                               (0.001  0.002  0.997)
                               (0.001  0      0.999)
                               (0       0      1)))".
```

```
Proved: "(CHECK-OUTCOMES SURG-COMP (DEATH PERF-BOWEL NO-COMP))".
Proved: "(CHECK-PRED-OUT-TYPES (ANES-DEATH TREATMENT)
                            ((ONE-OF DIE LIVE)
                             (ONE-OF LAPAROTOMY IVF-4 DO-NOTHING)))".
```

The following stochastic assessment has been found for node "SURG-COMP". Please review it and determine whether it is acceptable.

```
    Outcomes:       (DEATH PERF-BOWEL NO-COMP)

    Predecessors:   (ANES-DEATH TREATMENT)

    Distribution  ((1       0      0)
                   (1       0      0)
                   (0       0      1)
                   (0.001  0.002  0.997)
                   (0.001   0      0.999)
                   (0       0      1))
```

Is it acceptable? [Y/N]> _y_

```
Proved: "(CHECK-FULL-STOCH-ASSESSMENT SURG-COMP
                            (DEATH PERF-BOWEL NO-COMP)
                            (ANES-DEATH TREATMENT)
                            NIL
                            ((1       0      0)
                             (1       0      0)
                             (0       0      1)
                             (0.001  0.002  0.997)
                             (0.001   0      0.999)
                             (0       0      1)))".
Proved: "(ENTER-D-PRED SURG-COMP NIL)".
Proved: "(ENTER-NEW-C-PREDS SURG-COMP (ANES-DEATH TREATMENT)
                            ((ONE-OF DIE LIVE)
                             (ONE-OF LAPAROTOMY IVF-4 DO-NOTHING)))".
Proved: "(ENTER-OUTCOMES SURG-COMP (DEATH PERF-BOWEL NO-COMP))".
Proved: "(ENTER-DISTRIBUTION SURG-COMP ((1       0      0)
                             (1       0      0)
                             (0       0      1)
                             (0.001  0.002  0.997)
                             (0.001   0      0.999)
                             (0       0      1)))".
Proved: "(STOCHASTICALLY-ASSESSED SURG-COMP)".
Proved: "(ASSESSED SURG-COMP)".
```

Would you like to assess node "TREATMENT" by DIRECT-ASSESSMENT? [Y/N]> _n_

```
Proved: "(STOCHASTIC-ASSESSMENT TREATMENT
                           (LAPAROTOMY IVF-4 DO-NOTHING)
                           (IVF-ACCEPT)
                           ((ONE-OF ACCEPT NO-ACCEPT))
                           D-PRED
                           ((1  0  0)
                            (0  1  0)
                            (0  0  1)
                            (1  0  0)
                            (1  0  0)
                            (0  0  1)))".
```

Would you like to assess node "TREATMENT" by STOCHASTIC-ASSESSMENT? [Y/N]> y

> Note that although RACHEL has already found at least one possible
> STOCHASTIC-ASSESSMENT for node "TREATMENT", it still needs to check
> its suitability given previous assessments. Thus, it is possible
> that no actual STOCHASTIC-ASSESSMENTs will be attempted.

```
Proved: "(OK-FOR STOCHASTIC-ASSESSMENT TREATMENT)".
Proved: "(STOCHASTIC-ASSESSMENT TREATMENT
                           (LAPAROTOMY IVF-4 DO-NOTHING)
                           (IVF-ACCEPT)
                           ((ONE-OF ACCEPT NO-ACCEPT))
                           D-PRED
                            ((1  0  0)
                             (0  1  0)
                             (0  0  1)
                             (1  0  0)
                             (1  0  0)
                             (0  0  1)))".
Proved: "(CHECK-OUTCOMES TREATMENT (LAPAROTOMY IVF-4 DO-NOTHING))".
Proved: "(CHECK-PRED-OUT-TYPES (IVF-ACCEPT) ((ONE-OF ACCEPT NO-ACCEPT)))".
```

> The following stochastic assessment has been found for node "TREAT-
> MENT". Please review it and determine whether it is acceptable.

```
    Outcomes:       (LAPAROTOMY IVF-4 DO-NOTHING)

    Predecessors:   (D-NODE:MARSHA IVF-ACCEPT)

    Distribution:   ((1  0  0)
                     (0  1  0)
                     (0  0  1)
                     (1  0  0)
                     (1  0  0)
                     (0  0  1))
```

> Is it acceptable? [Y/N]> y

```
Proved: "(CHECK-FULL-STOCH-ASSESSMENT TREATMENT
                                     (LAPAROTOMY IVF-4 DO-NOTHING)
                                     (IVF-ACCEPT)
                                     D-PRED
                                     ((1  0  0)
                                      (0  1  0)
                                      (0  0  1)
                                      (1  0  0)
                                      (1  0  0)
                                      (0  0  1)))".
Proved: "(ENTER-D-PRED TREATMENT D-PRED)".
Proved: "(ENTER-NEW-C-PREDS TREATMENT (IVF-ACCEPT)
                                       ((ONE-OF ACCEPT NO-ACCEPT)))".
Proved: "(ENTER-OUTCOMES TREATMENT (LAPAROTOMY IVF-4 DO-NOTHING))".
Proved: "(ENTER-DISTRIBUTION TREATMENT ((1  0  0)
                                        (0  1  0)
                                        (0  0  1)
                                        (1  0  0)
                                        (1  0  0)
                                        (0  0  1)))".
Proved: "(STOCHASTICALLY-ASSESSED TREATMENT)".
Proved: "(ASSESSED TREATMENT)".
```

|| NOTE: Once again, Rachel updates its frontier node agenda.

```
Proved: "(FRONTIER D-MODEL:MARSHA ANES-DEATH)".
Proved: "(FRONTIER D-MODEL:MARSHA IVF-ACCEPT)".
Proved: "(FRONTIER D-MODEL:MARSHA IVF-IMPLANT)".
Proved: "(FRONTIER D-MODEL:MARSHA NUM-HOSP-DAYS)".
Proved: "(FRONTIER D-MODEL:MARSHA NUM-IVF-CYCLES)".
Proved: "(FRONTIER D-MODEL:MARSHA T-MUCOSA)".
Proved: "(FRONTIER D-MODEL:MARSHA T-WTHICK)".
```

```
Would you like to assess node "ANES-DEATH" by DIRECT-ASSESSMENT? [Y/N]> n
```

```
Proved: "(THNOT (HEAVY-DRINKER MARSHA))".
```

|| NOTE: To determine the probability of the patient dying from the effects of anesthe-
               sia (i.e., to establish the applicability of a particular expansion object for node

ANES-DEATH), Rachel needs to determine her ASA rating. This is an overall health rating developed by the American Society of Anesthesiologists (ASA), which is based, among other things, on whether the patient has any major illnesses and/or whether she drinks heavily [Klein, 1985]. Information about major illnesses is obtained below. However, Rachel has already determined that the patient does not drink heavily (while trying to estimate her remaining actuarial lifetime) and reuses this information here.

```
Is it true that "(NO-MAJOR-ILLNESSES MARSHA)"? [Y/N]> w

To establish that "(ASA-RATING MARSHA 2)".
 Major illnesses? [Y/N]> w
To establish that "(STOCHASTIC-ASSESSMENT ANES-DEATH
                                         $V683
                                         $V684
                                         $V685
                                         $V686
                                         $V687)".
 Major illnesses? [Y/N]> w
To establish that "(STOCHASTICALLY-ASSESSED ANES-DEATH)".
 Major illnesses? [Y/N]> w
To establish that "(ASSESSED ANES-DEATH)".
 Major illnesses? [Y/N]> w
To establish that "(^ASSESSED-ALL-FRONTIER-NODES D-MODEL:MARSHA)".
 Major illnesses? [Y/N]> w
To establish that "(FULLY-ASSESSED D-MODEL:MARSHA)".
 Major illnesses? [Y/N]> w
To establish that "(COMPLETE $MODEL)".
 Major illnesses? [Y/N]> w
Because you asked me.
 Major illnesses? [Y/N]> q


Is it true that "(NO-MAJOR-ILLNESSES MARSHA)"? [Y/N]> y


Proved: "(ASA-RATING MARSHA 2)".
Proved: "(STOCHASTIC-ASSESSMENT ANES-DEATH
                             (DIE LIVE)
                             (TREATMENT)
                      ((ONE-OF LAPAROTOMY IVF-4 DO-NOTHING))
                             NIL
                      ((0.001  0.999) (0.0005  0.9995) (0  1)))".


Would you like to assess node "ANES-DEATH" by STOCHASTIC-ASSESSMENT? [Y/N]> y
```

Note that although RACHEL has already found at least one possible
STOCHASTIC-ASSESSMENT for node "ANES-DEATH", it still needs to check
its suitability given previous assessments. Thus, it is possible
that no actual STOCHASTIC-ASSESSMENTs will be attempted.

Proved: "(OK-FOR STOCHASTIC-ASSESSMENT ANES-DEATH)".
Proved: "(THNOT (HEAVY-DRINKER MARSHA))".
Proved: "(ASA-RATING MARSHA 2)".
Proved: "(STOCHASTIC-ASSESSMENT ANES-DEATH
                           (DIE LIVE)
                           (TREATMENT)
                           ((ONE-OF LAPAROTOMY IVF-4 DO-NOTHING))
                           NIL
                           ((0.001 0.999) (0.0005 0.9995) (0 1)))".
Proved: "(CHECK-OUTCOMES ANES-DEATH (DIE LIVE))".
Proved: "(CHECK-PRED-OUT-TYPES (TREATMENT)
                           ((ONE-OF LAPAROTOMY IVF-4 DO-NOTHING)))".

The following stochastic assessment has been found for node
"ANES-DEATH". Please review it and determine whether it is
acceptable.

   Outcomes: (DIE LIVE)

   Predecessors: (TREATMENT)

   Distribution: ((0.001 0.999) (0.0005 0.9995) (0 1))

   Is it acceptable? [Y/N]> _y_

Proved: "(CHECK-FULL-STOCH-ASSESSMENT ANES-DEATH
                           (DIE LIVE)
                           (TREATMENT)
                           NIL
                           ((0.001   0.999)
                            (0.0005 0.9995)
                            (0   1)))".
Proved: "(ENTER-D-PRED ANES-DEATH NIL)".
Proved: "(ENTER-NEW-C-PREDS ANES-DEATH
                           (TREATMENT)
                           ((ONE-OF LAPAROTOMY IVF-4 DO-NOTHING)))".
Proved: "(ENTER-OUTCOMES ANES-DEATH (DIE LIVE))".
Proved: "(ENTER-DISTRIBUTION ANES-DEATH ((0.001   0.999)
                                 (0.0005 0.9995)
                                 (0   1)))".

```
Proved: "(STOCHASTICALLY-ASSESSED ANES-DEATH)"
Proved: "(ASSESSED ANES-DEATH)".
```

```
Would you like to assess node "IVF-ACCEPT" by DIRECT-ASSESSMENT? [Y/N]> n
```

```
Proved: "(INDICATED-ASSESSMENT IVF-ACCEPT
                        (ACCEPT NO-ACCEPT)
                        D-PRED
                        ((0  1) (0.5  0.5) (0  1)))".
```

NOTE: Up to this point, all nodes have been assessed indirectly—either stochastically or deterministically. In this case, Rachel has found an indicated assessment for node "IVF-ACCEPT". The assessment process follows the same three steps as before, except that no chance-node predecessors are added.

```
Would you like to assess node "IVF-ACCEPT" by INDICATED-ASSESSMENT? [Y/N]> y
```

Note that although RACHEL has already found at least one possible INDICATED-ASSESSMENT for node "ANES-DEATH", it still needs to check its suitability given previous assessments. Thus, it is possible that no actual INDICATED-ASSESSMENTs will be attempted.

```
Proved: "(OK-FOR INDICATED-ASSESSMENT IVF-ACCEPT)".
Proved: "(INDICATED-ASSESSMENT IVF-ACCEPT
                        (ACCEPT NO-ACCEPT)
                        D-PRED
                        ((0  1) (0.5  0.5) (0  1)))".
Proved: "(CHECK-OUTCOMES IVF-ACCEPT (ACCEPT NO-ACCEPT))".
```

The following indicated assessment has been found for node "IVF-ACCEPT". Please review it and determine whether it is acceptable.

   Outcomes: (ACCEPT NO-ACCEPT)

   Predecessors: D-NODE:MARSHA

   Distribution: ((0 1) (0.5 0.5) (0 1))

Is it acceptable? [Y/N]> y

```
Proved: "(CHECK-FULL-INDIC-ASSESSMENT IVF-ACCEPT
                              (ACCEPT NO-ACCEPT)
                              D-PRED
                              ((0  1) (0.5  0.5) (0  1)))".
Proved: "(ENTER-D-PRED IVF-ACCEPT D-PRED)".
Proved: "(ENTER-OUTCOMES IVF-ACCEPT (ACCEPT NO-ACCEPT))".
Proved: "(ENTER-DISTRIBUTION IVF-ACCEPT ((0  1) (0.5  0.5) (0  1)))".
Proved: "(ASSESSED-BY-INDICATION IVF-ACCEPT)".
Proved: "(ASSESSED IVF-ACCEPT)".
```

```
Would you like to assess node "IVF-IMPLANT" by DIRECT-ASSESSMENT? [Y/N]> n
```

```
Proved: "(STOCHASTIC-ASSESSMENT IVF-IMPLANT
                         (IMPLANT NO-IMPLANT)
                         (NUM-IVF-CYCLES)
                         ((ONE-OF 0 1 2 3 4))
                         NIL
                         ((0      1)
                          (1      0)
                          (0.41  0.59)
                          (0.34  0.66)
                          (0.1   0.9)))".
```

NOTE: It is interesting to see that contrary to intuition, the probability of producing an implantation through in-vitro fertilization (IVF) *decreases* as the number of IVF attempts *increases*. This decrease in the probability of implantation is a consequence of the rules that guide an IVF-4 regimen. These rules indicate that if the first IVF attempt is unsuccessful, a second IVF attempt will be routinely made. However, before making a third attempt following two consecutive failures, the patient's condition will be evaluated, and it is possible that no further attempts will be made. An even more rigorous evaluation will be made following a third unsuccessful attempt. Finally, according to the assumed regimen, no further IVF attempts beyond the fourth will be made.

It is worth noting that this distribution illustrates the view that probabilities reflect a state of information and not a state of nature. A more "objective" distribution based on the notion of "causality" may have taken quite a different form, since the greater the number of IVF attempts, the greater are the chances of "causing" an implantation. This point is discussed in more detail in Chapters 3 and 6.

Would you like to assess node "IVF-IMPLANT" by STOCHASTIC-ASSESSMENT? [Y/N]> y

> Note that although RACHEL has already found at least one possible STOCHASTIC-ASSESSMENT for node "IVF-IMPLANT", it still needs to check its suitability given previous assessments. Thus, it is possible that no actual STOCHASTIC-ASSESSMENTs will be attempted.

Proved: "(OK-FOR STOCHASTIC-ASSESSMENT IVF-IMPLANT)".
Proved: "(STOCHASTIC-ASSESSMENT IVF-IMPLANT
                             (IMPLANT NO-IMPLANT)
                             (NUM-IVF-CYCLES)
                             ((ONE-OF 0 1 2 3 4))
                             NIL
                             ((0   1)
                             (1   0)
                             (0.41 0.59)
                             (0.34 0.66)
                             (0.1   0.9)))".
Proved: "(CHECK-OUTCOMES IVF-IMPLANT (IMPLANT NO-IMPLANT))".
Proved: "(CHECK-PRED-OUT-TYPES (NUM-IVF-CYCLES) ((ONE-OF 0 1 2 3 4)))".

> The following stochastic assessment has been found for node "IVF-IMPLANT". Please review it and determine whether it is acceptable.

    Outcomes: (IMPLANT NO-IMPLANT)

    Predecessors: (NUM-IVF-CYCLES)

    Distribution: ((0   1)
                  (1   0)
                  (0.41 0.59)
                  (0.34 0.66)
                  (0.1   0.9))

> Is it acceptable? [Y/N]> y

Proved: "(CHECK-FULL-STOCH-ASSESSMENT IVF-IMPLANT
                             (IMPLANT NO-IMPLANT)
                             (NUM-IVF-CYCLES)
                             NIL
                             ((0   1)
                             (1   0)
                             (0.41 0.59)
                             (0.34 0.66)
                             (0.1   0.9)))".

```
Proved: "(ENTER-D-PRED IVF-IMPLANT NIL)".
Proved: "(ENTER-NEW-C-PREDS IVF-IMPLANT (NUM-IVF-CYCLES)
                                        ((ONE-OF 0 1 2 3 4)))".
Proved: "(ENTER-OUTCOMES IVF-IMPLANT (IMPLANT NO-IMPLANT))".
Proved: "(ENTER-DISTRIBUTION IVF-IMPLANT ((0      1)
                                          (1      0)
                                          (0.41  0.59)
                                          (0.34  0.66)
                                          (0.1   0.9)))".
Proved: "(STOCHASTICALLY-ASSESSED IVF-IMPLANT)".
Proved: "(ASSESSED IVF-IMPLANT)".
```

```
Would you like to assess node "NUM-HOSP-DAYS" by DIRECT-ASSESSMENT? [Y/N]> n
```

NOTE: Here again, Rachel queries the user for information to determine the validity of a given (stochastic) expansion object.

Experience shows that the patient's attitude toward recovery following surgery (e.g., her overall optimism—or pessimism—and her willingness to move despite a bit of pain and other forms of discomfort) greatly affects the length of time she will need to remain in the hospital. The more optimistic and active she is, the sooner she will be able to go home and the sooner she will recover from surgery.

```
Is it true that "(PATIENT-ATTITUDE MARSHA NORMAL)"? [Y/N]> w

To establish that "(STOCHASTIC-ASSESSMENT NUM-HOSP-DAYS
                                          $V825
                                          $V826
                                          $V827
                                          $V828
                                          $V829)".
  Normal attitude? [Y/N]> w
To establish that "(STOCHASTICALLY-ASSESSED NUM-HOSP-DAYS)".
  Normal attitude? [Y/N]> w
To establish that "(ASSESSED NUM-HOSP-DAYS)".
  Normal attitude? [Y/N]> q


Is it true that "(PATIENT-ATTITUDE MARSHA NORMAL)"? [Y/N]> y
```

```
Proved: "(STOCHASTIC-ASSESSMENT NUM-HOSP-DAYS
                        (0 4 6 8)
                        (SURG-COMP TREATMENT)
                        ((ONE-OF DEATH PERF-BOWEL NO-COMP)
                         (ONE-OF LAPAROTOMY IVF-4 DO-NOTHING))
                        NIL
                        ((0   1    0    0)
                         (0   1    0    0)
                         (1   0    0    0)
                         (0   0    0    1)
                         (0   0.2  0.8  0)
                         (1   0    0    0)
                         (0   0.4  0.6  0)
                         (1   0    0    0)
                         (1   0    0    0)))".
```

Would you like to assess node "NUM-HOSP-DAYS" by STOCHASTIC-ASSESSMENT? [Y/N]> y

> Note that although RACHEL has already found at least one possible
> STOCHASTIC-ASSESSMENT for node "NUM-HOSP-DAYS", it still needs to
> check its suitability given previous assessments. Thus, it is pos-
> sible that no actual STOCHASTIC-ASSESSMENTs will be attempted.

```
Proved: "(OK-FOR STOCHASTIC-ASSESSMENT NUM-HOSP-DAYS)".
Proved: "(STOCHASTIC-ASSESSMENT NUM-HOSP-DAYS
                        (0 4 6 8)
                        (SURG-COMP TREATMENT)
                        ((ONE-OF DEATH PERF-BOWEL NO-COMP)
                         (ONE-OF LAPAROTOMY IVF-4 DO-NOTHING))
                        NIL
                        ((0   1    0    0)
                         (0   1    0    0)
                         (1   0    0    0)
                         (0   0    0    1)
                         (0   0.2  0.8  0)
                         (1   0    0    0)
                         (0   0.4  0.6  0)
                         (1   0    0    0)
                         (1   0    0    0)))".
Proved: "(CHECK-OUTCOMES NUM-HOSP-DAYS (0 4 6 8))".
Proved: "(CHECK-PRED-OUT-TYPES (SURG-COMP TREATMENT)
                        ((ONE-OF DEATH PERF-BOWEL NO-COMP)
                         (ONE-OF LAPAROTOMY IVF-4 DO-NOTHING)))".
```

The following stochastic assessment has been found for node "NUM-HOSP-DAYS". Please review it and determine whether it is acceptable.

```
Outcomes:      (0  4  6  8)

Predecessors:  (SURG-COMP TREATMENT)

Distribution:  ((0   1     0     0)
                (0   1     0     0)
                (1   0     0     0)
                (0   0     0     1)
                (0   0.2   0.8   0)
                (1   0     0     0)
                (0   0.4   0.6   0)
                (1   0     0     0)
                (1   0     0     0))
```

Is it acceptable? [Y/N]> y

Proved: "(CHECK-FULL-STOCH-ASSESSMENT NUM-HOSP-DAYS
```
                (0 4 6 8)
                (SURG-COMP TREATMENT)
                NIL
                ((0   1     0     0)
                 (0   1     0     0)
                 (1   0     0     0)
                 (0   0     0     1)
                 (0   0.2   0.8   0)
                 (1   0     0     0)
                 (0   0.4   0.6   0)
                 (1   0     0     0)
                 (1   0     0     0)))".
```
Proved: "(ENTER-D-PRED NUM-HOSP-DAYS NIL)".
Proved: "(ENTER-NEW-C-PREDS NUM-HOSP-DAYS
```
                (SURG-COMP TREATMENT)
                ((ONE-OF DEATH PERF-BOWEL NO-COMP)
                (ONE-OF LAPAROTOMY IVF-4 DO-NOTHING)))".
```
Proved: "(ENTER-OUTCOMES NUM-HOSP-DAYS (0 4 6 8))".
Proved: "(ENTER-DISTRIBUTION NUM-HOSP-DAYS ((0   1   0   0)
```
                                    (0   1     0     0)
                                    (1   0     0     0)
                                    (0   0     0     1)
                                    (0   0.2   0.8   0)
                                    (1   0     0     0)
                                    (0   0.4   0.6   0)
                                    (1   0     0     0)
                                    (1   0     0     0)))".
```
Proved: "(STOCHASTICALLY-ASSESSED NUM-HOSP-DAYS)".
Proved: "(ASSESSED NUM-HOSP-DAYS)".

Would you like to assess node "NUM-IVF-CYCLES" by DIRECT-ASSESSMENT? [Y/N]> <u>n</u>

Proved: "(STOCHASTIC-ASSESSMENT NUM-IVF-CYCLES
                   (0 1 2 3 4)
                   (TREATMENT)
                ((ONE-OF LAPAROTOMY IVF-4 DO-NOTHING))
                 NIL
                 ((1   0   0   0   0)
                 (0 0.12 0.22 0.2 0.46)
                 (1 0   0   0   0)))".

Would you like to assess node "NUM-IVF-CYCLES" by STOCHASTIC-ASSESSMENT? [Y/N]> <u>y</u>

> Note that although RACHEL has already found at least one possible STOCHASTIC-ASSESSMENT for node "NUM-IVF-CYCLES", it still needs to check its suitability given previous assessments. Thus, it is possible that no actual STOCHASTIC-ASSESSMENTs will be attempted.

Proved: "(OK-FOR STOCHASTIC-ASSESSMENT NUM-IVF-CYCLES)".
Proved: "(STOCHASTIC-ASSESSMENT NUM-IVF-CYCLES
                   (0 1 2 3 4)
                   (TREATMENT)
                ((ONE-OF LAPAROTOMY IVF-4 DO-NOTHING))
                 NIL
                 ((1   0   0   0   0)
                 (0 0.12 0.22 0.2 0.46)
                 (1 0   0   0   0)))".
Proved: "(CHECK-OUTCOMES NUM-IVF-CYCLES (0 1 2 3 4))".
Proved: "(CHECK-PRED-OUT-TYPES (TREATMENT) ((LAPAROTOMY IVF-4 DO-NOTHING)))".

> The following stochastic assessment has been found for node "NUM-IVF-CYCLES". Please review it and determine whether it is acceptable.
>
> Outcomes: (0 1 2 3 4)
>
> Predecessors: (TREATMENT)
>
> Distribution: ((1 0   0   0   0)
>   (0 0.12 0.22 0.2 0.46)
>   (1 0   0   0   0))
>
> Is it acceptable? [Y/N]> <u>y</u>

```
Proved: "(CHECK-FULL-STOCH-ASSESSMENT NUM-IVF-CYCLES
                          (0 1 2 3 4)
                          (TREATMENT)
                          NIL
                          ((1   0      0     0    0)
                           (0  0.12  0.22  0.2  0.46)
                           (1   0      0     0    0)))".
Proved: "(ENTER-D-PRED NUM-IVF-CYCLES NIL)".
Proved: "(ENTER-NEW-C-PREDS NUM-IVF-CYCLES
                          (TREATMENT)
                          ((ONE-OF LAPAROTOMY IVF-4 DO-NOTHING)))".
Proved: "(ENTER-OUTCOMES NUM-IVF-CYCLES (0 1 2 3 4))".
Proved: "(ENTER-DISTRIBUTION NUM-IVF-CYCLES ((1   0      0     0    0)
                                            (0  0.12  0.22  0.2  0.46)
                                            (1   0      0     0    0)))".
Proved: "(STOCHASTICALLY-ASSESSED NUM-IVF-CYCLES)".
Proved: "(ASSESSED NUM-IVF-CYCLES)".
```

Would you like to assess node "T-MUCOSA" by DIRECT-ASSESSMENT? [Y/N]> y

NOTE: Up to this point, all frontier node assessments have been made from Rachel's knowledge base. Here, however, the physician user feels that the unique characteristics of the patient's medical circumstances can best be described by directly assessing the distribution of possible states of her tubal mucosa. In infertility medicine, these states are usually described as one of four categories: from 1:4 (the worst) to 4:4 (the best). For brevity, Rachel's knowledge base groups together categories 1:4 and 2:4 and labels them "BAD". Similarly, categories 3:4 and 4:4 are grouped together and are labeled "GOOD".

```
Proved: "(OK-FOR DIRECT-ASSESSMENT T-MUCOSA)".
```

Should the decision node (i.e., the node "D-NODE:MARSHA") be a direct predecessor of node "T-MUCOSA"? [Y/N]> n

```
Proved: "(CHECK-D-PRED T-MUCOSA)".
```

We now need to determine the outcomes of node "T-MUCOSA". Based on previous assessments, each outcome of this node must be an element of the following set (no repetitions allowed):

```
"(BAD GOOD)".
```

Please enter the outcomes of node "T-MUCOSA". To finish the list, please type "quit".

Outcome #1: [Set member]> _good_
Outcome #2: [Set member]> _bad_
Outcome #3: [Set member]> _quit_

The outcomes of "T-MUCOSA" have been set to: "(GOOD BAD)".

Proved: "(PRODUCED-OUTCOMES T-MUCOSA (GOOD BAD))".

The possible outcomes of node "T-MUCOSA" must now be assigned an unconditional probability distribution. Please enter specific probability values for each of this node's outcomes: "(GOOD BAD)".

No predecessors specified.

Enter a probability distribution as a list: _(0.67 0.33)_

Thank you, we are done entering a distribution for node "T-MUCOSA".

Proved: "(PRODUCED-DISTRIBUTION T-MUCOSA (0.67 0.33))".
Proved: "(DIRECTLY-ASSESSED T-MUCOSA)".
Proved: "(ASSESSED T-MUCOSA)".

Would you like to assess node "T-WTHICK" by DIRECT-ASSESSMENT? [Y/N]> _n_

Proved: "(STOCHASTIC-ASSESSMENT T-WTHICK
                        (THIN NORMAL THICK)
                        (T-MUCOSA)
                        ((ONE-OF BAD GOOD))
                        NIL
                        ((0.04 0.66 0.3)
                         (0   0.82 0.18)))".

Would you like to assess node "T-WTHICK" by STOCHASTIC-ASSESSMENT? [Y/N]> _y_

Note that although RACHEL has already found at least one possible STOCHASTIC-ASSESSMENT for node "T-WTHICK", it still needs to check its suitability given previous assessments. Thus, it is possible that no actual STOCHASTIC-ASSESSMENTs will be attempted.

Proved: "(OK-FOR STOCHASTIC-ASSESSMENT T-WTHICK)".
Proved: "(STOCHASTIC-ASSESSMENT T-WTHICK
                            (THIN NORMAL THICK)
                            (T-MUCOSA)
                            ((ONE-OF BAD GOOD))
                            NIL
                            ((0.04 0.66 0.3)
                              (0   0.82 0.18)))".
Proved: "(CHECK-OUTCOMES T-WTHICK (THIN NORMAL THICK))".
Proved: "(CHECK-PRED-OUT-TYPES (T-MUCOSA) ((ONE-OF BAD GOOD)))".

The following stochastic assessment has been found for node
"T-WTHICK". Please review it and determine whether it is acceptable.

    Outcomes: (THIN NORMAL THICK)

    Predecessors: (T-MUCOSA)

    Distribution: ((0.04 0.66 0.3)
                    (0   0.82 0.18))

Is it acceptable? [Y/N]> y

Proved: "(CHECK-FULL-STOCH-ASSESSMENT T-WTHICK
                            (THIN NORMAL THICK)
                            (T-MUCOSA)
                            NIL
                            ((0.04 0.66 0.3)
                              (0   0.82 0.18)))".
Proved: "(ENTER-D-PRED T-WTHICK NIL)".
Proved: "(ENTER-NEW-C-PREDS T-WTHICK (T-MUCOSA) ((ONE-OF BAD GOOD)))".
Proved: "(ENTER-OUTCOMES T-WTHICK (THIN NORMAL THICK))".
Proved: "(ENTER-DISTRIBUTION T-WTHICK ((0.04 0.66 0.3) (0 0.82 0.18)))".
Proved: "(STOCHASTICALLY-ASSESSED T-WTHICK)".
Proved: "(ASSESSED T-WTHICK)".

Proved: "(FULLY-ASSESSED D-MODEL:MARSHA)".

We have finished building a model for MARSHA's decision problem.
Please keep in mind that this model (or any model, for that matter) is
nothing more than a partial view of reality. It should be reviewed
carefully and modified if needed.

The model now needs to be evaluated (to obtain a formal recommendation) and appraised (to obtain other useful information, such as the
model's sensitivity to specific parameter values in the context of

the overall decision). For this purpose, Rachel will now automatically switch to the SUPERID environment. This environment provides full access to the influence diagram that constitutes the model for further analysis. In its current experimental implementation, Rachel does not have the ability to provide guidance beyond this point.

As a final check, Rachel will verify that the influence diagram that has been built for MARSHA's decision is internally consistent.

Would you like to proceed with this check? [Y/N]> y

CONGRATULATIONS! The decision model is internally consistent.

Proved: "(WELL-FORMED D-MODEL:MARSHA)".
Proved: "(COMPLETE D-MODEL:MARSHA)".

Welcome to SUPERID.   An experimental system for constructing, evaluating, and analyzing influence diagrams — *Rachel Version*

Type "?" to the "R>" prompt for help or "Q" to quit.

R> *Display*
    Nodename_Length: *2*

NOTE: This command generates a structural display of the influence diagram built by Rachel. When SUPERID produces displays like this one, it requires the length of all node names be truncated to a fixed number of characters (to two in this case) for the display to fit within the width of a page.

Since two-character names would be ambiguous in this diagram, the names of most nodes have been manually modified for this illustration. Some names have been extended to include their first three or four characters. Others are shown with their first and last characters separated by a pound (#) sign. Finally, nodes NUM-HOSP-DAYS and NUM-IVF-CYCLES are represented by their acronyms (NHD and NIC, respectively) instead of their names. Also, SUPERID indicates the value node with an asterisk (*).

D-MODEL:MARSHA

```
*V LI MOR MON THB I#R I#N I#B L#R L#N L#B IV-I NHD T-W NIC SU T-M AN TR IV-A DEC
<=-++
<=———+++
<=————— +++
<=—————— +++
    <=——————————————————————————————————————————————++
    <=—————————————————————————————————————————————————++
*V LI MOR MON THB I#R I#N I#B L#R L#N L#B IV-I NHD T-W NIC SU T-M AN TR IV-A DEC
    <==————————— +++
    <==——————————————— +++
    <==—————————————————————————————————————————————————++
      <==————————— +++
      <==————————————————————————+++
      <==——————————————————————————————————————————————++
*V LI MOR MON THB I#R I#N I#B L#R L#N L#B IV-I NHD T-W NIC SU T-M AN TR IV-A DEC
        <==—————————+++
        <==——————————————————————+++
        <==———————————————————————————————————————— ++
        <==———————————————————————————————————————————— ++
          <==———————————————————————————————————+++
          <==———————————————————————————————————+++
*V LI MOR MON THB I#R I#N I#B L#R L#N L#B IV-I NHD T-W NIC SU T-M AN TR IV-A DEC
          <==————————————————++++
            <==——————————————————+++
            <==—————————————— +++
              <==————————————————+++
              <==——————————————————————————— +++
              <===——————————+++
*V LI MOR MON THB I#R I#N I#B L#R L#N L#B IV-I NHD T-W NIC SU T-M AN TR IV-A DEC
                <== ——————————++
                <==————————————————————— ++
                <==—————————————+++
                <==—————————————— ++
                  <=———————++
                  <=————————— ++
*V LI MOR MON THB I#R I#N I#B L#R L#N L#B IV-I NHD T-W NIC SU T-M AN TR IV-A DEC
                          <=-++
                          <=-++++
                          <=————————+++
                          <===-+++
*V LI MOR MON THB I#R I#N I#B L#R L#N L#B IV-I NHD T-W NIC SU T-M AN TR IV-A DEC
```

NOTE: A more elaborate implementation of Rachel would clearly benefit from the use of better graphics than were available in the limited computer environment where it was developed.

Figure A.1 at the end of the Appendix provides a better illustration of the diagram and gives a hint of how better graphics could improve Rachel. In addition to the nodes included in the following structural display, Fig. A.1 contains two deterministic border nodes—labeled PT-ATTITUDE and ASA-RATING. Once assessed, a deterministic border node is just a constant and does not need to be explicitly included in its associated influence diagram. These nodes are shown in Fig. A.1 for completeness.

NOTE: Finally, the completed model is evaluated to yield a recommendation for action.

```
R> Maximize-Expected-Utility

IVF-MOR    Removed Deterministically
LAP-MOR    Removed Deterministically
MONEY      Removed Deterministically
MORBIDITY  Removed Deterministically

Removing IVF-MON  ...        ... IVF-MON Removed.
Removing LAP-MON  ...        ... LAP-MON Removed.
Removing LIFE  ...           ... LIFE Removed.
Removing NUM-HOSP-DAYS  ...  ... NUM-HOSP-DAYS Removed.
Removing THB  ...            ... THB Removed.
Removing IVF-THB  ...        ... IVF-THB Removed.
Removing LAP-THB  ...        ... LAP-THB Removed.
Removing SURG-COMP  ...      ... SURG-COMP Removed.
Removing ANES-DEATH  ...     ... ANES-DEATH Removed.
Removing IVF-IMPLANT  ...    ... IVF-IMPLANT Removed.
Removing NUM-IVF-CYCLES  ... ... NUM-IVF-CYCLES Removed.
Removing T-WTHICK  ...       ... T-WTHICK Removed.
Removing TREATMENT  ...      ... TREATMENT Removed.
Removing IVF-ACCEPT  ...     ... IVF-ACCEPT Removed.
Removing T-MUCOSA  ...       ... T-MUCOSA Removed.
Removing D-NODE:MARSHA  ...  ... D-NODE:MARSHA Removed.


(*) Assuming an exponential utility function with risk toler-
ance, R, equal to $5632.14

        Recommended Decision for Node:  D-NODE:MARSHA
        Optimal Treatment Choice:       LAPAROTOMY
        Certain Equivalent*:            $3723.22
```

```
(*) Assuming an exponential utility function with risk tolerance, R,
equal to $5632.14 .


R> g

Thank you for using Rachel.  Have a nice day.
```

NOTE: For brevity and simplicity, several features were left out of the current implementation of Rachel. For instance, the system does little to help the user
appraise the decision model. Rather, it simply places the user in the SU-
PERID environment where such analysis can be performed by issuing appropriate commands (not shown here). A more comprehensive implementation
of Rachel would not only display a recommendation for action, but would
also display such things as the profit (outcome) lotteries corresponding to
each alternative, a diagram of the most sensitive variables in the model, and
selected distributions of key uncertain model variables. In addition, Rachel
has no provision for automatically returning to the model formulation stage
after evaluation and appraisal. In a powerful-enough computer environment, any and all of these features would be relatively straightforward to
add to the current system.

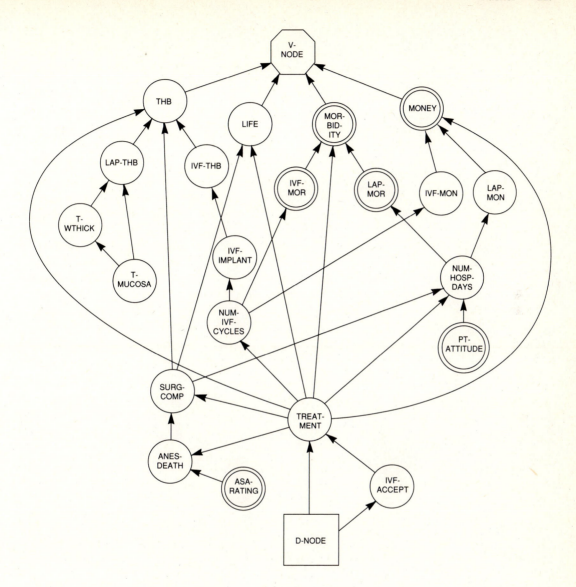

FIGURE A.1   Influence diagram built by Rachel for a patient with tubal blockage.

Glossary

This glossary defines many technical terms as they are used in the text. Whenever understanding a particular definition can benefit from referring to other terms in the glossary, the corresponding Glossary entries are noted. For simplicity, formal definitions have been avoided in favor of informal explanations supported by examples.

A

Abdominal

Pertaining to the abdomen, that portion of the body between the thorax and the pelvis.

Action

An irrevocable allocation of valuable resources. *See* Decision.

Action Axiom

An axiom that embodies a criterion for recommending action. Action axioms are of the form "IF a given condition holds, THEN the following should be done." Decision theory and, hence, decision analysis are based on the MEU action axiom. In general, the principle for action embodied by an action axiom (such as MEU) is highly defensible, and its scope is very broad. *See* Axiom, Maximum Expected Utility, and Norm.

Actuarial Expected Lifetime

An individual's statistically expected lifetime according to such parameters as age, sex, ethnic background, weight, occupation, and life-style habits, as found in current actuarial tables.

Adhesions

In infertility medicine, scar and other tissue that often develops as the result of pelvic inflammatory disease. These adhesions can have a deleterious effect on fertility by, for example, impairing the free movement of the fimbriae in one or both Fallopian tubes. Adhesions can be removed surgically and, sometimes, even as part of a laparoscopy. *See* Fallopian Tubes, Fimbriae, and Pelvic Inflammatory Disease.

Admissibility

A property of a formal criterion with respect to a normative theory. A given criterion is admissible with respect to a specific theory if (and only if) it abides by all the norms that underlie that theory. In particular, a necessary condition for a decision-making criterion to be admissible with respect to decision theory is that it never allow the decision-maker to willingly decrease his or her welfare for certain.

AI

Artificial intelligence.

Aleatory

Random; subject to chance.

Aleatory Variable

Uncertain variable. Strictly speaking, in decision analysis, an uncertain variable is called aleatory when it is explicitly modeled in probabilistic terms. An uncertain variable considered sufficiently unimportant to be represented deterministically is referred to as being *fixated*.

Algebra of Events

Basically, another name for set theory—a formal way for thinking about events, sets of events, and their properties. The algebra of events involves such concepts as *membership* (e.g., "heads" is a member of the set of possible outcomes of a fair coin toss), *union* (e.g., the set of events that constitute the human reproductive process is the union of the set of events in the male reproductive process and the set of events in the female reproductive process), and *intersection* (e.g., the intersection of the set of outcomes of the roll of a die and the set of even numbers is the set of numbers 2, 4, and 6).

Alternatives

Possible courses of action. Alternatives are often designed from more elementary decision variables. In decision analysis, making a high-quality decision requires that its decision basis contain a rich set of distinct alternatives. *See* Decision Basis and Decision Variable.

Amniocentesis [pl. Amniocenteses]
The withdrawal of a small amount of the fluid surrounding the fetus (amniotic fluid) obtained through a thin needle inserted through the abdominal wall. Amniocenteses are typically performed during the fourth month of pregnancy to test for certain birth defects and, less frequently, toward the end of the pregnancy to test for fetal maturity or blood type incompatibility between the fetus and the mother.

Ampulla [Ampullar Portion of the Fallopian Tube]
Trumpet-like, thin-walled portion of the Fallopian tube between the isthmic (narrow) portion and the fimbriated (finger-like) end of the tube. *See* Fallopian Tubes and Fimbriae.

Annuity
A stream of equal, yearly cash flows.

Appraisal
The third and last stage in using formal decision methods (and in decision analysis in particular). The objective of the appraisal stage is for the decision-maker to develop insight into the decision and determine a clear course of action. Much of the insight developed in this stage results from exploring the implications of the formal model of the decision developed during the formulation stage (i.e., from mining the model). Central to these implications is the formal recommendation for action calculated during the evaluation stage. Other implications include various forms of sensitivity of the recommendation to selected variables in the model. Additional insight is obtained by exposing key aspects of the reasoning that led to the formal decision model (i.e., by justifying the model). Possible actions following the appraisal stage include implementing the recommended course of action, revising the formal model and reevaluating it, or abandoning the analysis and doing something else. *See* Evaluation, Formulation, Justifying a Decision Model, and Mining a Decision Model.

Arteriogram
An X-ray (Roentgenogram) of an artery after injection of a radiopaque dye. *See* Radiopaque.

Artificial Intelligence (AI)
The subfield of computer science aimed at endowing computers with cognitive and perceptual abilities. Most current work in AI relies on the "physical symbol system" hypothesis—the idea that "intelligent" behavior can be automated by representing a particular domain (or, more accu-

rately, a theory about that domain) as a set of symbols and by manipulating these symbols in a way that is meaningful to the user of the AI system.

Assessment

In decision analysis, the assessment of a decision model element is the determination of its associated value or values. One speaks of assessing particular model parameters (e.g., probability distributions, risk-aversion coefficients, preference trade-off parameters) and of assessing nodes in an influence diagram.

Attention-Focusing Axiom

An axiom that embodies a criterion for focusing attention by ranking the elements of a formal decision model in order of importance. Attention-focusing axioms are of the folowing form: "Given a set of elements of a formal decision model and an objective function, the following is a ranking of the given model elements." For example, in decision analysis, deterministic sensitivity analysis (an attention-focusing method) ranks decision model elements according to the extent of their deterministic effect on the outcome of the decision (an attention-focusing axiom). *See* Attention-Focusing Method, Axiom, and Deterministic Sensitivity Analysis.

Attention-Focusing Method

An axiomatic system that contains at least one attention-focusing axiom. Deterministic sensitivity analysis, risk sensitivity, and time-preference sensitivity are attention-focusing methods in decision analysis. *See* Attention-Focusing Axiom, Deterministic Sensitivity Analysis, and Stochastic Sensitivity Analysis.

Axiom

A proposition regarded as self-evident. Although extensive reasons may be given to support the desirability of including a particular axiom in a formal system, any reasoning within the context of the formal system must view the axiom as self-evident.

Azoospermia

Absence of spermatozoa in the semen. Azoospermia is a common source of male sterility. *See* Oligospermia, Semen, Spermatozoa, and Sterility.

B

Backward Reasoning

Reasoning from conclusions to facts. *See* Forward Reasoning.

Basis Appraisal

The last of four phases in the traditional decision analysis cycle. During this phase of the cycle, the decision basis and its associated recommendation are interpreted in terms of their implications for action. At the end of this phase, the decision participants should determine whether a clear course of action has been identified or whether further analysis is necessary. *See* Appraisal, Decision Analysis Cycle, and Decision Basis.

Basis Development

The first of four phases in the traditional decision analysis cycle. The deterministic elements of the decision basis are formulated during this phase of the cycle. *See* Decision Analysis Cycle, Decision Basis, and Formulation.

Bernoulli Process

A random process consisting of a series of discrete, exchangeable trials (called Bernoulli trials), each of which can either succeed or fail with a common probability of success. If the probability of success is known, then the trials in a Bernoulli process are independent events. A common example of a Bernoulli process is a series of coin flips where, say, "heads" represents a success and "tails" a failure. In general, the probability of success in a Bernoulli process need not be one half (1/2) as in the case of a fair coin but can take any value from zero (0) to one (1).

Biopsy

The removal and examination of a small piece of tissue from the living body. As a rule, biopsies are performed to accurately establish a diagnosis.

Blastocyst

An early stage in the development of the embryo that results when fluid accumulates within the morula. The embryo reaches the blastocyst stage a few days after fertilization. *See* Morula.

Boolean Algebra

An algebraic representation of the algebra of events. The logic in most computers is based on Boolean algebra. Although there are more general formulations, most uses of Boolean algebra assume a binary domain and range, where variables and functions can only take one of two values: one (1) and zero (0). In Boolean algebra, connective operators such as AND, OR, and NOT are represented by algebraic operations. *See* Algebra of Events, Domain, and Range.

Border Node

In an influence diagram, a chance node with no direct chance predecessors. *See* Frontier Node and Influence Diagram.

Bottom-Up Reasoning

Reasoning from facts to conclusions. Same as forward reasoning.

C

Cash Flow

Net transfer of cash, accounting for both receipts (inward flows) and disbursements (outward flows) during a given period of time.

Certain Equivalent

The amount of a numeraire (e.g., money) that a decision-maker considers to be just equivalent to a given lottery on that numeraire. A certain equivalent reflects the decision-maker's values and his or her risk attitude. *See* Decision-Maker's Values, Lottery, Numeraire, and Risk Attitude.

Cervical Mucus

Secretion from the inside of the cervix produced during the menstrual cycle and during pregnancy. The consistency and composition of the cervical mucus allow it to discriminate well-formed spermatozoa from other potential entrants into the uterine cavity. In addition, its consistency and composition change drastically under hormonal action during the menstrual cycle to ensure that spermatozoa can only enter the uterine cavity at about the time of ovulation. During pregnancy, the cervical mucus serves as a plug, providing a physical and antibacterial barrier to the uterine cavity. *See* Cervix, Hormone, Menstrual Cycle, Spermatozoa, and Uterus.

Cervical Opening [Cervical Canal]

A passage inside the cervix connecting the vagina and the uterine cavity. *See* Cervix and Uterus.

Cervix

The lower constricted end of the uterus. The vagina is attached obliquely around the midportion of the cervix. *See* Uterus.

Chance Node

In an influence diagram, a node—usually drawn as an oval or a circle—that represents an uncertain variable. *See* Influence Diagram.

Chance Variable

Uncertain variable.

Circumstances

The information, constraints, and alternatives in a decision that are unique to a specific decision-maker.

Clairvoyant

A mythical character who can foretell the future, usually for a fee, provided he or she is given a well-defined question (one that passes the clarity test). The concept of the clairvoyant is useful in decision analysis for ensuring clarity of thought, particularly when assessing uncertainty. *See* Clarity Test and Wizard.

Clarity Test [Clairvoyant Test]

A test of how well a model element is defined. Although nothing (outside a formal system) can be completely defined, the clarity test allows the decision participants to determine whether such elements as variables, events, outcomes, and alternatives are sufficiently well defined to make the decision at hand. In general, a model element is well defined if a knowledgeable individual can answer questions about that model element without asking any further clarifying questions. For example, in the context of Rachel, the term *pregnancy* does not pass the clarity test, whereas the term *take-home baby* does. *See* Clairvoyant, Pregnancy, and Take-Home Baby.

Cleavage

The subdivision of the fertilized ovum into two (and then four, eight, sixteen, etc.) completely separate cells. *See* Ovum.

Coalescence

Property of formal decision models in which several parts of the model are either identical or very similar. Recognizing coalescence can greatly simplify and speed the assessment and evaluation of decision models.

Coitus

Heterosexual intercourse resulting in the introduction of semen into the female reproductive tract. *See* Semen.

Commensurate

To measure together (verb). Commensuration is a useful technique for comparing outcomes with a multitude of attributes. In practice, decision analysis depends on the ability of analysts to meaningfully commensurate complex outcomes. *See* Numeraire and Outcome.

Conception

Ill-defined term typically denoting fertilization and, possibly, implantation. *See* Fertilization and Implantation.

Condition-Recommendation Rule

A rule (i.e., a conditional statement) whose antecedent represents a narrowly defined state of the world and whose consequent represents a recommendation for action (e.g., IF you have a headache, THEN take aspirin). Although its scope is usually very limited (for instance, in comparison with MEU), a condition-recommendation rule is, strictly speaking, an action axiom. *See* Action Axiom, Conditional Statement, and Maximum Expected Utility.

Conditional Statement

A statement of the form "IF *a* THEN *b*", where *a* is referred to as its *antecedent* and *b* is referred to as its *consequent*. In artificial intelligence, conditional statements are often called rules.

Conditioning Arrow [Conditioning Arc]

In an influence diagram, an arrow that terminates on a chance node. A conditioning arrow indicates that the uncertain variable represented by the chance node at its head is probabilistically dependent on the outcome of the node at its tail. *See* Influence Diagram.

Constraints

In decision analysis, constraints are explicit limits imposed on the behavior (e.g., the possible values) of decision model elements. *Hard constraints* are inviolable; unless they are definitional in nature or they represent statements of principle, hard constraints are almost always simplifications of more elaborate soft constraints. *Soft constraints* are expressed in terms of an associated resource cost.

Context

The interrelated distinctions and interpretations that give meaning to a conversation. *See* Decision Context.

Cumulative Distribution Function

The integral of a probability density function. At any given point, r, in the range of the associated random variable, the value of the cumulative distribution function is the probability that the variable will take a value that is less than or equal to r. *See* Probability Density Function and Random Variable.

D

Data-Driven Reasoning

Reasoning from data to conclusions. Same as forward reasoning.

Decision

The commitment to irrevocably allocate valuable resources. The actual allocation of resources is an action. The verb *to decide* shares a Latin root (*caedere*, "to cut") with the word *scissors* and means "to cut down." *See* Action.

Decision Analysis (DA)

A discipline comprising the philosophy, theory, methodology, and professional practice necessary to formally address important decisions. Decision analysis includes many procedures, methods, and tools for identifying, clearly representing, and formally assessing the important aspects of a decision situation, for computing a recommended course of action by applying the MEU action axiom to a well-formed representation of the decision, and for translating the formal representation of a decision and its corresponding recommendation into insight for the decision-maker and other decision participants. *See* Appraisal, Decision Analysis Cycle, Decision Theory, Evaluation, Formulation, and Maximum Expected Utility.

Decision Analysis Cycle

Top-level procedure for carrying out a decision analysis. The traditional cycle consists of four phases: basis development, deterministic analysis, probabilistic analysis, and basis appraisal. A revised form of the cycle (discussed in Chapter 3) consists of an attention-focusing method followed by a decision method, each of which is composed of three stages: formulation, evaluation, and appraisal.

Decision Basis

The alternatives ("what you can do"), information ("what you know"), and preferences ("what you want") on which a decision is based. The decision basis constitutes a formal decision model.

Decision Context

The domain and situation of a decision. *See* Context, Decision, Domain, and Decision Situation.

Decision Domain

The domain of discourse within which a decision takes place; the generic aspects of a decision. For example, when buying a car, the fact that cars can have bench or bucket seats and that they typically run on either gasoline or diesel fuel are part of the decision domain. *See* Decision Situation.

Decision Equivalence

The relation between two influence diagrams that yield exactly the same recommendation for action and attain the same certain equivalent.

Decision-Maker

The individual responsible for allocating the valuable resources about which a decision is being made. For ethical reasons, decision analysis requires that the resources being allocated either belong to the decision-maker or that the decision-maker be empowered by their owner to allocate these resources in his best interests.

Decision-Maker's Values

Decision-maker's preferences over the possible outcomes of a decision. *See* Outcome, Preferences, and Value Model.

Decision Method

An axiomatic system that contains at least one action axiom. *See* Action Axiom.

Decision Node

In an influence diagram, a node—usually drawn as a retangle or a square—that represents a decision among possible alternatives.

Decision Participants

The individuals whose authority and knowledge make them participants in a given decision, including the decision-maker, his or her appointed experts, one or more decision analysts, and anyone else actively involved in the decision process.

Decision Situation

The specific circumstances and preferences of the decision-maker as they pertain to the decision; the unique aspects of a decision. For example, when buying a car, placing a higher value on safety than fuel efficiency and stating that the car must be useful on unpaved roads are elements of the decision situation. *See* Decision Domain.

Decision Support System (DSS)

An information-processing system designed specifically to address the information needs of decision-makers. Decision support systems evolved from data base and management information systems.

Decision System

A system that makes recommendations for action. Decision systems are typically implemented on a computer.

Decision Theory

An axiomatic system for representing decision situations and deducing a recommendation for action based on well-defined representations of decisions. Decision theory assumes the axioms of both logic and probability theory and augments them with a set of axioms about preferences (utility theory). Decision analysis is based on decision theory, much like engineering is based on physics or medicine is based on chemistry and biology. *See* Decision Analysis and Maximum Expected Utility.

Decision Tree

A graphical and mathematical representation of a decision problem. A decision tree is a connected tree with two types of nodes—decision and chance—and two types of branches between nodes—probabilistic (emanating from a chance node) and alternative (emanating from a decision node). Decision trees are well-defined mathematical structures that can be evaluated to produce a recommended course of action and to answer certain probabilistic and inferential questions. *See* Influence Diagram.

Decision Variable

A formal variable denoting the choice about a single element of a decision (e.g., budget level or whether to undergo surgery). An alternative is typically defined in terms of particular settings of several decision variables. For example, a car purchasing alternative may involve such decision variables as price, model, options, time of purchase, and choice of dealer. Some decision variables arise as a consequence of the domain in which the decision is being made, while others result from the decision-maker's unique circumstances. *See* Alternatives.

Decomposing a Node

The addition of direct predecessors (or direct predecessor relations by adding arrows) to a node in an influence diagram as a result of an indirect assessment. *See* Indirect Assessment and Influence Diagram.

Descriptive

A methodology, endeavor, or theory is descriptive when its primary function is to describe a view of the world (e.g., science). A descriptive methodology serves to issue statements involving the term *is* (e.g., a horse *is* a four-legged mammal; force *is* equal to mass times acceleration). *See* Normative and Prescriptive.

Deterministic

Not subject to chance. *See* Stochastic.

Deterministic Analysis

The second of four phases in the traditional decision analysis cycle. During this phase of the cycle, the decision basis is subjected to deterministic sensitivity analysis to identify those model elements worthy of probabilistic modeling. *See* Decision Analysis Cycle, Decision Basis, and Deterministic Sensitivity Analysis.

Deterministic Assessment

An indirect assessment that assigns a deterministic function to the node being assessed. Each argument of the assigned function corresponds to one of the variables represented by the node's direct predecessors. If these direct predecessors are not already part of the influence diagram, they are added as part of the deterministic assessment. *See* Deterministic, Indirect Assessment, and Stochastic Assessment.

Deterministic Model [Deterministic Basis]

A formal deterministic model of the decision situation at hand. The deterministic model maps possible outcome scenarios to a corresponding value of a single numeraire and is typically implemented as a computer program or, in simpler situations, as a table or a mathematical function.

The deterministic model includes the decision-maker's value model. *See* Deterministic, Numeraire, and Value Model.

Deterministic Sensitivity Analysis

Primary activity during the deterministic analysis phase of the decision analysis cycle. Deterministic sensitivity analysis is an attention-focusing method whose associated attention-focusing axiom ranks the elements of the decision basis according to how much the objective function (deterministic model) changes as these elements vary through their range of possible values. *See* Attention-Focusing Axiom, Attention-Focusing Method, Decision Basis, Deterministic Analysis, and Deterministic Model.

Direct Assessment

The unconditional assessment of a frontier node in an influence diagram. Directly assessing a node implies assigning either an unconditioned probability distribution or a single value to it. Direct assessments do not add structure (nodes and/or arrows) to the influence diagram and can be stored as rules in a knowledge base. *See* Frontier Node, Indirect Assessment, Knowledge Base, and Rule.

Distended

Enlarged or expanded from internal pressure.

Domain

In decision-making, the generic subject matter with respect to which a decision is being made. *See* Decision Domain. In mathematics, the domain of a function is the set of values its arguments can take. *See* Range.

Dominating Alternative

In a decision, an alternative that would be preferred given the vast majority of reasonable circumstances and preferences. Decision analysis is not particularly beneficial when there is an obvious dominating alternative.

DSS

Decision support system.

Dynamic

Time-dependent.

E

Ectopic Pregnancy [Tubal Pregnancy]

A pregnancy outside the uterine cavity, most commonly occurring in one of the Fallopian tubes. If it does not terminate by itself, an ectopic pregnancy usually needs to be terminated by surgery. (*Note*: New drugs may soon make surgery unnecessary for treating ectopic pregnancies.)

Ejaculation

Ejection of the seminal fluids from the urethra in the male. *See* Semen and Urethra.

Elasticity

In economics, the elasticity of demand for (supply of) a good is the percentage decrease (increase) in the volume of sales that would be induced by a 1 percent increase in price. For example, when elasticity is equal to one (1), the percentage changes in price and volume will equal each other.

Embryo

In humans, the stage of development between roughly the third day and the eighth week (inclusive) after fertilization. After the eighth week, the embryo is called a fetus. *See* Fetus.

Emission

The passage of semen and associated secretions into the urethra in preparation for ejaculation. *See* Ejaculation, Semen, and Urethra.

Endocrine

Pertaining to a gland that secretes a hormone directly into the blood stream; hormonal. *See* Hormone.

Endometrial Biopsy

Removal (excision) of a small portion of endometrial tissue for microscopic examination. The tissue is removed through the cervix with either local or no anesthesia. In a more extensive version of the endometrial biopsy, called *dilation and curettage* (D&C), a much larger portion of the endometrial tissue is removed under local, general, or spinal anesthesia. *See* Biopsy, Cervix, and Endometrium.

Endometrium

Mucous membrane lining the uterine cavity. From puberty to menopause, the endometrium is subject to the menstrual cycle within which it undergoes major changes—from a thin lining to a thick vascular membrane—on about a monthly basis. Besides blood, a large portion of the material expelled during menstruation consists of shedded endometrial tissue. *See* Menstrual Cycle, Menstruation, and Uterus.

Endoscopy

The visual inspection of any body cavity by means of an optical instrument called an endoscope. Many modern endoscopes use fiber-optic technology. *See* Fiber Optics.

Etiology

The study of the causes of disease.

Evaluation

The second and most algorithmic stage in using formal decision methods (and in decision analysis in particular). The objective of the evaluation stage is to produce a formal recommendation—and associated sensitivities—from a formal model of the decision situation. *See* Appraisal and Formulation.

Excess Distribution Function

A close relative of the cumulative distribution function. At any given point, r, in the range of the associated random variable, the value of the excess distribution function is the probability that the variable will take a value that is greater than or equal to r. The excess distribution function can be obtained by subtracting the cumulative distribution function from unity (1). *See* Cumulative Distribution Function, Probability Density Function, and Random Variable.

Expansion

One of two interrelated activities that take place in formulating decision models. Decision models are expanded in an attempt to include all pertinent aspects of a decision in its analysis. *See* Formulation and Reduction.

Expert System

A computer system designed to capture the skills and factual knowledge of one or more individuals. To achieve high levels of performance, expert systems typically combine traditional software engineering methods with techniques from artificial intelligence research and other advanced fields such as operations research and data base design. In addition, most large expert systems rely on techniques that are germane to their specific domain and that would typically not be associated with expert-system technology (e.g., simulation and digital signal processing). *See* Artificial Intelligence and Knowledge Engineering.

Exponential Utility Function

A utility function exhibiting constant risk aversion. The exponential utility function is the most commonly used utility function because it is a good model of risk attitude for most decision situations and because it is simple to assess. *See* Utility Function.

Extrapolability

A property of locally correct formal methods whose conclusions to complex problems (those not amenable to intuitive answers) are intuitively satisfactory from a belief that the reasoning embodied by the formal method remains valid as the size and complexity of the problem increases. *See* Local Correctness.

F

Fallopian Tubes

Two muscular passages that transport ova from the ovaries to the uterus and spermatozoa from the uterus to the ova. *See* Ampulla, Fimbriae, Ovaries, Ovum, Spermatozoa, and Uterus.

Fertilization

Impregnation of the ovum (the female germ cell) by a spermatozoon (the male germ cell). Usually takes place in the ampullar region of the Fallopian tube. Fertilization is a process that begins with the penetration of the ovum (called the secondary oocyte at this point in the reproduction process) by the spermatozoon and is completed with the fusion of the nuclei of these two cells. *See* Ampulla, Fallopian Tubes, Ovum, and Spermatozoa.

Fetus

In humans, the stage of development between the eighth week after fertilization and birth. Until the eighth week, the fetus is called an embryo. *See* Embryo.

Fiber Optics

An optical technology that allows light to be transmitted along a curved path. The technique relies on the use of thin, homogeneous, transparent glass fibers enclosed by another material with a lower index of refraction. These fibers can transmit light throughout their length by internal reflections.

Fimbriae [s. Fimbria]

Finger-like projections protruding from the ovarian end of the Fallopian tubes. The longest of these on each Fallopian tube, called the fimbria ovarica, is attached to the ovary located on the same side as that tube. *See* Fallopian Tubes and Ovaries.

First-Order Predicate Calculus (FOPC)

A restricted form of predicate calculus where quantified variables can take only the value of objects (e.g., a horse), not the value of functions (e.g., mother-of). *See* Predicate Calculus.

First-Order Prefix Predicate Calculus (FOPPC)

A form of first-order predicate calculus particularly amenable for use in computer applications. A statement like "*a* OR *b*" in more traditional *infix* notation would be stated as "(OR *a b*)" in *prefix* notation. *See* First-Order Predicate Calculus.

Follicle

A group of cells usually containing a fluid-filled cavity.

Follicle-Stimulating Hormone (FSH)

A hormone produced by the pituitary gland. In the female, FSH promotes the growth and development of the ovarian follicle and, with luteinizing hormone (LH), enhances secretion of the hormone estrogen by the ovary. In the male, together with the hormone testosterone, it promotes spermatogenesis. *See* Hormone, Ovarian Hormonal Secretions, Ovaries, and Spermatogenesis.

Follicular Phase [Proliferative Phase]

A phase of the menstrual cycle; specifically, the preovulatory or growth phase of the endometrium. *See* Endometrium and Menstrual Cycle.

FOPC

First-order predicate calculus.

FOPPC

First-order prefix predicate calculus.

Formulation

The first and often the most challenging stage in using formal decision methods (and in decision analysis in particular). The objective of the formulation stage is to develop a formal model of a given decision. *See* Appraisal, Evaluation, Expansion, and Reduction.

Forward Reasoning

Reasoning from facts to conclusions. *See* Backward Reasoning.

Frontier Node

A border node whose associated probability distribution has not been assessed. Until it is fully assessed, any influence diagram containing one or more frontier nodes is not well formed. *See* Border Node and Well-Formed Influence Diagram.

FSH

Follicle-stimulating hormone.

G

Genitalia

Reproductive organs.

Geometric Probability Mass Function

First-order Pascal probability mass function. *See* Pascal Probability Mass Function.

Goal-Directed Reasoning

Reasoning from goals to facts. Same as backward reasoning.

Graafian Follicle [Vesicular Follicle]

A mature vesicular follicle containing a nearly mature ovum (oocyte) that, upon rupture of the follicle, is discharged from the ovary. Between puberty and menopause, except during pregnancy, a Graafian follicle develops every menstrual cycle. *See* Follicle, Menopause, Menstrual Cycle, Ovaries, Ovum, and Puberty.

Graafian Stage

The last stage of an ovarian follicle. The Graafian stage occurs immediately prior to ovulation. *See* Graafian Follicle and Ovulation.

H
Heuristics

Rules of thumb. Practical guidelines for accomplishing specific tasks. Heuristics are often the result of individual or collective experience in a particular domain, and although they sometimes embody more general principles, they tend to deal with narrowly defined situations.

Hormone

A substance originating in an organ, gland, or other structure and conveyed through the blood to another part of the body, stimulating the latter by chemical action.

Hydrosalpinx [Hydrosalpinges]

Obliteration of the fimbriated end of the Fallopian tube by accumulation of fluid. The tube becomes distended (enlarged, balloon-like). *See* Fallopian Tubes and Fimbriae.

Hysterosalpingogram

X-Ray (Roentgenogram) of the uterus and Fallopian tubes. A hysterosalpingogram typically requires inserting a radiopaque dye through the cervix (a relatively painful procedure). *See* Cervix, Fallopian Tubes, Radiopaque, and Uterus.

I
ID

Influence diagram.

IDS

Intelligent decision system.

Implantation

Embedding of the developing blastocyst in the endometrium six or seven days following fertilization. Implantation can also occur at a place other than in the uterus, producing an ectopic pregnancy. *See* Blastocyst, Ectopic Pregnancy, Endometrium, Fertilization, and Uterus.

In Utero

Within the uterus.

In-Vitro Fertilization (IVF)

Fertilization outside the human body (literally, in glass). *See* Fertilization and Test-Tube Baby.

Inadmissible

Not admissible. *See* Admissibility.

Incidence

The fraction (or percent) of a population that satisfies a given criterion (e.g., the fraction of people affected with a given disease at a given time). *See* Prevalence.

Incipient Influence Diagram

A minimal influence diagram in which the value node has been assessed and a corresponding set of frontier nodes that are direct predecessors of the value node has been added to the diagram. Until it is fully assessed, an incipient influence diagram is not well formed. *See* Frontier Node, Influence Diagram, Minimal Influence Diagram, and Well-Formed Influence Diagram.

Income Stream

A series of net cash flows occurring over time. The income stream of an individual typically represents the magnitude, sign, and timing of his or her future earnings. *See* Cash Flow and Net Present Value.

Indicated Assessment

A type of direct (i.e., unconditional) assessment in which knowing that a particular set of preconditions holds is sufficient to assign an unconditional probability distribution or a single deterministic value to an uncertain variable represented by a frontier node. For example, knowing that someone we trust has asserted that a given coin is fair and knowing that the coin will be tossed by someone with no exceptional coin-tossing abilities may be sufficient to assign a probability of one half (1/2) that the coin flip will come out "heads." To be both valid and useful, an indicated assessment need not address all the possible cases of its associated preconditions (e.g., the above example need not address the case where the coin is known not to be fair). Indicated assessments do not add structure (nodes and/or arrows) to the influence diagram and can be stored as rules in a knowledge base. In an intelligent decision system, indicated assessments are looked up and then reviewed rather than being directly assessed by the user. *See* Direct Assessment, Frontier Node, Knowledge Base, and Rule.

Indicator Function

A function that maps the occurrence of a binary event (i.e., an event with two possible outcomes) onto the set {0, 1}. When the event occurs, the indicator function takes the value "one" (1); otherwise, it takes the value "zero" (0). An indicator function can also be constructed for events with more than two possible outcomes. In those cases, the range of the function must have a corresponding number of possible values.

Indirect Assessment

The *conditional* assessment of a frontier node in an influence diagram. An indirect assessment can be either deterministic—the frontier node is assessed through a deterministic function of its direct predecessors—or stochastic—the node is assigned a probability distribution conditioned on the outcomes of its direct predecessors. Indirect assessments add structure (nodes and/or arrows) to the influence diagram and can be stored as rules in a knowledge base. *See* Direct Assessment, Frontier Node, Knowledge Base, and Rule.

Inference Engine

A computer program that embodies one or more general-purpose problem-solving algorithms that are largely independent of any specific domain of discourse. Inference engines take various forms, but most can be viewed as implementing a deduction mechanism based on either propositional or predicate calculi. Typically, inference engines operate on associated knowledge bases. For instance, the computer language Prolog is mostly a knowledge representation language and an inference engine that operates on statements in that language. *See* Knowledge Base, Predicate Calculus, and Propositional Calculus.

Infertility

A greatly decreased capacity to reproduce. *See* Sterility.

Influence Diagram (ID)

A graphical and mathematical representation of probabilistic inference and decision problems. An ID is an acyclic, directed graph with two types of nodes—decision and chance—and two types of arrows (or arcs) between nodes—conditioning (ending on a chance node) and informational (ending on a decision node). Often, a single chance node in an ID is identified as its value node. In an ID, sets such as predecessors, successors, and direct (immediate) predecessors and successors of a node are defined in the obvious manner. Influence diagrams are hierarchical and can be defined either solely in terms of their structure or in greater detail in terms of the functional and numerical relation between diagram elements. An ID that is consistently defined at all levels—structure, function, and number—is a well-defined mathematical representation and is referred to as a well-formed influence diagram (WFID). When a WFID contains at least one decision node directly or indirectly influencing a value node, it is referred to as a well-formed decision influence diagram (WFDID). WFIDs can be evaluated using reversal and removal operations to yield answers to a large class of probabilistic, inferential, and decision questions. WFDIDs can also be evaluated to produce a recommended course of action. IDs are a generalization of decision trees. *See* Chance Node, Decision Node, Decision Tree, Removal, Reversal, and Value Node.

Information

The decision participants' knowledge of decision elements—both deterministic and stochastic—as it pertains to the decision at hand. This information is an essential part of a decision basis. In particular, a decision basis must incorporate information about the possible consequences of action. In the case of stochastic decision elements, this information must include a range of possible outcomes and a probability distribution over this range. *See* Decision Basis, Decision Participants, Probability Distribution, and Range.

Informational Arrow [Informational Arc]

In an influence diagram, an arrow that terminates on a decision node. An informational arrow indicates that the decision at its head is made with perfect knowledge of the outcome of the variable represented by the node at its tail. *See* Decision Node and Influence Diagram.

Inpatient

A patient who is hospitalized.

Intelligent Decision System (IDS)

A decision system that delivers expert-level decision analysis assistance. As part of this assistance, the IDS may provide access to a substantial knowledge base in the domain of the decision. *See* Decision Analysis, Decision System, and Knowledge Base.

Interarrival Time

In a Bernoulli or similar random process (e.g., Poisson), the number of trials (amount of time) between (and including) successes. The first-order interarrival time denotes the temporal distance between consecutive successes; the nth-order interarrival time denotes the temporal distance between a given success and the end of a series of n consecutive successes.

Internal Spermatic Vein Ligation (ISVL)

Ligation of the vein that supplies a scrotal varicocele. Scrotal varicoceles are most common on the left side of the scrotum. Internal spermatic vein ligation involves surgery under general anesthesia. Often referred to (somewhat incorrectly) as a varicocelectomy. *See* Ligation, Scrotal Varicocele, and Scrotum.

Invasiveness

In medicine, a procedure is invasive when it involves puncturing the skin or inserting an instrument into the body.

ISVL

Internal spermatic vein ligation.

IVF

In-vitro fertilization.

J

Justifying a Decision Model

Exploring and explaining the reasoning that led to the formulation of a particular decision model. *See* Appraisal and Mining a Decision Model.

K

KB

Knowledge base.

Knowledge Base (KB)

A collection of facts and rules describing a particular domain. Knowledge bases are written in a knowledge representation language (e.g., predicate calculus). A knowledge base—which contains mostly *declarative* knowledge about a given domain of discourse—is typically processed by an inference engine—which embodies mostly *procedural* knowledge about how to make logical deductions. *See* Inference Engine, Knowledge Representation Language, Predicate Calculus, and Rule.

Knowledge Engineering

The art of formalizing knowledge. Typically, the term *knowledge engineering* is used in reference to building expert systems. True to its name, the engineering of knowledge requires creativity and an appreciation for the specific context in which the knowledge will be used. *See* Context.

Knowledge Representation Language

A language for building knowledge bases. Knowledge representation languages can be based on one or more representation forms, including logical rules, frames, scripts, and semantic nets (or networks) [Nilsson, 1980; Charniak *et al.*, 1987], and on more traditional data structures like arrays and matrices. Influence diagrams are a knowledge representation language for decision problems. *See* Influence Diagram and Knowledge Base.

L

Laparoscopy

Internal exploration of the abdomen employing a type of fiber-optic endoscope called a laparoscope. Laparoscopy is invasive (entry is usually performed through the umbilicus or belly button) and constitutes a minor surgical procedure involving either local or general anesthesia. Besides a visual inspection, a laparoscopy usually involves inserting one or more tools to manipulate various abdominal structures. *See* Abdominal, Endoscopy, Fiber Optics, and Invasiveness.

Laparotomy

The surgical opening of the abdomen.

LH

Luteinizing hormone.

Ligation

The application of a thread or wire to constrict a vessel or other structure by tying it.

Local Correctness

A property of formal methods whose conclusions agree with intuition when both are used to address the same simple (toy) problems. *See* Toy Problem.

Lottery

An uncertain event whose outcome is obtained from a set of collectively exhaustive and mutually exclusive possibilities according to a corresponding probability distribution. *See* Probability Distribution.

Luteinizing Hormone (LH)

Hormone produced by the pituitary gland. Literally, "yellowing" hormone. In the male, LH stimulates the production of the hormone testosterone. In the female, it stimulates ovulation and the subsequent production of the hormone progesterone by the resulting corpus luteum (yellow body). *See* Hormone and Ovulation.

M

Maximum Expected Utility (MEU)

Maximum expected utility is the action axiom embodied by decision theory. As an axiom, MEU states the following: "IF you have a model of your decision in the language of decision theory (e.g., a decision tree or an influence diagram) that you believe adequately represents your decision problem, THEN you should act so as to maximize the expected value of your utility function as described in your model." *See* Action Axiom, Decision Theory, Decision Tree, Influence Diagram, and Utility Function.

Meiotic Division [Maturation Division, Meiosis]
Meiotic division is the process of germ cell formation. In human reproduction, there are two meiotic divisions. In the male, these divisions are part of the ongoing process of spermatogenesis and are completed before ejaculation. In the female, the first meiotic division ends at about the time of ovulation and produces the first polar body. (This division actually starts before birth, which could be over 40 years earlier.) The second meiotic division in the female takes place after the spermatozoon enters the ovum, producing the second polar body. *See* Ejaculation, Ovulation, Ovum, Polar Body, Spermatogenesis, and Spermatozoa.

Menopause
Cessation of menstruation.

Menstrual Cycle
Period extending from the onset of one menstruation to the onset of the next. The cycle is divided into several consecutive phases (menstrual, proliferative, and secretory) according to changes in the endometrium. *See* Endometrium and Menstruation.

Menstruation
Cyclic discharge of blood, mucus, and cellular debris from the uterus. Menstruation marks the readjustment of the uterus in preparation for the next ovulation and possible implantation. *See* Implantation, Ovulation, and Uterus.

MEU
Maximum expected utility.

Minimal Influence Diagram
A well-formed decision influence diagram (WFDID) with only a decision node directly influencing a value node. *See* Decision Node, Value Node, and Well-Formed Decision Influence Diagram.

Mining a Decision Model
Extracting information (e.g., sensitivity, value of information, and value of control) from a given decision model. *See* Appraisal and Justifying a Decision Model.

Modus Ponens [Rule of Detachment]
The logical syllogism that states the following: IF two sentences, a and b, are accepted as true, where a has the form of an implication and b matches

(strictly speaking, *unifies* with) the antecedent of *a*, THEN the consequent of *a*, which is a sentence (with its variables bound as needed to unify with *b*), may also be recognized as true. For example: *a* = for all *x*, IF *x* is a horse, THEN *x* is a mammal; *b* = Henry is a horse; therefore, using modus ponens, we can conclude that Henry is a mammal. *See* Syllogism.

Money Pump

A situation whereby an individual is made to willingly give away all his or her assets. A "money pump" situation can always be constructed for individuals with *intransitive* preferences (i.e., for whom preferring outcome *A* to outcome *B* and outcome *B* to outcome *C* does *not* imply that outcome *A* is preferred to outcome *C*). *See* Admissibility.

Morbidity

Strictly speaking, the quality of being caused by disease. The medical community sometimes uses this term more broadly to denote the frequency and degree of discomfort under a given set of circumstances. For example, we can speak of the morbidity associated with surgery, invasive testing, or drug therapies. The term is used in this broader sense in the book. *See* Invasiveness.

Morphology

Science of structure and form, without regard to function.

Mortality

The frequency of deaths under a given set of circumstances (e.g., from surgery or from car accidents).

Morula

An early stage in the development of the embryo. The morula is a mass of about fifty (50) to one hundred (100) cells that results from cleavage of the zygote. *See* Cleavage, Embryo, and Zygote.

Motile

Endowed with motility. The percentage of motile spermatozoa is an important measurement in semen analyses. *See* Motility, Semen Analysis, and Spermatozoa.

Motility

The ability to move spontaneously.

N
Neonatal Period

The first four weeks after birth.

Net Present Value (NPV)

The current value of a set of future outcomes. In finance, net present value is often computed on a series of positive and negative future cash flows (an income stream) by discounting them with appropriate powers of a discount (interest) rate. By using an appropriate numeraire, net present value techniques can be used to measure the value of future multiattribute outcome streams. *See* Income Stream and Numeraire.

No-Forgetting Arrows [No-Forgetting Arcs]

Arrows into decision nodes included in an influence diagram to satisfy the no-forgetting condition. *See* Influence Diagram and No-Forgetting Condition.

No-Forgetting Condition

The condition that whatever is known at the time a decision is made (i.e., choices at earlier decisions and/or values of observed uncertain variables) is remembered for subsequent decisions.

Norm

A principle of right action. *See* Normative.

Normative

A methodology, endeavor, or theory is normative when it is prescriptive and its prescriptions are based on a set of broadly applicable and highly defensible norms applied to a representation of the decision-maker's perception of the decision at hand (e.g., decision analysis and predicate logic). The norms in a normative methodology constitute one or more action axioms. *See* Action Axiom, Descriptive, Norm, and Prescriptive.

NPV

Net present value.

Numeraire

A unit of measure used as the basis for comparing a collection of distinct attributes. The most commonly used numeraire is "money"; other common numeraires include "remaining lifetime" and "utiles" or other dimensionless quantities. *See* Commensurate and Utiles.

O

Objective Function

Criterion for optimizing among a set of possible choices. In decision analysis, the objective function is the utility function applied to the value model. *See* Optimizing, Utility Function, and Value Model.

Oligospermia [Oligoazoospermia]

Low sperm concentration. Oligospermia is a common source of male infertility. *See* Azoospermia, Infertility, and Sperm Concentration.

Optimizing

Selecting the best from a set of possible options. Strictly speaking, the concepts of optimizing and optimal choice are only defined when the set of possible options and the criterion for selecting among them are formally defined. However, both terms are often used in common language to refer to seemingly good choices. *See* Objective Function and Satisficing.

Outcome

The state of the world after all decisions and uncertainties have been resolved (i.e., when an alternative has been selected for each decision and each uncertain variable has taken a particular value). In decision analysis, an outcome is described in terms of attributes about which the decision-maker has *direct* preferences. For instance, while a businessman about to introduce a new product would like to have a large market share, what he ultimately cares about is profits, on which he has a direct preference. (He only has an *indirect* preference on market share.) An important element of the philosophy of decision analysis is a distinction between decisions under uncertainty and outcomes. Thus, when decisions are made under uncertainty, a good (bad) decision *does not guarantee* a good (bad) outcome and vice versa. *See* Preferences.

Outpatient

A patient who receives medical care but is not hospitalized. *See* Inpatient.

Ovarian Hormonal Secretions

Hormones produced by the ovaries. The most important of these are estrogen (secreted by the follicles and corpus luteum) and progesterone (secreted by the corpus luteum). *See* Hormone and Ovaries.

Ovaries

Two plum-shaped glands in the female—one on each side of the uterus—that produce the female germ cell (the ovum) and many hormones (including estrogen and progesterone). *See* Hormone and Ovum.

Ovulation

Expulsion of the female germ cell (ovum) from a ruptured Graafian follicle. *See* Graafian Follicle.

Ovum [pl. Ova]

General term referring to the female germ cell at any stage of development.

Ovum Pickup

Passage of the ovum from the ovary to either Fallopian tube via its fimbriae. *See* Fallopian Tubes and Fimbriae.

Ownership

In decision analysis, ownership of a decision denotes a situation where the decision-maker has clarity of action and has made a commitment to act. In contrast, if the decision-maker feels the recommendation is merely someone else's choice, then he or she does not *own* the decision. Ownership is critical when the time comes to implement a decision. *See* Action and Decision.

P
Pascal Probability Mass Function
Probability of the number of Bernoulli trials required to produce the nth success. This number of trials is known as the nth-order interarrival (or waiting) time of the associated Bernoulli process. For example, the probability of the number of times we might need to flip a fair coin until we get a third "head" would be described by a third-order Pascal PMF, with probability of success equal to $1/2$. *See* Bernoulli Process, Interarrival Time, and Probability Mass Function. Also, see equation 8.4 in the text (Chapter 8) for a mathematical description.

Pathology
Study of the nature of disease. Strictly speaking, *pathology* refers to the study of abnormal structure, and *pathophysiology* refers to the study of abnormal function.

PDF
Probability density function.

Pedigree
The origin of an assertion or a declaration, including its source and the time when it was made. In the case of an assertion, the pedigree may also contain such other elements as certifications, justifications, disclaimers, and references. For example, the pedigree of a probability distribution (an assertion) consists of the name of the individual from whom the distribution was obtained, the time when it was obtained, and (optionally) a reference to any data used in the assessment. A pedigree may be either *pure* (when its source is a single individual) or *mixed* (when it is derived from statements made by several individuals). An assertion or a declaration is a *mongrel* when its pedigree is unknown or so mixed that its source is untraceable.

Pelvic Inflammatory Disease (PID)
Disorder occurring when infectious agents invade the uterus and spread to the Fallopian tubes, ovaries, and/or surrounding tissues. It is most common in young, sexually active women and may lead to blockage of one or both Fallopian tubes and prevent fertilization and/or implantation. *See* Fallopian Tubes, Fertilization, Implantation, Ovaries, and Uterus.

Physiology
The science of the function of cells, tissues, and organs of living organisms.

PID

Pelvic inflammatory disease.

Placenta

The vascular organ that unites the fetus to the maternal uterus. The placenta provides the primary means for the fetus to obtain nutrients from the mother and to discard waste products. *See* Fetus and Uterus.

PMF

Probability mass function.

Polar Body, First (Second)

A by-product of the first (second) meiotic division of the ovum. The first (second) polar body is a small cell containing half the usual number of chromosomes (a haploid number) and no cytoplasm; it disintegrates shortly after it is produced. *See* Meiotic Division and Ovum.

Postcoital Test

Test performed to determine whether one or more spermatozoa have been able to penetrate the cervical mucus. The test is performed by observing a sample of the female's cervical mucus under the microscope from a few hours to a couple of days after intercourse. For best results, the postcoital test is performed one or two days before the woman's expected ovulation date. A positive postcoital test is an indication of male fertility and a positive, albeit weaker, indication of proper hormonal function in the female partner. *See* Cervical Mucus, Hormone, Ovulation, and Spermatozoa.

Predicate Calculus

A language (syntax and grammar) that extends the propositional calculus by adding quantification: "For All *x*..." (universal quantification) and "There exists an *x*..." (existential quantification). The predicate calculus helps us formalize statements like: "All horses are mammals" and "At least one horse is named Henry." Most applications of the predicate calculus use a restricted form—called the first-order predicate calculus. *See* First-Order Predicate Calculus and Propositional Calculus.

Preferences

A statement of the satisfaction one receives from particular states of the world. Formally, one prefers state *A* to state *B* if, given a deterministic choice between these two states, one would choose *A*. Preferences can be either *direct* (when they pertain to attributes that directly constitute the outcomes of a decision) or *indirect* (when they pertain to attributes that only indirectly relate to the outcomes of a decision). For example, while a patient undergoing surgery may have only indirect preferences over the type of anesthetic to be used, he or she has direct preferences over the discomfort, monetary effects, and length-of-life effects that might result from the chosen anesthetic. Decision theory requires that preferences over the possible outcomes of a decision be *transitive* (i.e., if *A* is preferred to *B* and *B* is preferred to *C*, then *A* is preferred to *C*). *See* Decision Theory, Deterministic, and Outcome.

Pregnancy

Ill-defined term denoting the condition of a woman carrying a live embryo or fetus. Depending on the context, the onset of pregnancy can be defined as either fertilization, implantation (the most common definition), or the time when fetal growth produces a noticeable outside change in the mother's body. *See* Embryo, Fertilization, Fetus, and Implantation.

Prescriptive

A methodology, endeavor, or theory is prescriptive when its primary function is to direct action (e.g., engineering, decision analysis). A prescriptive methodology serves to issue statements with the term *should* or *ought* (e.g., a bridge *should* be built to withstand strong winds; an event *should* be well-defined prior to assessing a corresponding probability distribution) and must include at least one action axiom. *See* Action Axiom, Descriptive, and Normative.

Presenting

In medicine, a patient is said to *present with* a particular condition when this condition is his or her main reason for seeking medical help. This condition is referred to as the patient's *presenting condition*.

Prevalence

The number of individuals in a population that satisfy a given criterion (e.g., the number of people affected with a given disease at a given time). *See* Incidence.

Probabilistic Analysis

The third of four phases in the traditional decision analysis cycle. During this phase, the elements of the decision basis worthy of probabilistic modeling are probabilistically assessed and a formal decision-theoretic (MEU) recommendation (with associated sensitivities) is derived from the resulting probabilistic model. *See* Decision Analysis Cycle, Decision Basis, Evaluation, and Maximum Expected Utility.

Probability Density Function (PDF)

A function of a continuous uncertain variable whose integral over an interval gives the probability that the variable's outcome will fall within that interval. When the uncertain variable is a random variable (i.e., when its range is strictly numerical), two related functions are defined with respect to this integral: for semi-infinite intervals bounded on the top, the integral is referred to as the variable's *cumulative distribution function*; for semi-infinite intervals bounded on the bottom, the integral is referred to as the variable's *excess distribution function*. *See* Cumulative Distribution Function, Excess Distribution Function, Random Variable, and Uncertain Variable.

Probability Distribution

Strictly speaking, a probability mass function. In practice, the term probability distribution is often used to denote both probability mass functions and probability density functions. The term is used in this broader sense in the book. *See* Probability Density Function and Probability Mass Function.

Probability Mass Function (PMF)

A function of a discrete uncertain variable whose value for each possible outcome of the variable is the probability that the outcome will obtain. *See* Uncertain Variable.

Probability Theory

A branch of mathematics concerned with measuring and reasoning about uncertainty. Probability theory was first formalized by Laplace and later axiomatized by Kolmogoroff. Lindley and others have shown that probability is the only sensible way to measure uncertainty for decision-making.

Profit Lottery [Outcome Lottery]

A lottery over the numeraire of a decision model given a particular set of choices (usually the optimal set) for the model's decision variables and reflecting all the uncertainties represented in the model. A profit lottery is typically depicted in the form of a cumulative distribution function. See Cumulative Distribution Function, Decision Variable, Lottery, and Numeraire

Proliferative Phase

Follicular phase.

Propositional Calculus

A language (syntax and grammar) that embodies the algebra of events. The propositional calculus helps us formalize statements like the following: "IF it is true that Tweety is a bird and he is either hungry or thirsty, THEN it is also true that he is either a hungry bird or a thirsty bird"; or "IF it rained last Monday, THEN it rained last week." *See* Algebra of Events.

Puberty

The period during which an individual attains the capability of sexual reproduction. Besides genital organ maturation, puberty involves the development of secondary sexual characteristics (e.g., pubic hair) and, in the female, the onset of menstruation. *See* Genitalia and Menstruation.

R
Radiopaque

Property of materials that are opaque to X-rays.

Random Variable

An uncertain variable whose range is strictly numerical. *See* Range and Uncertain Variable.

Range

The range of a function or a variable is the set of its possible values. *See* Domain.

Reduction

One of two interrelated activities that take place in formulating decisions. Decision models are reduced to make them both intuitive and tractable. *See* Expansion and Formulation.

Removal

One of two elementary operations in evaluating well-formed influence diagrams (WFIDs). Node A can be removed into *chance* node B when:

1. A and B have an identical set of direct predecessors (except for A's arrow into B)—conditioning arrows may be added as needed to achieve this condition, as long as no cycles are created;

2. B is the only direct successor of A.

Mathematically, removal corresponds to different operations when A is a chance node and when A is a decision node.

- For general WFIDs, removal is only defined when A is a chance node—removing it into B corresponds to integrating A's associated probability distribution into B's.

- However, when the diagram is a well-formed *decision* influence diagram (WFDID) and B is its value node, removal is defined both when A is a chance node and when A is a decision node.

  a. When A is a chance node, in addition to integrating A's associated probability distribution into B's, removing A involves calculating the decision-maker's expected utility with respect to A.

  b. When A is a decision node, removing A corresponds to maximizing the decision-maker's expected utility with respect to A.

Removing A deletes it from the evaluated diagram. *See* Chance Node, Decision Node, Probability Distribution, Reversal, Value Node, Well-Formed Decision Influence Diagram, and Well-Formed Influence Diagram.

Reversal

One of two elementary operations in evaluating well-formed influence diagrams. An arrow between chance nodes A and B can be reversed when both nodes have an identical set of direct predecessors (except for A's arrow into *B*). Arrows may be added as needed to achieve this condition, as long as no cycles are created. Arrows involving a decision node cannot be reversed. Mathematically, reversing an arrow from node *A* to node *B* corresponds to applying Bayes' theorem to their associated probability distributions. The graphical direction of the arrow from *A* to *B* is reversed following a reversal operation. *See* Chance Node, Decision Node, Probability Distribution, Removal, and Well-Formed Influence Diagram.

Risk

A commonly misused term. Risk refers to the possibility of loss or injury.

Risk Attitude

The decision-maker's attitude toward taking risks. Most people are risk averse and therefore willing to pay a premium to avoid risk. Risk proneness, although allowed within decision theory, is rarely encountered in practice and can be viewed as an indicator of a less-than-fully developed decision model. *See* Decision Theory.

Risk-Aversion Coefficient

The only parameter in the exponential utility functional form. As its name implies, the risk-aversion coefficient measures the degree to which the decision-maker is averse to taking risks; the larger the coefficient, the more risk aversion is represented by the corresponding utility function. *See* Exponential Utility Function, Risk Attitude, and Utility Function.

Risk Sensitivity

A measurement of the effect that risk attitude has on the optimal decision and on its associated certain equivalent. *See* Certain Equivalent and Risk Attitude.

Risk Tolerance [Risk-Tolerance Coefficient]

The inverse of the risk-aversion coefficient.

Robustness

Characteristic of a method or a system that performs properly despite wide variations in its inputs and its environment.

Roentgenogram

X-ray.

Rule

A conditional statement. Rules provide a very useful language for representing many kinds of complex knowledge in a computer. *See* Conditional Statement, Knowledge Engineering, and Knowledge Representation Language.

S

Salpinges

Fallopian tubes.

Satisficing

Selecting any option from a set of possibilities as long as it satisfies all pertinent constraints. In general, *satisficing* means settling for a good option as opposed to *optimizing*, which means finding the best option. *See* Optimizing.

Scrotal Sac

Scrotum.

Scrotal Varicocele

Enlargement of the veins of the spermatic cord, commonly occurring on the left side of the scrotum. *See* Scrotum.

Scrotum

In the male, skin and muscle sac containing the testes. *See* Testes.

Search Algorithms

Systematic means for finding a desired object (goal) within a space of possibilities (search space). Formal search algorithms can be categorized in terms of their *completeness* (a complete algorithm always reaches its goal in finite time, given the goal can be reached at all within the search space), their *efficiency* (an efficient algorithm will require a small number of attempts to reach its goal), and their *admissibility* (for some optimality criterion, an admissible algorithm will search along an optimal path). Well-known search algorithms include depth-first, breadth-first, branch-and-bound, best-first, minimax, alpha-beta, *A** ("*A*"-star), and *AO** ("*AO*"-star) [Nilsson, 1980].

Secondary Stage

That stage of ovum maturation following the separation of the first polar body. *See* Ovum and Polar Body.

Secretory Phase [Luteal Phase]

Phase of the endometrium within the menstrual cycle; specifically, the time between ovulation and the onset of menstruation. *See* Endometrium, Menstrual Cycle, Menstruation, and Ovulation.

Semen

Viscous, whitish fluid containing spermatozoa and secreted by the prostate, testes, and other reproductive glands. Its primary function is to transport spermatozoa during ejaculation. *See* Ejaculation, Spermatozoa, and Testes.

Semen Analysis

Analysis of several key semen parameters to determine male fertility. Included in the analysis are measurements of seminal volume, sperm count, sperm motility, motile sperm count, sperm morphology, and seminal acidity (pH). *See* Semen, Sperm Concentration, Sperm Morphology, and Sperm Motility.

Sensitivity Analysis

A measurement of the effect that the elements of a model have on the implications of the overall model. In decision analysis, we distinguish between deterministic and stochastic sensitivity analyses. *See* Deterministic Sensitivity Analysis and Stochastic Sensitivity Analysis.

Situation

The elements of a decision that are unique to the decision-maker and that would not typically pertain to other decisions in the same domain. *See* Decision Situation and Domain.

Sperm

Spermatozoon or spermatozoa.

Sperm Concentration

Density of spermatozoa in the semen. Number of spermatozoa in a unit of semen (typically a square centimeter on a microscope slide). *See* Semen and Spermatozoa.

Sperm Count

Sperm concentration.

Sperm Morphology

Shape of spermatozoa. Common abnormal shapes include multiple tails, multiple bodies, misformed head, curled tail, and anomalies in size. *See* Morphology and Spermatozoa.

Sperm Motility

Ability of spermatozoa to move spontaneously. Sperm motility is often measured as a percentage of spermatozoa moving spontaneously under the microscope. *See* Spermatozoa.

Spermatic Vein

Vein that drains blood from the testes. In infertility, the spermatic vein can be ligated to alleviate the effects of a scrotal varicocele. *See* Ligation, Scrotal Varicocele, Scrotum, and Testes.

Spermatogenesis

The formation of spermatozoa.

Spermatozoa [s. Spermatozoon]

Mature male germ cells formed within the testes. *See* Testes.

Stationarity

A process or a model is said to be stationary when its properties stay constant with respect to a given dimension—typically time and/or space—or a set thereof. All concepts and distinctions are ultimately based on an assumption of stationarity at some level of abstraction.

Stationary Process

A process is stationary when its key parameters (e.g., flow rate, frequency, magnitude) either do not vary at all or vary so slowly (compared to the process itself) that one can safely assume they do not vary. *See* Stationarity.

Sterility

The total absence of reproductive capacity. *See* Infertility.

Stochastic

Uncertain; subject to chance.

Stochastic Assessment

An indirect assessment that assigns a conditional probability distribution to the node being assessed. This probability distribution is conditioned on the node's direct predecessors. If these direct predecessors are not already part of the influence diagram, they are added as part of the stochastic assessment. *See* Deterministic Assessment and Indirect Assessment.

Stochastic Sensitivity Analysis

An important activity during both the probabilistic analysis and basis appraisal phases of the decision analysis cycle. Stochastic sensitivity analysis is the generic name for a collection of attention-focusing and model-validation methods. One of these methods (probabilistic sensitivity) ranks the elements of the probabilistic model according to how much the objective function changes as they vary through their range of possible values. Other forms of stochastic sensitivity include constructing and analyzing profit lotteries and carrying out risk sensitivity, value-of-information, and value-of-control calculations. *See* Attention-Focusing Method, Basis Appraisal, Decision Analysis Cycle, Objective Function, Probabilistic Analysis, Profit Lottery, Risk Sensitivity, Value of Control, and Value of Information.

Sunk Cost

Cost incurred in the past; a sunk cost should not affect future decisions except in terms of its effect on the decision-maker's state of information and availability of resources.

Syllogism

A formal rule for deducing a conclusion from a set of premises (as in "Every woman is a mammal; Sally is a woman; therefore Sally is a mammal"). Modus ponens is an example of a syllogism. *See* Modus Ponens.

T

Take-Home Baby (THB)

A live human infant, four weeks after birth. Although most babies go home considerably before the end of their fourth week of life, the technical term take-home baby is used to denote a clear-cut marker for the success of an infertility treatment. *See* Clarity Test, Conception, and Pregnancy.

Test-Tube Baby

Popular term used to describe babies conceived through in-vitro fertilization. *See* In-Vitro Fertilization.

Testes [s. Testis]

Two male reproductive glands located in the scrotum. Testes produce the male germ cells (spermatozoa) and the hormone testosterone. *See* Hormone and Scrotum.

Testicles

Testes.

THB

Take-home baby.

Time Preference

The desire most of us have to receive good things as soon as possible and bad things as late as possible. In finance and decision analysis, time preference is often described by discounting the value—positive or negative—of future outcomes. *See* Net Present Value.

Top-Down Reasoning

Reasoning from goals to facts. Same as backward reasoning.

Toxicity

The quality of being poisonous.

Toy Problem

Narrowly defined problem area that, despite its usually small size, reflects many of the key features of a larger, more realistic problem domain. Well-known toy problems in decision analysis include the "Party Problem" [Howard 1981b] and the "Used Car Buyer" [Howard and Matheson, 1983–1984]; well-known toy problems in artificial intelligence include the

"Blocks World" [Winston, 1977] and the "Monkey and Bananas Problem" [Feldman and Sproull, 1977]. A toy problem is also referred to as a *microcosm*.

Transmission Network

In probability theory, a graph consisting of a set of nodes—representing events—connected by uncertain links—representing dependencies between events. Transmission networks can be useful for modeling random processes where some events depend on collections of other concurrent (e.g., parallel) and sequential (e.g., serial) events. For example, transmission networks are well suited for modeling such physiological processes as human reproduction.

Tubal Blockage

Mechanical obstruction in one or both Fallopian tubes impeding the movement of the ovum and/or spermatozoa inside the tube(s). Tubal blockage is a common, major source of infertility. *See* Fallopian Tubes, Infertility, Ovum, and Spermatozoa.

Tubal Mucosa

Mucous membrane lining the inside of the Fallopian tubes; its ciliated (finger-like) surface helps the ovum move through the tube. The tubal mucosa undergoes cyclic changes similar to those of the endometrium. *See* Endometrium, Fallopian Tubes, and Ovum.

U

Uncertain Variable

A stochastic element in a formal model of a decision or of an inferential problem (e.g., length of life or future stock price). In decision models, some uncertain variables arise as a consequence of the domain in which the decision is being made, while others result from the decision-maker's unique information and circumstances. *See* Circumstances, Domain, and Stochastic.

Unkunk

Short for *unknown unknown*; an unkunk typically refers to an uncertainty that was unanticipated and, hence, unaccounted for in a formal model. Unkunks could also refer to unanticipated decision variables, although this usage is less common.

Urethra

Canal for discharging urine; it extends from the bladder to the outside. In the female, its external orifice lies in the area between the vagina and the clitoris; in the male, its orifice is located at the tip of the penis. In the male, the urethra serves as the passage for both urine and semen. *See* Semen.

Uterine Cavity

The inside of the uterus.

Uterus [Womb]

Female organ for containing and nourishing the embryo and then the fetus from the time of implantation to the time of birth. The uterus is a hollow, muscular, pear-shaped structure inside the lower abdomen; it is lined on the inside by the endometrium. *See* Embryo, Endometrium, Fetus, and Implantation.

Utiles

Units of utility. A dimensionless quantity that is relatively meaningless but nonetheless useful for assessing utility functions. Utiles are particularly useful in domains where measuring outcomes in terms of a monetary or a lifetime equivalent is awkward. *See* Numeraire and Outcome.

Utility Function

A mathematical function that maps the set of possible outcomes of a decision to a dimensionless quantity (called the utility of these outcomes) and expresses the decision-maker's attitude toward taking risks. *See* Risk Attitude.

V

Value Model

A formal model of the decision-maker's direct preferences over the possible outcomes of a decision. *See* Outcome and Preferences.

Value Node

In an influence diagram, a node—usually drawn as an octagon or a diamond (rhombus)—that represents the decision-maker's preferences.

Value of Control [Value of Wizardry]

A quantitative measure of the value of controlling the outcome of an uncertain variable. Decision theory provides a means for calculating the value of both perfect and imperfect control. The former value, informally known as the value of wizardry, is an upper bound for the latter. Obtaining meaningful value-of-control measurements requires an awareness of important restrictions (concerning the nature of free will and the meaning of counterfactual statements) on the validity of this kind of analysis. *See* Wizard.

Value of Information [Value of Clairvoyance]

A quantitative measure of the value of knowing the outcome of an uncertain variable prior to making a decision. Decision theory provides a means for calculating the value of both perfect and imperfect information. The former value, informally known as the value of clairvoyance, is an upper bound for the latter. Obtaining meaningful value-of-information measurements requires an awareness of important restrictions (concerning the nature of free will) on the validity of this kind of analysis. *See* Clairvoyant.

Values of a Variable
Possible settings that a decision or chance variable can take within a given formal model.

Varicocelectomy
Incorrect term commonly used to refer to an internal spermatic vein ligation (ISVL). *See* Internal Spermatic Vein Ligation.

Vasectomy
Sterilization of the male by surgical removal of a portion of each of the two vasa deferentia (s. vas deferens), which are the ducts that carry sperm out of the testicles—or, more accurately, out of the epididymis—prior to ejaculation. *See* Sterility.

Vesicular Follicle
Graafian follicle.

W

Well-Formed Decision Influence Diagram (WFDID)
A well-formed influence diagram with at least one decision node directly or indirectly influencing a value node and satisfying the no-forgetting condition. *See* Influence Diagram and No-Forgetting Condition.

Well-Formed Influence Diagram (WFID)
A syntactically correct, completely assessed influence diagram whose nodes have fully consistent distributions and outcomes. *See* Influence Diagram.

WFDID
Well-formed decision influence diagram.

WFID
Well-formed influence diagram.

Wince Factor
The engineering heuristic that states that "if a designer can easily tell where to invest an extra unit of effort to improve the design, then the design is not properly balanced."

Wisdom Base

In an intelligent decision system, that portion of its knowledge that embodies fundamental—and, hence, portable—principles of good decision-making. The system's wisdom base is distinguished from its more traditional knowledge bases, which contain domain-specific knowledge. *See* Decision Analysis, Intelligent Decision System, and Knowledge Base.

Wizard

A mythical character who can change the future, usually for a fee, provided he is given a well-defined request (one that passes the clarity test). The concept of the wizard is useful in decision analysis for assessing deterministic preferences by eliminating the complexity added by uncertainty. *See* Clairvoyant and Clarity Test.

Y

Yin-Yang

Set of concepts (usually a pair) that, although different, cannot exist without each other (e.g., light and darkness, good and bad)—from the Chinese terms for male and female. Also refers to the two sides of an issue.

Z

Zygote

Cell produced when the male germ cell (spermatozoon) fertilizes the female germ cell (ovum). *See* Ovum and Spermatozoa.

Bibliography

Abdelmassih, R.; S. Fujisaki; and A. Faúndes. 1982. Prognosis of varicocelectomy in the treatment of infertility, based on pre-surgery characteristics. *International Journal of Andrology* 5:452–460.

Ackoff, R. L. 1987. Presidents' symposium: OR, a post mortem. *Operations Research* 35, no. 3 (May–June): 471–474.

Aikins, J. S.; J. C. Kunz; E. H. Shortliffe; and R. J. Fallat. September 1982. PUFF: An expert system for interpretation of pulmonary function data. *Report No. Stan-CS-82-931*. Stanford, Calif.: Department of Medicine and Computer Science, Stanford University.

Amelar, R. D., and L. Dubin. 1975. Male infertility: Current diagnosis and treatment. *Urology* 1 (January):1–31.

Austin, C. R. 1972. The ethics of manipulating human reproduction. In *Reproduction in Mammals*. Vol. 5: *Artificial Control of Reproduction*. Edited by D. R. Austin and R. V. Short. London: Cambridge University Press.

Bain, J. 1981. Male infertility: Selected clinical and investigative parameters. In *Oligoazoospermia: Recent Progress in Andrology*. Edited by G. Frajese. New York: Raven Press.

Barr, A.; P. R. Cohen; and E. A. Feigenbaum, eds. 1981–1983. *The Handbook of Artificial Intelligence*. 3 vols. Los Altos, Calif.: William Kaufmann.[1]

Beck, R. J.; J. P. Kassirer; and S. G. Pauker. 1982a. A convenient approximation of life expectancy (the "DEALE")—I. Validation of the method. *The American Journal of Medicine* 73 (December):883–888.

Beck, R. J.; S. G. Pauker; J. E. Gottlieb; K. Klein; and J. P. Kassirer. 1982b. A convenient approximation of life expectancy (the "DEALE")—II. Use in medical decision-making. *The American Journal of Medicine* 73 (December):889–897.

Behrman, S. J., and R. W. Kistner, eds. 1968. *Progress in Infertility*. Boston: Little, Brown.

Bellman, L. R. 1957. *Dynamic Programming*. Princeton, N.J.: Princeton University Press.

Bernoulli, D. 1738. Specimen theoriae novea de mensora sortis. *Papers of the Imperial Academy of Sciences in Petersburg* 5:175–192.

Black, R. B. 1979. The effects of diagnostic uncertainty and available options on perceptions of risk. *Birth Defects: Original Article Series* XV-5C: 341–354.

Bonczek, R. H.; C. W. Holsapple; and A. B. Whinston. 1981. *Foundations of Decision Support Systems*. New York: Academic Press.

The Boston Women's Health Book Collective. 1979. *Our Bodies Ourselves: A Book by and for Women*. 2nd ed. New York: Simon and Schuster.

Breese, J. S. 1987. Knowledge representation and reasoning in intelligent decisions systems. Ph.D. dissertation. Stanford, Calif.: Department of Engineering-Economic Systems, Stanford University.

Breese, J., and S. Holtzman. 1984. *SUPERID: Influence diagram processing environment—User's guide*. Stanford, Calif. Department of Engineering-Economic Systems, Stanford University.

Buchanan, B. G., and E. A. Feigenbaum. 1978. DENDRAL and Meta-DENDRAL: Their applications dimension. *Journal of Artificial Intelligence* 11:5–24.

Buchanan, B. G., and E. H. Shortliffe. 1984. *Rule-Based Expert Systems*. Reading, Mass.: Addison-Wesley.

Bursztajn, H.; R. I. Feinbloom; R. M. Hamm; and A. Brodsky. 1981. *Medical Choices, Medical Chances: How Patients, Families, and Physicians Can Cope with Uncertainty*. New York: Delta/Seymour Lawrence Book.

---

[1] This reference actually consists of three volumes edited by different pairs of editors on different dates. However, these three volumes constitute a single unit and are referenced thus. The actual editors and dates for each volume are A. Barr, and E. A. Feigenbaum, Vol. 1, 1981; A. Barr, and E. A. Feigenbaum, Vol. 2, 1982; P. R. Cohen, and E. A. Feigenbaum, Vol. 3, 1982.

Bustos-Obregón, E.; A. Guadarrama; A. Thumann; F. Zegers; and C. Barros. 1981. Normal semen values and sperm fertilizing ability. In *Oligoazoospermia: Recent Progress in Andrology*. Edited by G. Frajese. New York: Raven Press.

Capra, F. 1975. *The Tao of Physics*. New York: Bantam Books.

Carnap, R. 1958. *Introduction to Symbolic Logic and Its Applications*. New York: Dover.

Cazalet, E. G.; C. E. Clark; and T. W. Keelin. 1978. Costs and benefits of over/under capacity in electric power system planning. EPRI EA-927, *Research Project 1107, Final Report*. Palo Alto, Calif.: Electric Power Research Institute.

Chalk, R.; M. S. Frankel; and S. B. Chafer. 1980. *AAAS professional ethics project: Professional ethics activities in the scientific advancement of science*. Washington, D.C.: AAAS Committee on Scientific Freedom and Responsibility.

Charniak, E.; C. K. Riesbeck; and D. V. McDermott. 1980. *Artificial Intelligence Programming*. Hillsdale, N.J.: Lawrence Erlbaum Associates, Publishers.

Charniak, E.; C. K. Riesbeck; D. V. McDermott; and J. R. Meehan. 1987. *Artificial Intelligence Programming*. 2nd ed. Hillsdale, N.J.: Lawrence Erlbaum Associates, Publishers.

Chen, K., and G. T. Patton. 1967. Branch-and-bound approach for decision-tree analysis. *SRI Project 188531-172*. Menlo Park, Calif.: Stanford Research Institute.

Christensen-Szalanski, J. J. J. 1984. Discount functions in the measurement of patients' values: Women's decisions during childbirth. *Medical Decision-Making* 4, no. 1:47–58.

Ciampi, A.; M. Silberfield; and J. E. Till. 1982. Measurement of individual preferences: The importance of "situation-specific" variables. *Medical Decision-Making* 2, no. 4:483–495.

Clancey, W. J., and R. Letsinger. 1981. NEOMYCIN: Reconfiguring a rule-based expert system for application to teaching. *Proceedings of the International Conference on Artificial Intelligence*. 7:829–836.

Clancey, W. J., and E. H. Shortliffe, eds. 1984. *Readings in Medical Artificial Intelligence: The First Decade*. Reading, Mass.: Addison-Wesley.

Collins, J. A.; W. Wrixton; L. B. Janes; and E. H. Wilson. 1983. Treatment-independent pregnancy among infertile couples. *The New England Journal of Medicine* 39, no. 20 (November):1201–1206.

Copeland, T. E., and J. F. Weston. 1979. *Financial Theory and Corporate Policy*. Reading, Mass.: Addison-Wesley.

Cox, R. T. 1946. Probability, frequency, and reasonable expectation. *American Journal of Physics* 14, no. 1 (January–February):1–13.

Cramer, D. W.; A. M. Walker; and I. Schiff. 1979. Statistical methods in evaluating the outcome of infertility therapy. *Fertility and Sterility* 32, no. 1:80–86.

Dantzig, G. B. 1951. Maximization of a linear function of variables subject to linear inequalities. In *Cowles Commission Monograph*. Vol. 13. Edited by T. C. Koopmans. Chapter XXI of *Activity Analysis of Production and Allocation*. New York: Wiley.

_____ . 1963. *Linear Programming and Extensions*. Princeton, N.J.: Princeton University Press.

Davis, R.; B. Buchanan; and E. Shortliffe. 1977. Production rules as a representation for a knowledge-based consultation program. *Artificial Intelligence*. 8:15–45.

Davis, R., and D. Lenat. 1982. *Knowledge-Based Systems in Artificial Intelligence*. New York: Academic Press.

de Finetti, B. 1937. La prévision: Ses lois logiques, ses sources subjectives. *Annales de l'Institut Henri Poincaré* 7:1–68.

_____ . 1968. Probability: Interpretations. In *International Encyclopedia of the Social Sciences*. New York: Macmillan, pp. 496–505.

de Kleer, J. A. 1986. An assumption-based truth maintenance system. *Artificial Intelligence* 28, no. 2:127–162.

Dempster, A. P. 1968. A generalization of Bayesian inference. *Journal of the Royal Statistical Society, Series B* 30:205–247.

Dorfman, R. 1972. *Prices and Markets*. 2nd ed. Englewood Cliffs, N. J.: Prentice-Hall.

Dorland's Illustrated Medical Dictionary. 1981. 26th ed. Philadelphia: Saunders.

Doyle, A. C. 1982. *Adventures of Sherlock Holmes*. New York: Buccaneer Books.

Drake, A. W. 1967. *Fundamentals of Applied Probability Theory*. New York: McGraw-Hill.

Duda, R. O.; J. Gaschnig; and P. E. Hart. 1979. Model design in the PROSPECTOR consultant system for mineral exploration. In *Expert Systems in the Micro-electronic Age*. Edited by D. Michie. Edinburgh: Edinburgh University Press, pp. 153–167.

Duda, R. O.; P. E. Hart; P. Barrett; J. G. Gaschnig; K. G. Konolige; R. Reboh; and J. Slocum. 1978. Development of the PROSPECTOR Consultation System for Mineral Exploration. *Final Report, SRI Projects 5821 and 6415*. Menlo Park, Calif.: SRI International.

Duda, R. O.; P. E. Hart; and N. J. Nilsson. 1976. Subjective Bayesian methods for rule-based inference systems. Presented at the National Computer Conference. Menlo Park, California: Stanford Research Institute.

Duda, R. O.; P. E. Hart; N. J. Nilsson; R. Reboh; and J. Slocum. 1977. Development of a computer-based consultant for mineral exploration. *Annual Report, SRI Projects 5821 and 6415*. Menlo Park, Calif.: SRI International.

Duda, R. O.; P. E. Hart; R. Reboh; J. Reiter; and T. Risch, 1987. Syntel: Using a Functional Language for Financial Risk Assessment. IEEE Expert. Fall, 1987, pp. 18–31.

Duda, R. O., and R. Reboh 1984. AI and decision-making: The PROSPECTOR experience. In *Artificial Intelligence Applications for Business*. Edited by W. Reitman. Norwood, N. J.: Ablex, pp. 111–147.

Edmonds, D. K.; K. S. Lindsay; J. F. Miller; E. Williamson; and P. J. Wood. 1982. Early embrionic mortality in women. *Fertility and Sterility* 38:447.

Eliasson, R. 1981. Sperm count and fertility: Facts and myths. In *Oligoazoospermia: Recent Progress in Andrology*. Edited by G. Frajese. New York: Raven Press.

Eraker, S. A., and H. C. Sox, Jr. 1981. Assessment of patients' preferences for therapeutic outcomes. *Medical Decision-Making* 1, no. 1:29–39.

Erman, L. D.; F. Hayes-Roth; J. R. Lesser; and D. Raj Reddy. 1980. The HEARSAY-II speech understanding system: Integrating knowledge to resolve uncertainty. *Computing Surveys* 12, no. 2:213–253.

Erman, L. D., and V. R. Lesser. 1980. The HEARSAY-II speech understanding system: A tutorial. In *Trends in Speech Recognition*. Edited by W. Lea. Englewood Cliffs, N.J.: Prentice-Hall, pp. 361–381.

Feigenbaum, E., and P. McCorduck. 1983. *The Fifth Generation: Artificial Intelligence and Japan's Computer Challenge to the World*. Reading, Mass.: Addison-Wesley.

Feldman, E. A., and R. F. Sproull. 1977. Decision theory and artificial intelligence II: The hungry monkey. *Cognitive Science* 1, no. 2:158–192.

Fikes, R. E.; P. Hart; and N. J. Nilsson. 1972. Learning and executing generalized robot plans. *Artificial Intelligence*. 3:251–288.

Fikes, R. E., and N. J. Nilsson. 1971. STRIPS: A new approach to the application of theorem proving to problem solving. *Artificial Intelligence* 2:189–208.

Freedy, A.; K. B. Davis; R. Steeb; M. G. Samet; and P. C. Gardiner. 1976. Adaptive computer aiding in dynamic decision processes: Methodology, evaluation and applications. *Technical Report, No. PFTR-1016-76-8/30*. Woodland Hills, Calif.: Perceptronics, Inc.

Gautier, T., and H. Berlioz. 1968. Les nuits d'été. London: The Decca Record Company Ltd. From *Poésies Diverses*, originally published by T. Gautier under the title *Comédie de la Mort*, 1938. Original translation from the French.

Genesereth, M. R., and N. J. Nilsson. 1987. *Logical Foundations of Artificial Intelligence.* Los Altos, Calif.: William Kaufmann.

Ginsberg, A. S. 1969. Decision analysis in clinical patient management with an application to the pleural effusion problem. Ph.D. dissertation. Stanford, Calif.: Department of Engineering-Economic Systems, Stanford University.

Ginsberg, A. S., and F. L. Offensend. 1968. An application of decision theory to a medical diagnosis-Treatment problem. *Transactions on Systems Science and Cybernetics.* SSC-4, no. 3 (September):355–362.

Goldman, L.; D. L. Caldera; S. R. Nussbaum; F. S. Southwick; D. Krogstad; B. Murray; D. S. Burke; T. A. O'Malley; A. H. Goroll; C. H. Caplan; J. Nolan; B. Carabello; and E. E. Slater. 1977. Multifactorial index of cardiac risk in noncardiac surgical procedures. *New England Journal of Medicine* 297, no. 16 (October 20):845–850.

Good, I. J. 1962. Subjective probability as the measure of a non-measurable set. In *Logic, Methodology and Philosophy of Science*. Edited by E. Nagel, P. Suppes, and A. Tarski. Stanford, Calif.: Stanford University Press, pp. 319–329.

Gorry, G. A., and G. O. Barnett. 1968. Experience with a model of sequential diagnosis. *Computers and Biomedical Research.* 1:490–507.

Gorry, G. A.; J. P. Kassirer; A. Essig; and W. B. Schwartz. 1973. Decision analysis as the basis for computer-aided management of acute renal failure. *American Journal of Medicine.* 55:473–484.

Gove, P. B., ed. 1971. *Webster's Third New International Dictionary of The English Language*, Unabridged. Springfield, Mass.: G. and C. Merriam Company.

Guzick, D. S.; D. S. Bross; and J. A. Rock. 1982. A parametric method for comparing cumulative pregnancy curves following infertility therapy. *Fertility and Sterility* 37, no. 4 (April):503–507.

Guzick, D. S., and J. A. Rock. 1981. Estimation of a model of cumulative pregnancy following infertility therapy. *American Journal of Obstetrics and Gynecology.* 140, no. 5 (July):573–758.

Hall, G. H. 1967. The clinical application of Bayes' theorem. *Lancet* (September):555–556

Harmon, P., and D. King. 1985. *Expert Systems: Artificial Intelligence in Business.* New York: Wiley.

Harron, F.; J. Burnside; and T. Beauchamp. 1983. *Health and Human Values: A Guide to Making Your Own Decisions.* New Haven, Conn.: Yale University Press.

Hatcher, R. A.; G. K. Stewart; F. Stewart; F. Guest; N. Joseph; and J. Dale. 1982. *Contraceptive Technology: 1982–1983.* 11th rev. ed. New York: Irvington Publishers.

Hayes-Roth, F.; D. A. Waterman; and D. B. Lenat, eds. 1983. *Building Expert Systems.* Reading, Mass.: Addison-Wesley.

Heidegger, M. 1962. *Being and Time.* New York: Harper & Row.

Hellerstein, D. 1983. Overdosing on medical technology. *Technology Review* (August–September):13–17.

Henrion, M., and B. Fischhoff. 1986. Assessing uncertainty in physical constants. *American Journal of Physics.* 54, no. 9 (September):791–798.

Hertz, J.H. 1960. *The Pentateuch and the Haftorahs.* London: Soncino Press.

Higgins, R. C. 1977. *Financial Management.* Chicago: Science Research Associates, Inc.

Hillier, F. S., and G. J. Lieberman. 1967. *Operations Research.* 2nd edition. San Francisco: Holden-Day, Inc.

Hofstadter, D. R. 1979. *Gödel, Escher, Bach: An Eternal Golden Braid.* New York: Basic Books.

Holtzman, S. 1980. Non-uniform time-sale modification of speech. E.E.-S.M. thesis, Cambridge, Mass.: Department of Electrical Engineering and Computer Science, M.I.T.

_____ . 1981. A model of the decision analysis process. Stanford, Calif.: Department of Engineering-Economic Systems, Stanford University.

_____ . 1983a. Academic economics. Stanford, Calif.: Department of Engineering-Economic Systems, Stanford University.

_____ . 1983b. A decision aid for patients with end-stage renal disease. Stanford, Calif.: Department of Engineering-Economic Systems, Stanford University.

_____ . 1984. On the use of formal methods for decision-making. Presented at the ORSA/TIMS 17th Joint National Meeting. San Francisco, California. May, 1984. Stanford, Calif.: Department of Engineering-Economic Systems, Stanford University.

_____ . 1985a. Intelligent decision systems. Ph.D. dissertation. Stanford, Calif.: Department of Engineering-Economic Systems, Stanford University. Reprinted by University Microfilms International. Number 8511317. Ann Arbor, Mich.

_____ . 1985b. Rachel: An intelligent decision system for infertile couples. Presented at the ORSA/TIMS 20th Joint National Meeting. Atlanta, Georgia. November 1985. Department of Engineering-Economic Systems, Stanford University, Stanford, Calif.

_____ . 1985c. An architecture for intelligent decision systems. Presented at the ORSA/TIMS 20th Joint National Meeting. Atlanta, Georgia. November 1985. Stanford, Calif.: Department of Engineering-Economic Systems, Stanford University.

_____ . 1986. Analyst: An intelligent decision system for new microcomputer product introduction. Stanford, Calif.: Department of Engineering-Economic Systems, Stanford University.

Holtzman, S., and J. Breese. 1986. Exact reasoning about uncertainty: On the design of expert systems for decision support. In *Uncertainty in Artificial Intelligence*, Edited by J. F. Lemer and L. N. Kanal. Amsterdam: North-Holland, pp. 339–345.

Howard, R. A. 1966. Decision analysis: Applied decision theory. In *Proceedings of the Fourth International Conference on Operations Research*. Edited by D. B. Hertz and J. Melese. New York: Wiley-Interscience, pp. 55–71.

_____ . 1968. The foundations of decision analysis. *IEEE Transactions on Systems Science and Cybernetics*. SSC4, no. 3 (September):1–9.

_____ . 1970. Risk preference. In *Readings on the Principles and Applications of Decision Analysis*. Edited by R. A. Howard and J. E. Matheson. Vol. II (1984). Menlo Park, Calif.: Strategic Decisions Group, pp. 626–663.

_____ . 1971. *Dynamic Probabilistic Systems*. 2 vols. New York: Wiley.

_____ . 1973. Decision analysis in systems engineering. In *Systems Concepts: Lectures on Contemporary Approaches to Systems*. Edited by R. F. Miles. New York: Wiley.

_____ . 1979. Life and death decision analysis. Research Report No. EES-DA-79-2. Stanford, Calif.: Department of Engineering-Economic Systems, Stanford University.

_____ . 1980a. On making life and death decisions. In *Societal Risk Assessment*. Edited by R. C. Schwing and W. A. Albers, Jr. New York: Plenum, pp. 89–113.

_____ . 1980b. An assessment of decision analysis. *Operations Research* 28, no. 1:4–27.

_____ . 1981a. *EES 221—Probabilistic Analysis.* Stanford, Calif.: Department of Engineering-Economic Systems, Stanford University.

_____ . 1981b. *EES 231—Decision Analysis*. Stanford, Calif.: Department of Engineering-Economic Systems, Stanford University.

_____ . 1983. The evolution of decision analysis. In *Readings on the Principles and Applications of Decision Analysis*. Edited by R. A. Howard and J. E. Matheson. Vol. I (1983). Menlo Park, Calif.: Strategic Decisions Group, pp. 5–16.

_____ . 1984. On fates comparable to death. *Management Science* 30, no. 4:407–422.

_____ . 1987a. Knowledge maps. Stanford, Calif.: Engineering-Economic Systems Department, Stanford University. Submitted to *Management Science.*

_____ . 1987b. Progress and promise in decision analysis. Stanford, Calif.: Engineering-Economic Systems Department, Stanford University. Submitted to *Management Science.*

Howard, R. A., and J. E. Matheson. 1981. Influence diagrams. In *Readings on the Principles and Applications of Decision Analysis*. Edited by R. A. Howard and J. E. Matheson. Vol. II (1984). Menlo Park, Calif.: Strategic Decisions Group, pp. 719–762.

Howard, R. A. and J. E. Matheson, eds. 1983–1984. *Readings on the Principles and Applications of Decision Analysis*. 2 vols. Menlo Park, Calif.: Strategic Decisions Group.

Howard, R. A.; M. W. Merkhofer; A. C. Miller; and S. N. Tani. 1975. A preliminary characterization of a decision structuring process for the task-force commander and his staff. *SRI International Technical Report, MSD-4030.* Menlo Park, Calif.: SRI International.

Huff, D. 1954. *How to Lie with Statistics*. New York: Norton.

Hughes, E. C., ed. 1972. *Obstetric-Gynecologic Terminology*. Philadelphia: F. A. Davis Company.

Jaffe, A. J., and H. F. Spirer. 1987. *Misused Statistics: Straight Talk for Twisted Numbers.* New York: Decker.

Kahneman, D.; P. Slovic; and A. Tversky, eds. 1982. *Judgment Under Uncertainty: Heuristics and Biases*. London: Cambridge University Press.

Kahneman, D., and A. Tversky. 1979. Prospect theory: An analysis of decision under risk. *Econometrica* 47, no. 2 (March): 263–291.

Kapleau, P. 1967. *Three Pillars of Zen.* Boston: Beacon.

Kassirer, J. P. 1983. Adding insult to injury: Usurping patients' prerogatives. *New England Journal of Medicine* 308:898–901.

Kassirer, J. P.; A. J. Moskowitz; J. Lau; and S. G. Pauker. 1987. Decision analysis: A progress report. *Annals of Internal Medicine* 106, no. 2:275–291.

Keeler, E. B., and S. Cretin. 1983. Discounting of life-saving and nonmonetary effects. *Management Science* 29 (March):300–206.

Keelin, T. W. 1977. A protocol and procedure for assessing multiattribute preference functions. Ph.D. dissertation. Stanford, Calif.: Engineering-Economic Systems Department, Stanford University.

_____ . 1981. A parametric representation of additive value functions. *Management Science* 27, no. 10:1200–1208.

Keen, P. G. W., and M. S. Scott Morton. 1978. *Decision Support Systems: An Organizational Perspective.* Reading, Mass.: Addison-Wesley.

Keeney, R. L., and H. Raiffa. 1976. *Decisions with Multiple Objectives: Preferences and Value Tradeoffs.* New York: Wiley.

Kessler, R. 1984–1985. Private communications.

Klein, S. L. 1985. *A Glossary of Anesthesia and Related Terminology.* New York: Medical Examination Publishing Company.

Kolata, G. 1986. What does it mean to be "rare" or "likely?" *Science* 234 (October 31, 1986):542.

Kolmogoroff, A. 1933. *Grundbegriffe der Wahrscheinlichkeitsrechnung.* Berlin: Springer.

_____ . 1950. Foundations of the Theory of Probability. New York: Chelsea Publishing Co.

Kong, A. M.; G. O. Barnett; F. Mosteller; and C. Youtz. 1986. How medical professionals evaluate expressions of probability. *New England Journal of Medicine* 315, no. 12:740–744.

Korsan, R. J., and J. E. Matheson. 1978. Pilot automated influence diagram decision aid. *SRI International Technical Report No. 7078.* Menlo Park, Calif.: SRI International.

Kuhn, T. S. 1962. *The Structure of Scientific Revolutions.* Chicago: University of Chicago Press.

Kulikowski, C., and S. Weiss. 1982. Representation of expert knowledge for consultation: The CASNET and EXPERT projects. In *Artificial Intelligence in Medicine,* ed., P. Szolovitz. Boulder, Colo. Westview Press, pp. 21–55.

Kunz, J. R. M., ed. 1982. *The American Medical Association Family Medical Guide*. New York: Random House.

Lamb, E. J. 1972. Prognosis for the infertile couple. *Fertility and Sterility* 23, no. 5 (May):320–325.

————. 1983-1984. Private communications.

Lamb, E. J. and A. L. Cruz. 1972. Data collection and analysis in an infertility practice. *Fertility and Sterility* 23, no. 5 (May):310–314.

Lamb, E. J., and V. E. Waechter. 1981. Guide for infertile patients. Introductory pamphlet for patients, gynecology and obstetrics clinic. Stanford, Calif.: Stanford University.

Laplace, P. S., Marquis de. 1812. *Théorie Analytique des Probabilités*. Reprinted by Impression Anastaltique, Culture et Civilization, Brussels, 1967.

————. 1951. *A Philosophical Essay on Probabilities*. 6th edition. New York: Dover.

Leaper, D. J.; J. C. Horrocks; J. R. Stoniland; and P. T. DeDombal. 1972. Computer-assisted diagnosis of abdominal pain using "estimates" provided by clinicians. *British Medical Journal* 4 (November 11):350–354.

Lenat, D. B. 1981. The nature of heuristics. *Heuristic Programming Project, Report No. HPP-81-22*. Stanford, Calif.: Department of Computer Science, Stanford University.

Lenat, D. B., and J. S. Brown. 1983. Why AM and EURISKO appear to work. In *Proceedings of the Second National Conference on Artificial Intelligence*, p. 236. Menlo Park, Calif.: American Association for Artificial Intelligence.

Lenat, D. B.; R. Davis; J. Doyle; M. R. Genesereth; I. Goldstein; and H. Schrabe. 1981. Meta-cognition: Reasoning about knowledge. *Heuristic Programming Project, Report No. HPP-81-21*. Stanford, Calif.: Department of Computer Science, Stanford University.

Lindley, D. V. 1982. Scoring rules and the inevitability of probability. *International Statistical Review* 50:1–26.

Lindsay, R.; B. G. Buchanan; E. A. Feigenbaum; and J. Lederberg. 1980. *Applications of Artificial Intelligence for Organic Chemistry: The DENDRAL Project*. New York: McGraw-Hill.

Lubs, M. L. 1979. Does genetic counseling influence risk attitudes and decision making? *Birth Defects: Original Article Series* XV-5C:335–367.

Luenberger, D. G. 1973. *Introduction to Linear and Non-Linear Programming*. Reading, Mass.: Addison-Wesley.

_____ . 1979. *Introduction to Dynamic Systems: Theory, Models and Applications*. 2 vols. New York: Wiley.

Matheson, J. E. 1970. Decision analysis practice: Examples and insights. In *Proceedings of the Fifth International Conference on Operational Research, Venice*. London: Tavistark Publications, pp. 677–691.

_____ . 1986. Private communications.

Matheson, J. E., and R. A. Howard. 1968. An introduction to decision analysis. In *Readings on the Principles and Applications of Decision Analysis*. Edited by R. A. Howard and J. E. Matheson. Vol. I (1983). Menlo Park, Calif.: Strategic Decisions Group, pp. 17–55.

Matheson, J. E., and W. J. Roths. 1967. Decision analysis of space projects: Voyager Mars. In *Readings on the Principles and Applications of Decision Analysis*. Edited by R. A. Howard and J. E. Matheson. Vol I (1983). Menlo Park, Calif.: Strategic Decisions Group, pp. 445–475.

McCarthy, J. 1980. Circumscription—a form of non-monotonic reasoning. *Artificial Intelligence* 13:27–39.

_____ . February 1984. Private correspondence.

McCosh, A. M., and M. S. Scott Morton. 1978. *Management Decision Support Systems*. New York: Wiley.

McDermott, J. 1980a. R1: A rule based configurer of computer systems. *Technical Report CMU-CS-80-119*. Pittsburgh: Department of Computer Science, Carnegie-Mellon University.

_____ . 1980b. R1: An expert in the computer systems domain. *Proceedings of the American Association for Artificial Ingelligence* 1:269–271.

_____ . 1980c. R1: An expert configurer. *Technical Report CMU-CS-80-119*. Pittsburgh: Computer Science Department, Carnegie-Mellon University.

_____ . 1982. R1: A rule-based configurer of computer systems. *Artificial Intelligence* 19, no. 1:39–88.

McNamee, P., and J. Celona. 1987. *Decision Analysis for the Professional—with Supertree.* Redwood City, Calif.: Scientific Press.

McNeil, B. J., and S. J. Pauker. 1979. The patient's role in assessing the value of diagnostic tests. *Radiology* 132 (September):605–610.

McNeil, B. J.; S. J. Pauker; H. C. Sox; and A. Tversky. 1982. On the elicitation of preferences for alternative therapies. *New England Journal of Medicine* 306, no. 21:1259–1262.

McNeil, B. J.; R. Weichselbaum; and S. J. Pauker. 1978. Fallacy of the five-year survival in lung cancer. *New England Journal of Medicine* 299, no. 25: 1397–1401.

_____ . 1981. Speech and survival. *New England Journal of Medicine* 305, no. 17: 982–987.

Meistrich, M. L., and C. C. Brown. 1983. Estimation of the increased risk of human infertility from alterations in semen characteristics. *Fertility and Sterility* 40, no. 2 (August):220–230.

Melzack, R., ed. 1983. *Pain Measurement and Assessment*. New York: Raven Press.

Menke, M. M.; J. Gelzer; and J. P. Pezier. 1981. Evaluating basic research strategies. *Long Range Planning* 14:44–57.

Merkhofer, M. W. 1987. Quantifying judgmental uncertainty: Methodology, experiences, and insights. *IEEE Transactions on Systems, Man, and Cybernetics* SMC-17, no. 5 (September/October):741–752.

Merkhofer, M. W., and E. B. Leaf. 1981. A computer-aided decision structuring process—final report. *SRI International Technical Report 1513*. Menlo Park, Calif.: SRI International.

Merkhofer, M. W.; B. E. Robinson; and R. J. Korsan. 1979. A computer-aided decision structuring process. *SRI International Technical Report 7320*. Menlo Park, Calif.: SRI International.

Miller, A. C., III; M. W. Merkhofer; R.A. Howard; J.E. Matheson; and T. R. Rice. 1976. Development of automated computer aids for decision analysis. *SRI International Technical Report 3309*. Menlo Park, Calif.: SRI International.

Miller, A. C., III, and T. Rice. 1983. Discrete approximations of probability distributions. *Management Science* 26 (March):352–362.

Minsky, M. 1980. A framework for representing knowledge. In *Mind Design: Philosophy, Psychology and Artificial Intelligence*. Edited by J. Haugeland. Montgomery, Ala.: Bradford Books.

Moses, J. 1975. *A MACSYMA Primer*. Math Lab Memo No. 2. Cambridge, Mass.: Computer Science Laboratory, M.I.T.

Moto-oka, T, ed. 1981a. *Fifth Generation Computer Systems: Proceedings of the International Conference on Fifth Generation Computer Systems*. Amsterdam: North-Holland.

Moto-oka, T. 1981b. Keynote speech: Challenge for knowledge information processing systems. In *Fifth Generation Computer Systems: Proceedings of the International Conference on Fifth Generation Computer Systems*. Edited by T. Moto-oka. Amsterdam: North-Holland, pp. 1–89.

Newell, A.; J. C. Shaw; and H. A. Simon. 1960. A variety of intelligent learning in a general problem solver. In *Self Organizing Systems*. Edited by M. C. Yovits and S. Cameron. New York: Pergamon, pp. 153–189.

Newell, A., and H. A. Simon. 1963. GPS, a program that simulates human thought. In *Computers and Thought*. Edited by E. A. Feigenbaum and J. Feldman, New York: McGraw-Hill, pp. 279–293.

Nilsson, N. J. 1980. *Principles of Artificial Intelligence*. Palo Alto, Calif.: Tioga Publishing Company.

Nofziger, M. 1982. *The Fertility Question*. Summertown, Tenn.: The Book Publishing Company.

North, D. W. 1968. A tutorial introduction to decision theory. *IEEE Transactions on Systems Science and Cybernetics SSC4*, no. 3 (September):200–210.

Odell, W. D., and D. L. Moyer. 1971. *Physiology of Reproduction*. Saint Louis: Mosby.

Olmsted, S. M. 1982. SUPERTREE-decision tree processing program. Menlo Park, Calif.: Strategic Decisions Group.

————. 1983. On representing and solving decision problems. Ph.D. dissertation. Stanford, Calif.: Engineering-Economic Systems Department, Stanford University.

Orwell, G. 1946. *Animal Farm*. New York: Harcourt Brace Jovanovich.

————. 1949. *Nineteen Eighty Four*. New York: Harcourt Brace Jovanovich.

Overstreet, J. W., and W. F. Blazak. 1983. The biology of human male reproduction: An overview. *American Journal of Industrial Medicine* 4:5–15.

Owen, D. L. 1978. The use of influence diagrams in structuring complex decision problems. *Proceedings of the Second Lawrence Symposium on Systems and Decision Sciences*, October 3–4. In *Readings on the Principles and Applications of Decision Analysis*. Edited by R. A. Howard and J. E. Matheson. Vol. 2 (1984). Menlo Park, Calif.: Strategic Decisions Group, pp. 763–771.

Owen, D. L.; J. E. Matheson; and R. A. Howard. 1978. The value of life and nuclear design. Presented at the American Nuclear Society Topical Meeting, "Probabilistic Analysis of Nuclear Reactor Safety" May 8–10, 1976. In *Readings on the Principles and Applications of Decision Analysis*. Edited by R. A. Howard and J. E. Matheson. Vol. 2 (1984) Menlo Park, Calif.: Strategic Decisions Group, pp. 507–519.

Owen, P. A. 1979. Decisions that affect outcomes in the distant future. Ph.D. dissertation. Stanford, Calif.: Department of Engineering-Economic Systems, Stanford University.

Pauker, S. G.; G. A. Gorry; J. P. Kassirer; and W. B. Schwartz. 1976. Towards the simulation of computer cognition: Taking a present illness by computers. *American Journal of Medicine.* 60 (June):981–996.

Pauker, S. G., and J. P. Kassirer. 1987. Decision Analysis. *New England Journal of Medicine* 316, no. 5:250–258.

Pearl, J. 1984. *Heuristics.* Reading, Mass.: Addison-Wesley.

Pearn, J. H. 1973. Patient's subjective interpretation of risks offered in genetic counseling. *Journal of Medical Genetics* 10, no. 2:129–134.

Pinckney, C., and E. R. Pinckney. 1982. *The Patient's Guide to Medical Tests.* New York: Facts on File Publications.

Plante, D. A.; J. P. Kassirer; D. A. Zarin; and S. G. Pauker. 1986. Clinical decision analysis service. *The American Journal of Medicine* 80:1169–1176.

Pliskin, J. S.; D. S. Shepard; and M. C. Weinstein. 1980. Utility functions for life years and health status. *Operations Research* 28, no. 1:206–224.

Polansky, F. 1984. Private communications.

Pollard, A. B. 1969. A normative model for joint time/risk preference decision problems. Ph.D. dissertation. Stanford, Calif.: Department of Engineering-Economic Systems, Stanford University.

Polya, G. 1945. *How to Solve It: A New Aspect of the Mathematical Method.* Princeton, N.J.: Princeton University Press.

Pople, H. 1977. The formation of composite hypotheses in diagnostic problem solving—an exercise in synthetic reasoning. *Proceedings of the International Joint Conference on Artificial Intelligence* 15:1030–1037.

————. 1982. Heuristic methods for imposing structure on ill-structured problems: The structuring of medical diagnosis. In *Artificial Intelligence in Medicine.* Edited by P. Szolovitz. Boulder, Colo. Westview Press, pp. 119–190.

Rabiner, L. R., and R. W. Schafer. 1978. *Digital Processing of Speech Signals.* Englewood Cliffs, N.J.:Prentice-Hall.

Raiffa, H. 1970. Decision Analysis: Introductory Lectures on Choices Under Uncertainty. Reading, Mass.: Addison-Wesley.

Read, J. L.; R. J. Quinn; D. M. Berwick; H. V. Fineberg; and M. C. Weinstein. 1984. Preferences for health outcomes: Comparison of assessment methods. *Medical Decision-Making* 4:315–329.

Rota, G. C. 1973. The end of objectivity. Unpublished verbatim report of a three-part lecture series. Cambridge, Mass.: M.I.T.

Rousseau, W. R., and J. E. Matheson. 1967. Computer programs for decision analysis: Generation and analysis. *SRI Project 188531-168*. Menlo Park, Calif.: Stanford Research Institute.

Sackett, D. L., and G. W. Torrance. 1978. The utility of different health states as perceived by the general public. *Journal of Chronic Diseases* 31: 697–704.

Sadow, J. I. D. 1980. *Human Reproduction: An Integrated View*. Chicago: Yearbook Medical Publishers.

Savage, L. J. 1972. *The Foundations of Statistics*. New York: Dover.

Schwartz, W. B.; G. A. Gorry; J. P. Kassirer; and A. Essig. 1973. Decision analysis and clinical judgment. *American Journal of Medicine* 55 (October):459–472.

Shachter, R. D. 1986a. Evaluating influence diagrams. *Operations Research* 34, no. 6 (November–December):871–882.

_____ . 1986b. DAVID: Influence diagram processing environment for the Macintosh. In *Proceedings of the RCA/AAAI Workshop on Uncertainty and Probability in Artificial Intelligence*, pp., 243–248.

Shafer, G. 1976. *A Mathematical Theory of Evidence*. Princeton, N.J.: Princeton University Press.

Shortliffe, E. H. 1976. *Computer-Based Medical Consultations: MYCIN*. New York: American Elsevier.

Shortliffe, E. H., and B. Buchanan. 1975. A model of inexact reasoning in medicine. *Mathematical Biosciences* 23:351–379.

Shortliffe, E. H.; B. G. Buchanan; and E. A. Feigenbaum. 1979. Knowledge engineering for medical decision making: A review of computer-based clinical decision aids. *Proceedings of IEEE* 67, no. 9:1207–1224.

Shortliffe, E. H.; A. Carlisle; M. B. Bischoff; A. B. Campbell; W. Van Melle; and C. D. Jacobs. 1981. ONCOCIN: An expert system for oncology protocol management. *Proceedings of the International Joint Conference on Artificial Intelligence* 7:876–881.

Siegelman, E. Y. 1983. *Personal Risk: Mastering Change in Love and Work*. New York: Harper & Row.

Silber, S. J. 1980. *How to Get Pregnant*. New York: Scribner.

Simon, H. A. 1976. *Administrative Behavior*. 3rd edition. New York: Free Press.

_____ . 1977. *The New Science of Management Decision*. Rev. ed. Englewood Cliffs, N.J.: Prentice-Hall.

_____ . 1982. *The Sciences of the Artificial*. 2nd edition. Cambridge, Mass.: The M.I.T. Press.

Singer, I. B. 1982. *The Collected Stories of Isaac Bashevis Singer*. New York: Farrar-Strauss-Giroux.

Smith, C. A. B. 1961. Consistency in statistical inference and decision. *Journal Royal Statistical Society*, Series B 23:1–25.

Solbel, D. S., and T. Ferguson. 1985. *The People's Book of Medical Tests*. New York: Summit Books.

Sox, H. C., Jr. 1987. Decision analysis: a basic clinical skill? *New England Journal of Medicine* 316, no. 5: 271–272.

Sox, H. C., Jr.; C. H. Sox; and R. K. Tauphins. 1973. The training of physician's assistants. *New England Journal of Medicine* 288: 818–824.

Spencer-Brown, G. 1972. *Laws of Form*. New York: Dutton.

Spetzler, C. S., and C. A. S. Staël von Holstein. 1975. Probability encoding in decision analysis. *Management Science* 22:340–358.

Staël von Holstein, C. A. S. 1973. A tutorial in decision analysis. Presented at the Third Research Conference on Subjective Probability Values and Decision Making, London, September 1971, revised July 1973. In *Readings on the Principles and Applications of Decision Analysis*. Edited by R. A. Howard, R. A. and J. E. Matheson. Vol. I (1983). Menlo Park, Calif.: Strategic Decisions Group, pp. 130–157.

Staël von Holstein, C. A. S., and C. S. Spetzler. 1973. A manual for encoding probability distributions. *SRI Project Report MSD-1408-105*. Menlo Park, Calif.: SRI International.

Steinberger, E., and L. J. Rodriquez-Rigau. 1981. Treatment of male infertility. In *Oligoazoospermia: Recent Progress in Andrology*. Edited by G. Frajese. New York: Raven Press.

Steinberger, E.; L. J. Rodriquez-Rigau; and K. D. Smith. 1981. The interaction between the fertility potentials of the two members of an infertile couple. In *Oligoazoospermia: Recent Progress in Andrology*. Edited by G. Frajese. New York: Raven Press.

Strull, W. M.; B. Lo; and G. Charles. 1984. Do patients want to participate in medical decision making? *Journal of the American Medical Association* 252, no. 21 (December):2990–2994.

Swerdloff, R. S., and S. P. Boyers. 1982. Evaluation of the male partner of an infertile couple: An algorithmic approach. *Journal of the American Medical Association* 247, no. 17 (May):2418–2422.

Szolovitz, P., ed. 1982. *Artificial Intelligence in Medicine*. AAAS Selected Symposium. Boulder, Colo.: Westview Press.

Szolovitz, P., and S. G. Pauker. 1978. Categorical and probabilistic reasoning in medical diagnosis. *Artificial Intelligence* 11:115–144.

Tani, S. N. 1975. Modeling and decision analysis. Ph. D. dissertation. Stanford Calif.: Department of Engineering-Economic Systems, Stanford University.

Tarski, A. 1965. *Introduction to Logic and to the Methodology of Deductive Sciences*. New York: Oxford University Press.

Thomas, C. L., ed. 1977. *Taber's Cyclopedic Medical Dictionary*. 13th edition. Philadelphia: F. A. Davis Company.

Thompson, J. S., and M. W. Thompson. 1980. *Genetics in Medicine*. Philadelphia: Saunders.

Tribus, M. 1969. *Rational Descriptions, Decisions, and Designs*. New York: Pergamon.

Tversky, A., and D. Kahneman. 1974. Judgment under uncertainty: Heuristics and biases. *Science* 185 (September 27):1124–1131.

_____ . 1981. The framing of decisions and the psychology of choice. *Science* 211 (January 30):453–458.

U. S. Bureau of the Census, Department of Commerce. 1977. *The U. S. Factbook, the American Almanac*. New York: Grosset & Dunlap.

Van Horne, J. C. 1986. *Financial Management and Policy*, 7th ed. Englewood Cliffs, N.J.: Prentice-Hall.

Van Melle, W.; A. C. Scott; J. S. Bennett; and M. Peairs. 1981. The EMYCIN manual. *Report No. STAN-CS-81-885*. Stanford, Calif.: Department of Computer Science, Stanford University.

Veatch, R. M. 1978. The definition of death: Ethical, philosophical, and policy confusion. In *Medical Ethics*. Edited by N. Abrams and M. D. Buckner. Cambridge, Mass.: M.I.T. Press.

Vermeulen, A. 1981a. Endocrine exploration of male infertility. In *Oligoazoospermia: Recent Progress in Andrology*. Edited by G. Frajese. New York: Raven Press.

_____. 1981b. Hormonal treatment of male infertility. *Oligoazoospermia: Recent Progress in Andrology*. Edited by G. Frajese. New York: Raven Press.

von Neumann, J., and O. Morgenstern. 1947. *Theory of Games and Economic Behavior*. Princeton, N.J.: Princeton University Press.

Wallsten, T. S., and D. V. Budescu. 1983. Encoding subjective probabilities: A psychological and psychometric review. *Management Science* 29, no. 2 (February):151–173.

Warner, H. R.; A. F. Toronto; L. G. Veasy; and R. Stephenson. 1961. A mathematical approach to medical diagnosis: Application to congenital heart disease. *Journal of the American Medical Association* 177 (July):177–183.

Weaver, D. D., and L. F. Escobar. 1987. Twenty-four ways to have children. *American Journal of Medical Genetics* 26:737–740.

Webber, B. L., and N. J. Nilsson. 1981. *Readings in Artificial Intelligence*. Palo Alto, Calif.: Tioga Publishing Co.

Weizenbaum, J. 1976. *Computer Power and Human Reason: From Judgement to Calculation*. San Francisco: Freeman.

Wiener, N. 1964. *God and Golem, Inc*. Cambridge, Mass.: The M.I.T. Press.

Winograd, T., and F. Flores. 1986. *Understanding Computers and Cognition: A New Foundation for Design*. Norwood, N.J.: Ablex.

Winston, P. H. 1977. *Artificial Intelligence*. Reading, Mass.: Addison-Wesley.

Winston, P. H., and B. K. P. Horn. 1980. *LISP*. Reading, Mass.: Addison-Wesley.

Zadeh, L. A. 1978. Fuzzy sets as a basis for a theory of possibility. *Fuzzy Sets and Systems* 1:3–28.

_____ . 1981. Fuzzy probabilities and their role in decision analysis. In *Proceedings of the 4th MIT/ONR Workshop on Command, Control and Communication*. M.I.T., pp. 159–179.

_____ . 1983. The role of fuzzy logic in the management of uncertainty in expert systems. *Fuzzy Sets and Systems* 11:199–227.

Index

Page numbers in boldface indicate a glossary entry. Bold page numbers within brackets denote secondary glossary entries. The definition of an entry can be found on italic page numbers.